Like Roses Rising from Concrete:

52 Reflections on Christ, the Black
Church and Urban Culture

GREGORY E. BRYANT

authorHOUSE®

AuthorHouse™
1663 Liberty Drive
Bloomington, IN 47403
www.authorhouse.com
Phone: 1 (800) 839-8640

Published by AuthorHouse 10/24/2018

ISBN: 978-1-5462-6507-8 (sc)
ISBN: 978-1-5462-6506-1 (e)

Library of Congress Control Number: 2018912605

Print information available on the last page.

Acknowledgements

As a preacher and pastor who loves God's church, whenever I write for long, extended periods of time, the Apostle Paul comes to mind. In my solitude, I think about how the one-time Pharisee of Pharisees, labored feverishly to start and establish congregations. Paul wrote legendary letters of various length, filled with church doctrine, Christological revelation, and references to practical ecclesiastical matters, all of which were intended to glorify God, and edify God's first century followers of the Christ. I imagine Paul writing, hunched over in prison cells, with bad smells; and in small houses, modest synagogues, and flimsy tents, sometimes near hills and high places, other times, in valleys, near the shorelines of tributaries. In many settings, I imagine Paul penning or dictating, all that the Holy Spirit had burned in his soul to share. I thank God for Paul, because besides Jesus, David, and the Apostle John, his words have blessed me in many midnight hours. Although, on occasion, I have also argued with Paul, more often than not, I have been inspired and comforted by what the Holy Spirit gave to him to share with us. He is a constant conversation partner, as I seek to become a better pastor, preacher, theologian, and writer, for the glory of God and the good of God's people.

As I think about the nature of this project, I also praise God for two Detroit preachers – contemporaries. A father and son team. The Reverends Dr. Charles Gilchrist Adams, and Charles Christian Adams, Senior Pastor, and Co-Pastor, of the Hartford Memorial Baptist Church, respectively. Charles Gilchrist Adams has modeled and helped reaffirm for me what the pastor, as theologian, looks like; the son has too. Both have been caring colleagues, and the son, a dear friend. From the father, among many things, I have learned the importance of using the weekly bulletin, for something more than simply a document dedicated for a few announcements and the record of the order of service. In Hartford's Sunday bulletin, Dr. Adams submits a powerful, meaty, and fairly lengthy, pastoral reflection, based on the lectionary texts for each week, according to the liturgical calendar. Each meditation is thoughtful, evidencing expert hermeneutical training, and a Holy Ghost inspired anointing. His son, and successor, exhibits these same gifts in his role as pastor, scholar, and gifted preacher, in his own right. It is because of what I saw in those Hartford bulletins, about four years ago, that I started including a weekly pastoral reflection in the United Christian Church of Detroit's bulletins.

I also want to thank God for Ms. Rosa Randall, our church's office administrator. Sister Randall is a gifted administrator, with an attention to detail. She is the one who, among many other tasks, compiles our nine to ten-page bulletin, and helps to keep our information channels flowing smoothly. While composing bulletins, that I redesigned, a couple of years ago, she said to me, "Pastor, my brother, who is also a pastor, really likes reading United's bulletins when I send them to him. He said he especially enjoys reading your pastoral meditations on the sermon text for the week. Pastor, they are a blessing, and people need to read them." This comment helped plant the seed for me to begin to organize and filter through a couple of years' worth of reflections, so that I could put them in book form. She was also very helpful in taking a look at an early draft of the book and providing additional editorial eyes for the project.

I am also thankful to God for the congregation I serve. The prayers and support of so many faithful members have helped to give me the focus and tenacity to keep plumbing God's word, so that I might live and teach God's word, with sincerity and humility.

I am most grateful for my family - my wife, Crystal, our three children, and my extended family. Together, it seems they have held secret meetings and colluded to keep me thoroughly grounded, in the knowledge that I am loved unconditionally. Outside of Christ, no one has been more helpful in encouraging me to be the best pastor and writer I can be, other than my wife. I am grateful that with the encouragement she has given me over the years, she has also given me the space to enjoy seasons of solitude. With patience, she has allowed me to have times when my books and notes, and laptop, are spread out on the floor, in a section of our living room, as God and I hammer out what the Spirit has brewing in my soul. I thank God for the love, space and grace she has given and continues to give.

The wilderness and the dry land shall be glad; and the desert shall rejoice and blossom as the rose. It shall blossom abundantly, and rejoice even with joy and singing...

(Isaiah 35:1-2a)

Did you hear about the rose that grew from a crack in the concrete? Proving nature's laws wrong, it learned to walk without having feet. Funny, it seems by keeping its dreams, it learned to breathe fresh air. Long live the rose that grew from concrete when no one else even cared.

Tupac Shakur

We wouldn't ask why a rose that grew from the concrete had damaged petals, in turn we would all celebrate its tenacity; we would all love its will to reach the sun; well, we are the roses, this is the concrete and these are my damaged petals; don't ask me why, thank God, and ask me how.

Tupac Shakur

Now on the first *day* of the week Mary Magdalene went to the tomb early, while it was still dark, and saw *that* the stone had been taken away from the tomb...Peter therefore went out, and the other disciple, and were going to the tomb. So they both ran together, and the other disciple outran Peter and came to the tomb first...Then Simon Peter came, following him, and went into the tomb; and he saw the linen cloths lying *there*, and the handkerchief that had been around His head...For as yet they did not know the Scripture, that He must rise again from the dead.

(Verses from John 20:1-9)

Table of Contents

Part 4
Ordinary Time

Part 5
Advent and Christmas

Introduction: Tupac, Concrete, and Roses

At various times in his short adult life, Tupac Shakur, the late rapper, poet, and actor, shook off his *Thug-Life* persona and spoke and wrote very powerfully and prophetically about the struggles of black people in general, and black youth in particular. Though it would be a mistake to call him a prophet of Christian orthodoxy in the traditional sense, because Tupac was not one whose persona displayed the overall character, insight and message of Jesus Christ[1], upon careful review of his work, it is clear that Shakur, whose parents were members of the Black Panther Party, proved himself to be a keen observer of black life and black pain. He was a young man who had ancestral and experiential knowledge of black outrage and grief – gifts and the curse which enabled him to speak convincingly and powerfully about the harsh conditions which have made it difficult for people of color to survive poverty, crime, violence, and racism. Though not a Christian prophet, in the fullness of what that description means, at times, he observed, pontificated and challenged American society to see what the sins of racism, and classism have done to mar the black and brown aspects of humanity. In this limited, and yet very important way, we can say that there were moments during his short life, when Tupac spoke prophetically to the masses about the conditions of black folk.

If one were to carefully wade and cut through the multivalent layers of his rap lyrics - lyrics often infused with rebellion, a gangster bravado,

---

[1] Though not a prophet of Christ, ironically, and bizarrely, Shakur depicted himself as a crucified, Christ- figure, on the CD cover he had just completed at the time of this death; a CD, entitled, *The Don Killuminati: Seven Day Theory)*

threats of violence and revenge, and an occasional propensity for sexual misbehavior and misogyny - one would discover that there was something else there too; there were times when the flowering of a powerful, needed-to-be-spoken, seed of truth would break through his more stereotypical gangster lyrics. There were times when Tupac spoke cogently, persuasively and metaphorically, about the indomitable nature of the human spirit; there were times when he was, in a sense, *preaching*; and when he sermonized he was preaching to two audiences – *one which knew intimately* of the pain, oppression and dysfunction about which he spoke, and another *which had not experienced* the world with which black people were acquainted all too well. His music and lyrics reached from the poorest ghettos to the whitest and wealthiest suburbs.

Thematically, though Tupac often rapped about the tragedy of life experienced and viewed through the window of shattered dreams, at times, he would raise our awareness of the potential triumphs that people who were down-trodden could experience, if they would only hold on to important spiritual virtues like *love* and *hope*. For example, the listeners of his music know that his song, *Brenda's Got a Baby*, captures the sad aspects of the life of a young urban mother who lacks righteous and healthy boundaries; consequently, because of bad choices, her life is lived without much earthly hope and ends tragically. The song was a lesson, a warning, to those who might be inclined to choose similarly self-destructive paths. Conversely, his song, *Dear Momma*, reflects the incomparable resiliency of a mother's love, against the backdrop of a sometimes, wayward son's rebellious attitude which is ameliorated to some degree by his deep gratitude. The mother-figure in his text, though not without her own faults, is one who attempts to set boundaries for her wayward son, as she raised him with tough love:

> Hugging on my mama from a jail cell
> And who'd think in elementary? Hey! I'd see the penitentiary, one day
> And running from the police, that's right. Mama catch me, put a whooping to my backside

This song also offers the possibility of reconciliation between the two protagonists - a mother and her son, who are struggling to survive in the urban jungle. One can hear an even stronger rhapsodic tone in the repeating hook of Tupac's urban anthem, *Keep Your Head Help.* This "sermonic" offering is a mix of bitter and sweet; a prophetic indictment against irresponsible black men; and a soothing reminder offered to often maligned women, to keep looking upwards and beyond one's immediate misery. It begins with Tupac serving up some powerful social commentary about the inherent, irrationality, of far too many men who abuse women. He quickly and poignantly asks a series of penetrating truth-laced questions, which seem to flow from the Spirit:

> And since we all came from a woman…I wonder why we take from our women; why we rape our women; do we hate our women? I think it's time to…heal our women, be real to our women. And if we don't we'll have a race of babies, that will hate the ladies, that make the babies…

It is because of Shakur's penchant for articulating in the raw, the plight of many struggling, socially oppressed African Americans (often forgotten and maligned Americans, who are trying to rise above the oppressive conditions of a sometimes dangerous, anti-black, and anti-God world), that we see in the best of his work a glimpse of powerfully rhymed, and uncensored truths that must be answered -- truths about the conditions of a sin-sick world, where realized dreams are rare. At his best, Shakur often describes a world that breaks God's heart, because it breaks the hearts of God's children. A world filled with people who are trying to rise above the boundaries, barriers and ceiling limitations – the concrete which seems designed by nefarious forces, both social and spiritual, to keep people depressed and suppressed. We hear in Tupac's most optimistic lyrics, an unfettered hope shining and rhyming through the grimy walls of a world that is sometimes unyielding and unforgiving. When this gift, born of hope, shines through, the improbable, and even the miraculous happens – *a rose grows, pushing up, out, and through hard barriers, against the odds!* In many ways, this offering of hope and victory is one of the main roles of Christian preaching; and many of us preachers hope that the instillation of hope and a sense of victory over evil, is one of the main effects our pulpit pronouncements are having on our listeners.

In a sense, Tupac was a young, tragically flawed, impulsive, but gifted, "street preacher," who sermonized on the human condition in urban America, profanely, hypocritically, and prophetically, through the medium of rap. But as much as his fame was rooted in rap, ironically, one of the greatest Shakur thematic tropes, and creative contributions, is not found in the lyrics of any of his rap songs. In my estimation, his strongest verses appear in one of his poems; a poem, which seems to have captured the unspoken strivings and aspirations of the universal throngs of people who have faced hard adversity, and yet have also been graced by the Creator to rise above life's inherent limitations. For me, the imagery invoked in what is his most famous poem, *The Rose that Grew from Concrete,* reflects the very best of his hopeful sermonizing. The content of it reflects those elements which make up some of the core tenets of the Christian faith - foundational teachings like grace, faith, and a hopeful, resurrection-like perseverance – all shining forth, against the backdrop of life's sometimes suffocating structures of oppression and death. His key metaphor of a flowering rose which grows up through cracks and manifests its intense beauty, despite its surrounding hard concrete streets, seems to echo the Christian truth of how the Spirit of God can cause hope, faith, love, achievement, success, and purpose, to inexplicably ascend through the lives of many who, seemingly, should never rise above their depressing and oppressive conditions. Through grace, God causes persons, who appear to the world to be throwaways, to be filled with a spiritual dynamism that helps them rise above hard, harsh, brutal, cold, and dead situations. Variations of his poem (apparently, Tupac crafted at least two popular versions) are studied and analyzed in classrooms all over the nation, especially in our urban centers. One of the most popular versions has experienced a resurgence, as it was recently featured in a popular Gatorade commercial, which stars the former Chicago Bulls' guard, Derek Rose. Through Tupac's lines, the listener is probed and prompted to reflect on the miracle of how beauty, life, inspiration, and even success can emerge (ala Derek Rose's basketball gifts and career), despite the presence of forces that often suppress and suffocate such gifts; we are probed and prompted to celebrate the miracle of such a grace. With the right ears, one can hear in Tupac's verses, the timeless reminder of how God can take the seed of what appears to be a life destined for ridicule, misadventure and total failure; and God can infuse such a life with an amazing ability to blossom, even when it is located and planted in harsh contexts – conditions seemingly meant to stop life from *living*. In the cold context of the proverbial concrete, something as beautiful as a rose can emerge with deep red petals, damaged, but intact. This is not just the story of the many nameless, persevering African American youths who populate this country; this is not just the tale of athletes, like Derek Rose, who have come of age in dangerous ghettos, and triumphed to reach rare heights of success; this is even more than a testimony of the "successful part" of Tupac's own life. As a great metaphor for life-rising-above its hostile conditions, is this not ultimately the story of Jesus of Nazareth, the Son of God, who was born in, and traversed through, and ministered in, various corridors of sin, hate, demonic attacks, poverty, violence, immorality, religious rigidity, ethnic prejudices, and Roman imperialism? Regardless of the spiritual and social opposition that he faced, Jesus flourished beyond any other life. As the *Son of God*, he manifested a profound connection with God, and a power over evil, before, during and after the crucifixion. As the *Son of Humanity*, he was vulnerable and exposed to the nocturnal and negative side of human existence, which temporarily seemed to get the best of him, but failed to stop him.

Is not this tale of a rising rose, the story of every person born into dire social and spiritual conditions; who by God's grace has been born a second time and made brand new? Is this rose trope, not also the story of too many African Americans to name, who survived the Middle Passage, auction blocks, whips, hot sun and hard ground of North Carolina's tobacco fields, Mississippi's cotton fields, the Jim Crow South, and the trek northward to lands unknown; as they made their way into the hard and segregated ghettos of our Northern industrial cities, to start banks and credit unions; to ascend to the heights of various business and social endeavors; more than a few receiving a variety of advanced academic degrees; with many more building up society from the church house to the court house; erecting powerful spiritual centers of healing, social help, and economic and political empowerment?

As a preacher of the good news of Jesus Christ, and as one who has often trumpeted how God continues to infuse God's people with the power to keep rising, over and over again, even when circumstances, people, and devils, seem to want to dance triumphantly upon our freshly dug graves;

when I think of great women and men of American history, who made their marks; along with the countless, potential W.E.B. Duboises, Howard Thurmans, Gardner C. Taylors, Percy L. Julians, Mary Mcloud Bethunes, Mahalia Jacksons, Dr. Kings, Thurgood Marshalls, Cornel Wests, Michael E. Dysons, Oprah Winfreys, T.D. Jakeses, Vashti Mckenzies; of the potential, Serena and Venus Williamses, Michael Jordans, Kobes, and Lebrons, I hear in Tupac's rose-rising-up-through-concrete metaphor, an undeniable echo of the gospel of Jesus Christ and the power of the Holy Spirit to cause rebirths, and to change so much tragedy, into so much triumph. This is why I have tagged this series of reflections and meditations, *Like Roses Rising Up from the Concrete: Reflections on Christ, the Church, Urban Culture, and Tupac.*

The "Rose" trope that Tupac employs, is an apt gospel trope, as we consider the main purposes for pastoral reflections. Historically speaking, the gospel of Jesus has always empowered those who live in our industrial centers, in America, with a word of hope. For me, this rose-metaphor mirrors one of the main functions of Christian reflection and meditation, which is to help those who are weary and worn by personal and systemic sins, to find forgiveness, empowerment, and a resurrection hope, through the words and presence of Christ. It is my hope that the contents of this book will encourage Christians and spiritual seekers alike, to study the word of God, and meditate on the presence and spirit of Christ, as they reflect on how the gospel-spirit has impacted black history, urban culture, the world, this preacher, and many other spiritual travelers, along life's journey. Tupac's words about a rising rose describe what theological reflection, Christian preaching, musings on the messiah, praying, worship, writing, trusting, and even questioning, empowers people to do -- which is to eventually, flower and blossom upwards, towards the *Son-shine*, rising above some very hard realities.

The Layout of this Book

What makes up the content of this book is a collection of fifty-two pastoral reflections, which I originally wrote for members and guests of the United Christian Church of Detroit. These meditations and essays have been assembled and modified, sometimes expanded, and sometimes reduced from their original form and size. They have been selected from a larger corpus of reflections, that were created and collected over a three-year period.

It has been one of my disciplines as the Pastor of United, to provide a weekly, pastoral meditation for publication in our Sunday Bulletins. Each weekly meditation is based on the sermonic scripture text/texts for Sunday morning's worship service. Each is also rooted in my spiritual and theological musings about the text/texts, earlier in the week. Since it is my practice to craft each pastoral meditation *before* I start to formally construct and write the Sunday sermon (I start writing my sermons on Thursdays), none of the pastoral thoughts published here are sermon manuscripts. In fact, these meditations are different in structure, flow, and in terms of points of practical application, from the sermon manuscript, from which I will preach. The purpose for having a pastoral reflection published in our bulletins each week, is to offer a kind of free-flowing, food-for-thought, preview, of the sermonic text; it is designed to whet our church attendees' appetites for the biblical text, before and after the preaching moment on Sunday. They are designed to give attendees an opportunity to meditate on some aspect of the text that might provide additional spiritual fodder for their coming week. I would like to believe that the actual sermon is much tighter in structure, and more sharply focused as it presents the main theological issue, often with a counter argument, then a synthesis, and practical application/options that *might* lead the listener to spiritual solutions and resolutions. The ultimate goal of each sermon is to point the listener to the God revealed in Christ, the One who can solve, or resolve, whatever is the social situation or theological dilemma. More specifically, each entry in this book, reflects my musings, as an African American Christian, situated in what has been the most impoverished, big city in America. Despite its immense struggles, Detroit is an amazing and dynamic city, with both a glorious, and tragic history, collapsed into its story.

Like many rust belt cities, Detroit fell victim to a combination of years of racist political policies, real estate redlining, coupled with the loss of countless manufacturing jobs to overseas relocation. This problematic combination decimated the city's economic prosperity, tax base, and its black citizens' hopes of continuing to enjoy the fruits of a middle class, social status, that many whites enjoyed. But, despite its thorny history, and its current spiritual and social context of grief, anger, racism, poverty, substance abuse; human trafficking; violence, aimlessness, and hopelessness, there are also beautiful leaves and rose petals, which continue to defiantly push upward and outward, through the social and spiritual malaise, which tries to suppress the common good. Each essay not only captures a bit of my own optimism about life and the city of Detroit, but also the optimism of our congregation's membership – citizens of Detroit – who have been buoyed by the optimism of God, as revealed through the many promises of God, located in hundreds of biblical texts. Many Detroiters are a resilient and optimistic bunch; this is seen in the faces of praying grandmothers, who are believing that their children and grandchildren will end up well; this is evidenced by strong fathers who are working two jobs, to provide material sustenance for their families; this is revealed in how the city planners and private sector developers are investing a lot of financial and energy capital into new businesses and architectural projects – the stuff of dreams, in the downtown and mid-town areas. These are a few of the evidences of the fighting spirit of Detroiters, coupled with the workings of God's grace, and of a powerful resurrection hope. Thus, many of the following pastoral meditations contain evidences of a hope that starts in in the heart of worshipers, but which works its way up from the bottom as a search for meaning and purpose in the God, who originally gives us seeds of hope.

I consider all fifty-two essays to be tools to help the student of the scriptures, the seeking church member, and the contemplative church leader/preacher, to think more deeply about the inspiring things God has done and is doing in our history, and world. My hope is that as the reader wrestles with a designated reflection, she/he would meditate on the themes present in the main scripture text/texts for that week, cross-referencing the main text with other scriptures, and supplemental reading material. I also acknowledge that there also might be greater wisdom in the reader wrestling with one essay per day, using the book as a spiritual devotional help for *fifty-two days* instead of fifty-two weeks. Whatever one's comfort level is in shaping one's reading schedule, my ultimate hope is that the reader would be guided by the Spirit to hear and weigh what Christ is revealing to them, through the scriptures, words, imagery, general history, black history, and questions (**With some of the entries from Epiphany, Black History, Lent, Holy Week, and Advent, I have provided study questions for discussion, and for a deeper reflection**). It is my deep conviction that as we draw closer to the Christ of the Bible, God will shed light on how we are to love, serve, live, move, and have our being in the world. In addition, for those of us who have been called to do Christian ministry in an urban setting, I hope this book will inspire the reader to think about Christian ministry in a way that is relevant, informed, and culturally sensitive, to the plight of a people who have had concrete barriers erected over their heads; barriers that *can only be* penetrated, and transcended, with help from God!

As our congregation and I have journeyed and sojourned together, our faith community has struggled to make aspects of the reign of God become a reality in our part of the world. We have worshiped, prayed, laughed, cried, evangelized, served, given, hoped, and dreamed, that our part of Detroit would become infused with village values (characteristics of God's kingdom/kin-dom). Although a few of these reflections draw from memories, stories, and testimonies which predate my time and experiences in Detroit -- times and experiences which recall years lived in Chicago, in Hawkins (Texas), and in Indianapolis – I think it is significant that all these meditations were given their final shape and form, amongst the sounds, sights, smells, soils, and yes *concrete*, of the Motor City. This has been my assigned garden for more than seven years; this has been where our congregation has tried to plant God's goodness, in the hope of helping people to push up through what seems like impenetrable forces of spiritual and social resistance.

A last word about this book: These fifty -two entries cover a variety of subjects. They are presented in the chronology of the kind of sermon topics I normally cover during the course of a year, as I follow (albeit, rather loosely) the key liturgical celebrations of the church calendar. These topics and themes represent some of the seasonal markers observed in many African American mainline congregations: *Epiphany*, Black History Month, the weeks of *Lent, Easter*, Mother's Day, *Pentecost*, Father's Day, Women's Day, *Ordinary Time,* Youth Sundays, Stewardship Month, Senior's Day, Laity Sunday, Men's Day, *Advent, Christmas*, Kwanzaa and Watch Night. By highlighting Epiphany, in the first few protracted pastoral musings, the reader is invited to consider how an encounter with the vision of Jesus Christ can become our all-encompassing vision; a vision which moves us to inner transformation. My personal testimony is included in the first essay. After Epiphany, February is in view. The next collection of reflections show-cases the importance of believers celebrating the history, purpose and legacy of the black church, in American society. Next, with the Lenten season in view, there are various critical meditations about how the tragedy of Christ's suffering, self-denial, and crucifixion, transmutes gloriously into the power of the resurrection – giving all of us who have felt crucified, and crushed, by death-dealing forces, a strong resurrection hope in God, which helps us to keep serving, loving, and being. After the Lenten essays, I share several Easter reflections which encapsulate and set the tone for all *rose-rising-from- concrete*, motifs. As my tracking of the Christian year progresses, I also share thoughts about the priceless gifts we have in our parents, which are revealed through the scriptures and meditations I wrote for Mother and Father's Day worship services; then, with Pentecost Sunday in view, I share several reflections about the mind-blowing, and life-empowering gift we have in the presence and power of the Holy Spirit. As the reader approaches the section which marks Ordinary Time (The Season of the Christian Year which follows Pentecost Sunday, and lasts until Advent, and is marked, liturgically, by the color green), I cover a variety of subjects with which we must grapple in the day-to-day living out of our faith: Our romantic lives in light of our faith; the institution of marriage; dating; sexuality; God's call on our youth; the importance of our financial stewardship; the criticality of our need to practice nourishing and sustaining spiritual disciplines, like prayer and scripture journaling. I also cover topics like worship, spiritual warfare, evangelism, service, social and racial justice, charity, forgiveness, and mercy. In recognition that ordinary time continues into the Fall and early winter months, reflections associated with our congregation's Friends and Family Day celebrations (normally held in September) are shared under this heading; next, Stewardship Month is celebrated in our congregation in October, so I have included several entries which deal with what God says about how God's children ought to handle their resources. As we move toward Thanksgiving, thoughts about what it means to live lives of gratitude are included. With the approach of the season of Advent and

Christmas, I share pastoral thoughts that should help the reader to *consider anew, what the almighty can do* (as worded in the classic hymn, *Praise to the Lord, the Almighty*), in light of the fact that according to Matthew's Gospel, God has come "down forty, and two generations," to tabernacle with humanity, most powerfully and palpably, via the birth of Jesus Christ; and that God has promised to come again as Savior and Judge, ushering in the eschatological reign and domain of God on earth, as it is in heaven. Finally, no black church liturgical calendar is complete, without the nearly ubiquitous presence of the Watch Night worship service,[2] on New Year's Eve. In our congregation, we celebrate Kwanzaa on this night, as we reflect upon our liberation from enslavement, along with the seven principles of Kwanzaa, in the context of our faith, while donning African, or African influenced clothing, and hosting a Karamu meal afterwards. Again, the main themes of these end/beginning of the year Watch Night reflections, center on our giving thanks to God for strengthening our ancestors in the fight for freedom, as we anticipate the availability of God's continued strength and prosperity, as we move into the New Year.

Again, my ultimate hope is that these pastoral essays, like roses ascending and pushing through hard barriers, will point the reader toward the beauty of Christ, the strength of faith, the power of the word of God, and the fascinating story of what God has done and is doing in the world, black culture, the black church, and the Church Universal. It is my personal testimony, along with the testimonies of countless others that the love, mercy, and empowerment of God, can cause those who have been counted out, to rise above, bloom, and be counted in.

In many ways, my life has become a rose that grew up through the concrete. Having grown up on the Southside of Chicago, and pastored churches in rough Indianapolis and Detroit neighborhoods, I know something about concrete; it is unyielding and can be brutally hard. As a pre-teen and teen, I played endless hours of lot-baseball on hard dirt, and pick-up and tournament basketball, on concrete. As a teen, I have stood on many-a-porch stoop, and in many-a-alleyway, drinking and smoking on

---

[2] The origin of the Watch Night service purportedly dates back to December 31, of 1862, when enslaved African Americans were waiting for the New Year to come; they were anticipating the beginning of 1863, the year when the Emancipation Proclamation would become the law of the land.

concrete; I have run from robbers and gangs on concrete; I have whistled at, and tried to court young ladies, while on concrete. Although I was raised in a typical, middle-class home and neighborhood, replete with hard-working home owners, local businesses and business owners, fairly decent schools, wonderful athletic leagues, beautiful parks and needed park district community programs for youth and seniors, and of course strong churches, our neighborhood like many others in the city, had a very hard side; and though, like some of my friends did, I never joined one of the dreaded street gangs of Chicago, our section of town was still rife with gangs, violence, and the many vices that flourished in more impoverished sections of our city. The thing was, our homes might have looked a little nicer than some others, and lawns might have been kept neater than some other areas, but we still moved and lived in the context of real concrete. If we wanted trouble, it was always only a half-a mile away, or the next couple of streets over. Because of the hard realities of racism, segregation, and inferior systems of education, along with an unhealthy dose of urban hedonism and escapism, much of Black and Brown Chicago was a fast-paced, often beautiful and densely populated environment, that had very dangerous elements added to its concrete mix – fast cars, fast bikes, fast people, drug sales, gun-violence, human trafficking, criminals and gangs. But, despite my social setting, God, who knew the address of my soul, knocked on the door of my heart when I was 18 years old; a time when I did not have a clear and calming sense of purpose; on a day when I was high on marijuana and brandy, and filled with inner fears. Through a television preacher, God planted a seed of peace, forgiveness and love within in me that was rooted in the salvific work of Jesus Christ on Calvary's cross. From that day, thirty-four years ago, until now, God has pushed me, coaxed me, and corrected me toward growth, like a branch on a vine; often upwards, and sometimes even outwards and briefly downwards, around turns and twists, and then upwards again --- growing, with damaged petals -- growing toward healing and wholeness in the Son-light. The presence of the Son-light is that key ingredient in life that makes growth possible. This is why I preach, pastor, and write.

Part 1
Epiphanies

1. Looking to Jesus

Then God said, "Let there be light"; and there was light. And God saw the light, that it was good; and God divided the light from the darkness. God called the light Day, and the darkness He called Night...Then God said, "Let the earth bring forth grass, the herb that yields seed, and the fruit tree that yields fruit...Then God said, "Let there be lights in the firmament of the heavens...Then God said, "Let the waters abound with an abundance of living creatures, and let birds fly above the earth...Then God said," Let the earth bring forth the living creature according to its kind: cattle and creeping thing and beast of the earth...and it was so.

(Selected verses from Genesis 1)

God, who at various times and in various ways spoke in time past to the fathers by the prophets, has in these last days spoken to us by His Son, whom He has appointed heir of all things, through whom also He made the worlds, who being the brightness of His glory and the express image of His person...

(Hebrews 12:1-3a)

I remember vividly the early 1980s. It was the period when I was in my middle to late teens and growing up on the exciting and sometimes dangerous, South Side of Chicago. This time marked the last vestige of

1

that awkward stage between childhood and adulthood. My teenage friends and I, spent a lot of time enjoying new found freedoms: hanging out with acquaintances; taking in the sights and sounds at the Evergreen Park Mall (once located on the far South Westside of the city before it was demolished a couple of years ago); going to the Pro-Am Summer League basketball games, which were primarily held at Chicago State University and the Illinois Institute of Technology[3]; going to backyard cookout, after cookout; and then occasionally attending parties at *Sauers*, which was probably the most popular dance club for African American teens and young adults, on the South Side, between 1980-1982; and also venturing to some back-alley drug pick-up spot, in what we used to call, *"The Low End"* (an area in and around the Englewood Community on Chicago's Southside) to purchase marijuana. I fondly remember that around '84, my friends and I would travel northward and get into the more sophisticated dance clubs for the *over-twenty-one* crowd. These cherished nocturnal adventures to the other side of the city were beyond exciting for an 18, and 19-year-old teen. The near Northside of the city was the glitzy, nightclub, avant-garde district, where we could see how the *other side* lived. All of these places made up the geography and social topography of our new playgrounds.

At the time, I claimed no strong spiritual moorings and no religious affiliation. I considered myself to be free of such ideological and behavioral weights and constraints. Many of us were beginning to enjoy our first real taste of independence from parental and religious oversight. With our parents' cars, or cars of our own, and a year or two of college under our belts; with part-time, and even full-time jobs, we had a little spending money, and access to freedoms, previously unknown; a freedom with which we could go and explore the length, width, and breadth of our city, and our vices.

Summers spent venturing to the near North Side of Chicago, around

---

[3] The Pro-Am Summer League basketball tournaments were a series of summer tournaments which included professional, college, and top high school basketball players from the Chicagoland area. Usually, there were two games played an evening. In one day, one might see a game which featured the NBA stars, Isaiah Thomas, Mark Aguire, and Reggie Theus, playing with top Division 1 and 2 college players, and the most celebrated High School players in the area. Occasionally, the Bulls' newly acquired, Michael Jordan would "lace them up" and show what kind of athletic genius he was on the courts. These games were big social events for African American young adults.

Rush Street[4], and certain areas close to the Lakefront, were wonders that had to be seen. I remember that beginning around 10 p.m., on many Fridays, we would fill up our cars with gas, and our bodies and minds with our choice of alcohol, marijuana, and other chemical substances, as we ventured out to places like, the afore-mentioned, Rush Street, to see the strange and exotic sites that the city had to offer. *We were often on a vision quest.* We percolated with hopes of seeing and connecting with new people and exciting experiences. Once we would arrive around the northern portion of Rush Street, close to Division Street, our lowered eye-lids would widen just a bit. We would be dazzled by the large crowds walking up and down this nocturnal entertainment corridor for blocks and blocks. Try to envision a half mile or so of city blocks, framed by the dark border of the night sky, swarming with people and peppered with alluring dance clubs which were just opening for the night; bumper-to- bumper traffic, high-end luxury and sports cars, trendily dressed women and men - some dressed preppy, others dressed in new-wave style clothing, and yet others dressed like punk rockers. This eclectic city scene was multi-racial: blacks, whites, Hispanics, and Asians (this was a rarity at the time, given that most of the other parts of Chicago, other than the Hyde and Lincoln Park neighborhoods, were extremely racially segregated). Historically, Chicago has been one of the most segregated cities in the nation, but in those days Rush Street was not, especially on the weekends. It was not just multi-racial, but also multi-cultural on a variety of levels: straights, gays, bi-sexuals, transvestites, gangsters/thugs, skateboarders, break dancers, video gamers, athletes, the wealthy, and the not-so-wealthy, were all there; in fact, all expressions of young humanity seemed to be there, at the height of the cocaine era. Most of the those who made up this thronging spectacle, seemed to be no older than forty years old. The disco-soul and Italo-soul dance music blaring from our car stereos was a youthful loud. The colors were dark, yet vibrant. The aromas were legion, and the vision, amazing and pulsating with energy.

---

[4] Rush Street was named after Benjamin Rush, one of the signers of the Declaration of Independence. It is primarily a one-way street on the Near North Side of Chicago. It starts at the Chicago River. Beginning in the 1960s, Rush Street was the center of Chicago nightlife, for decades. The section between Oak Street and Chicago Avenue was the most popular section of the street.

I can remember that in one night, we might encounter a big-time NBA player, who was out on a date with his significant other, with rows of luxury cars parked on the curbs outside of the establishment they were entering. We might also see people dancing in a packed, two story bar/ club – an establishment that had an entire external wall, and a first story ceiling, which doubled as a second story floor, made of glass, so onlookers, walking by on the sidewalks outside, could look in and see inside (literally through a looking glass) the partygoers on the first and second floors, seemingly having the time of their lives. While high, we might enter a building that housed and was filled with computer games, where throngs of young gamers would play Space Invaders, Donkey Kong, and Pac-Man, all night long. On any given weekend, we might see women kissing other women, or men whistling at other men, as we neared the Gay and Lesbian night club district. But, with much of our voyeurism and touring, in retrospect, there seemed to be a superficiality and artificialness. Upon reflection, I would liken our irreligious quests to that of a band of nomadic sea-shell collectors, who, while on beaches, might tour rows of glistening, strange, exotically colored shells that are wonderful and amazing (and sometimes shocking) to look at, but once opened, what was revealed was either the shell's emptiness or a dying, or dead mollusk inside. We were in search for *meaningful epiphanies, but much of what we witnessed was superficial, empty and smelled of spiritual decay.*

As I think about those times, I can now see more clearly than ever that in our lustful wanderings and watching; in our hazy drug experimentations, there was no substantial and enduring satisfaction at the core of our experiences. Sure, at times, we had moments of great fun – fantastic fun! but after the initial titillation of the experience, we had not experienced much that could be counted as an enduring good which was worth our viewing and experiential pleasures. After the car-riding, sexual-encounter-chasing, with the pulsating dance music in our ears; after the people-gawking, the alcohol use, the marijuana smoking, the pill-popping, game-rooming, the club-hopping, and the many attempts to locate true, or not-so-true romance, there was nothing tangible and lasting to show for all of our moving about this dark kaleidoscope which was this part of Chicago. There was no enduring quality of goodness to show and celebrate for the money spent and brain cells sacrificed. No doubt, we had temporary fun; we enjoyed the glitz and the spectacle, but at what cost? Sure, we saw exciting sights, and heard strange sounds, but had what our eyes and ears experienced satiated us? Did these experiences give any of us a sense that we could and would accomplish something meaningful in life as black youths who were trying to make sense of a world – a world which seemed organized to systematically hold black folk down? We were coming of age in one of the most segregated cities in America. What was happening on and around Rush Street, was not the normative experience of Chicagoans all over the city. It was a weekend fantasy. Since the time of the first Richard Daley's administration as mayor, the city had been run by politicians who benefited politically and socially from a racially segregated city – a city controlled by city planners who made sure that blacks, and Hispanics, were red-lined into certain geographical and school district boundaries, away from white Chicagoans. Did our escapism and viewing pleasures give us any real motivation to aspire to become change agents? Or were we just drinking in the entire scene as escaping, young hedonists, marching through a world of unreality?

The older me that I have become, clearly recognizes that in our late teens we were not concerned about bigger pictures. We were just trying to have youthful fun. This is understandable. We were young and energetic. We were exploring. We were trying to discover our likes, loves and limits. This is what young people do. We were not trying to grapple with the larger issues of life. Barring extreme and terrible circumstances, such as having to grow up in a war-torn context; or trying to come of age while enduring unfortunate levels of abuse and violence; or the worst forms of abject poverty; barring these dire situations, many (though certainly not enough) children and youth are graced with a blossoming spring season in their lives when they are free to enjoy the freedoms of growing up and living without many responsibilities lurking overhead. Most of those in my circle were either lower-middle, to solidly middle-class, youths. And we were living out what the writer of Ecclesiastes noted when the writer wrote that *there is a season for all things*; thusly, we believed that there was a season for youthful fun; maybe even for hedonistic epiphanies.

We were young and carefree, living life in the big city, without a spiritual or moral compass but with a thirst for mind altering experiences. Although we occasionally talked among ourselves about the evidences of the stubborn existence of that demon called, *racism*, we did not talk much about black history, spirituality or religion (maybe, a little, when we were under the influence of alcohol or a narcotic). On one rare occasion, I can remember sitting in the basement of a good friend's home. Mike's basement bedroom was like a separate apartment from the rest of his parent's home. On this particular night, he and I were drinking wine, and smoking cigarettes (the places to buy marijuana were "dry," this night). As we sat, listening to music, we began talking a little psychology. Mike and I were musing about the validity and merits of whether someone could be hypnotized. Soon, the conversation shifted, and we started talking about spirituality, race and religion; and as we talked, we discussed the virtues of such powerful leaders like the Reverend Dr. Martin Luther King Jr., and above all, Jesus. This conversation is easy for me to remember, because as I look back, it was a rarity. Normally, our main interests included going to the Northside, the Lakefront, playing basketball, purchasing marijuana, beer, and harder liquor, "chasing women" (often, without catching), and trying to make it to a party. We did not normally analyze or exult about the power of Dr. King, or Jesus, or any other transcendent figure for that matter; but on this one rare evening, we did.

In retrospect, I think our ordinary weekend vision quests told the real tale of what was going on in our hearts, and on our minds. We respected the virtuous, moral, and spiritual aspects of life, but we did not understand the true beauty of those dynamics yet. My friends and I hungered for a vision of life which was secular, expensive, escapist, expansive, materialistic, diverse, fun, exciting, *and meaningful*. We were looking for something we did not quite possess yet – for something which we did not know truly existed for us. I think, subconsciously, we were looking to be a part of a magical movement larger than ourselves; some thrilling journey that could placate and guide us, but not convict us spiritually, socially, or challenge us to think seriously about our lives; or to change directions regarding our sinful pursuits.

The Genesis of All Visions.

What I did not know at this point in my life was how the Spirit of God, when coupled with revelation in the Bible, could facilitate, fuel, and inspire the seeking mind to dream of, and *picture* a glorious, purposeful and exciting direction in life; a glorious vision rooted in the genesis of all things. In Genesis 1, the author paints a vivid cosmic, primordial, and prehistoric picture, of a time, before recorded time. This vision of creation which Christians and Jews traditionally believe was given either to Moses, or to an author/authors who had heard the oral history of the Jewish creation narrative; a vision that was ultimately birthed by the creative brilliance and revelation of God, in my view. In the first chapter of the Hebrew Bible, God shows us how things came to be. God is shown to be the mysterious and creative Genius Who speaks vision into reality -- out of God's mouth. God envisions, speaks, and things happen! God imagines and speaks the world as good, colorful, breath-taking in beauty, vibrant, lush, free, and complex in its scope, detail, and structure; yet God speaks *it out,* paradoxically simple in symmetry and order. God speaks out light, and the cosmos, galaxies, stars, and planets form. The earth is settled, the primordial waters are divided from atmosphere and space --- from out of the watery chaos, order emerges, seeds grow, birds fly, animals roam, and insects appear. From what we have in the narrative, when God envisions and speaks something into being, God first spoke to the raw materials from which the new creation would emerge. God spoke to the sea, for the production of the sea creatures; God spoke to the earth, for the emergence of animals and insects. But, as God begins to fashion the crown of God's creation, God speaks to God's self: "Let us, make humanity!" God is the source (the being) from which God will form the hidden and visible part of humankind. Of this knowledge, most of my friends and I were ignorant.

Genesis 1:26 - 27, unveils the crown of God's creative vision --- human beings made in God's image and after God's likeness; beings planted in the region of Africa and Mesopotamia, who can dream, imagine, and speak out goodness and greatness, or rebellion and sin; beings who can envision today, what might be tomorrow, and who then can work to make that tomorrow--vision a concretized reality today. After creating the world and the natural order, God is depicted as sharing the divine self with these special beings who are made in God's image and likeness. God breathes into these creatures and makes them for God's purposes; and God begins this creative action in the region of Africa and Mesopotamia for a purpose.

Humankind originates in this region. Therefore, all humankind should have a great respect, and a sense of awe, for the *motherland* of us all.

God has placed us in the context of a lush and exciting world; God made humankind so that we might see, experience and enjoy the cosmos, the Garden of Eden, other people and beings, and the layout of the world, as we enjoy the visiting presence and life of God. The God portrayed in the Hebrew scriptures is not one who is so lonely and desperate, that God *had to* create humanity to be complete. In divine freedom, and mystery, God is depicted as the One who desires to *share* God's image and authority with creatures made in God's image, as a selfless act, which benefits the human creation. In God's freedom, we were made to reflect God's image in a world of wonder, amazement, and even evil and danger. We were made to have dominion over the good and the bad --- an authoritative and caretaking presence over everything on the planet, because, like no other terrestrial creatures, we can imagine dreams and then, consciously, plan to fulfill those dreams as we honor our Creator. Out of the warm region of North Africa and the Middle East, we were made to be the original gardeners, lovingly tending to all that God had envisioned and spoken into existence; as we too learn to envision, speak, and create.

I believe that in various ways, my friends and I, when we were teens and young adults with hungry and thirsty eyes, we were unconsciously, and misguidedly trying to reconnect with this original vision of humanity's potential and purpose for being placed on this planet; we were looking for that mysterious and *exciting something* which we thought would help satisfy our vision quests for purpose, authority, excitement, creativity, and beauty. As we ambled about Rush Street, and the unformed terrain of our lives, we wanted to be a part of something/Someone larger – something/Someone who would make our hearts come alive and give us a purpose to which we could aspire. Trips to the crowded Rush street, and places like it, were our best irreligious attempts to see and connect with all of the exciting aspects and benefits of the expansive, diverse, beautiful and fun gifts inherent in God's creation; in other words, without God, *we were trying to explore and enjoy creation, its content, and all of its novel and exciting potential, to the fullest.* Little did we know, we were fishing in the wrong pond, and looking through a window facing a wall. In just a few years, I would discover that it is through God's gracious self-disclosure and the act of gazing upon the divine image (via meditating on God's nature, actions, wonders, miracles, teachings, testimonies, and promises, as revealed through the scriptures), and by following God's leadings in the world, through the Spirit, as we worship, fellowship, love, play, plan, create, evangelize, engage in charity and justice work, and love some more, that we are eventually empowered to see more clearly, the beauty and excitement of God's genius. And as we gaze upon God, we are affected and influenced. It is through the multi-faceted, biblically rooted image of God's creative and redeeming presence at work in the world, that our hearts can begin to be lifted, and our talents used to re-create the Beloved Community. How? As we peer into the window of the divine image, we also see a reflection of our potential, and the potential of our world – our eyes are opened in the best sense.

Contemplating and meditating on the love, creativity, generosity, diversity and holiness of God is a profound enough consideration to hold our attention, and to spur us on to acts of loving service. There is a sense in which when we *see* the essence of God; the essence of who God is, and what God is about; and when we do, not only do we see immeasurable goodness, beauty, and amazement, beyond description, but we also simultaneously get a glimpse of our best selves (because we have been made in God's image), and our worst selves (because we are sinners). When we perceive God through Scripture and in nature, initially we should be inspired and awe-struck, but also utterly overwhelmed and astonished, like the Prophet Isaiah was in Isaiah 6. When we have an epiphany of the purity and glory of God's love and God's intentions, we also then clearly see ourselves – our true motives, shady dealings, and selfish intentions. Isaiah was not necessarily horrified by the awesomeness of God, but of the image of himself, after seeing God. In contrast to a vision of God's profound beauty and holiness, Isaiah saw himself as wretched, in need of emergency help! The good news is that after this epiphany, cleansing, healing, and inspiration come to Isaiah, and Isaiah becomes one of the most remarkable "seers" in all of history, and he helps change his society and our world, for the better.

When we initially encounter God, we are overwhelmed by God's holiness, and completely underwhelmed by our pettiness and lack of holiness. Such revelations of God, over against ourselves, aided by the gift of repentance, can move us from self-dread, to launching us toward powerful and promising future possibilities. Moved by a compelling vision of God, God's movement in the world, and our redeemed selves, we are then freed up, along with a vast sea of other seers, to speak with creative authority against the dream-dashing forces of spiritual darkness. With God in sight, through the mediums of God's Word and Spirit, we become glorious actors, in the drama of life, surrounded by others who have historically occupied the stage, long before us. Along with a great cloud of witnesses, both historical and contemporary, we become visionaries, and spiritual conduits of the ever living, ever moving, Spirit; witnessing how God is moving to change the world, as we sing our terrestrial and celestial music of praise, while running toward victory against forces of evil resistance, is the task at hand.

The sad thing about all of this is that many people, much older than we were as late teens and young adults, seem to go through life never desiring to see, or chase this kind of vision – a vision of our Creator, the loveliness of creation, and the truth about who we were created to be. Far too many seem satisfied to only witness and peer at what we were looking for when we were young adults -- a vision of empty, glitter and glitz; a place of lights and shadows, represented by what's found in a nightclub district, like that one located in 1980s Chicago.

This lack of hunger for greater and more substantive visions, might point to the problem of a church which sometimes seems to have not seen God. If the church is blind; blinded by dead religious traditions and congregational and denominational infighting and politics, then how can the church articulate and show that which is awesome and compelling about God? If the church is suffering from myopia, then how can the church paint a picture that attracts others to God's beatific Kingdom? But in spite of these questions, irrepressibly, God keeps working to reveal the glorious truth of God's love, holiness, and creativity, to both seekers and to those who do not seem to have a clue.

The Most Profound Epiphany Begins with Seeing Christ

In the common Greek of the first century (Koine Greek), the word *epiphainein* means to have a vision or revelation of God. In Jewish and Christian thought and writings, God is revealed as the initiator of all visions of God; human beings are on the receiving end of what God initiates. God chooses to disclose God's presence and nature, through God's word. It is a vision given by virtue of The Word. We do not merit God's self- disclosure; we cannot force God to disclose to us Who God is, but in love, for God's purposes, God chooses to do so; in God's freedom and love, God elects to speak to us. Throughout the sacred texts of scripture, God reveals God's presence and power to women, men, boys and girls, who cry out for God's saving presence (and even to those who are not searching for God). In each instance of divine revelation, Yahweh (the One Whom Jesus calls *The Father*) is manifested only when Yahweh chooses to condescend and show out and up. Thankfully, God has promised to do so, when our hearts cry out in earnest for God. But even in our crying out, we cannot shout loud enough, or climb mountains high enough to see God; We can't dance hard enough, or clap loud enough, or shout passionately enough, or fast and pray long enough, or practice dead religious rituals earnestly enough to force God to do what we want God to do. But the great news which shouts from our Judeo-Christian heritage is that the One True God is precisely the kind of God who *desires* to be known by us. Jesus reveals One to us Who wants us to ask, seek, knock, and find (Matthew 7:7). God is seeking those who are open, even in small ways, to the revelation of God. The One True God is the kind of God Who *desires* to reveal God's Self to a broad diversity of peoples – a throng of witnesses of all racial and cultural backgrounds; the despised and rejected, as well as the empty and disaffected; persons who were once liars and cheaters; sex addicts and drug merchants; abusers and misusers, but who, because of grace and visions, are made priests, poets, community organizers, dream architects, community guardians, benefactors, liberators and prophets – all witnesses of God and God's reigning presence in the earth! In the Beatitudes[5] Jesus said that the pure in heart will see God. God purifies us as we meditate on God's visions for humanity and creation, which are revealed in God's word.

The Biblical record testifies that the God revealed to the Patriarchs,

---

[5] The beatitudes are a set of principles which lead to a state of blessedness that Jesus said people would enjoy if they practiced or manifested eight characteristics or principles that are connected to the kingdom of God. These statements of the Lord, if put into practice, will assure a state of peace and joy before God; they are found in the Sermon on the Mount, as depicted in Matthew's Gospel, beginning in chapter 5.

Moses, Joshua, and all of God's prophets, is the One True God – the God who desires to cut covenants with us. Through miracles and strong acts of love, Yahweh is Whomever Yahweh desires to be *for us* – and thanks be to God, Yahweh desires to be our covenant keeping Helper! Yahweh is the Great *I Am*, a very present Help in a time of trouble. Yahweh is the Most-High, the One Who is always at work to save, liberate, and lift us up. Many rappers can be heard in various songs describing how they are *too high* above their competition to be *"seen."* This is just lyrical bragging and verbal posturing and posing, but Yahweh is so awesomely immanent and truly transcendent, that in truth we cannot fully *see* Yahweh's *full glory* and live to tell it. Fully seeing God, in our flesh, would be a dangerous, if not an all together fatal enterprise; and yet, because of God's desire to be known, God allows us to catch accurate *glimpses* of God's glory (seeing through a glass darkly), like in the case of Moses, as he was shielded in the cleft of the rock, as God passed by. Gentiles, pagans, minorities, teens, single mothers, construction workers, convenience store cashiers, dope addicts, prostitutes, those enslaved by human traffickers, and incarcerated mothers and fathers have all been enraptured, elevated and transformed, at the core by seeing God. Why? Because God is transcendent and immanent love, which means God's love blows our minds, and yet, it is conceivable and comforting to the human heart.

The wonderful news is that this chasm, which has prevented our visual perception of God, has been removed in Christ, and he has opened up the way to God, forever. The message of the book of Hebrews is that for at least the last two millennia, God has chosen to decisively and emphatically reveal the Divine presence of Yahweh, in Jesus Christ of Nazareth, the Son, the ultimate High Priest, through whom **we see the face and heart of God**. *In Christ, young and old alike, can see God as Holy love - the creative, suffering, nature-commanding, demon-expelling, sickness-healing, sin-forgiving, soul-liberating, and covenant- keeping Presence, who desires to reconcile and restore us.*

In the Son, who died while forgiving us, and rose to love and empower us, we have the hope of everlasting life. Through the Holy Spirit, prayer and frequently visiting the Gospel narratives, the New Testament Epistles, and the First Testament stories; and through reaching out to serve and love our neighbors, we have unfettered access to the image and presence of God!

It is a vision so astounding in its love-brilliance, holiness, and humility, that it leaves all other visions in the shadows; its luminosity becomes more and more brilliant as we study, obey, serve and gaze upon the Lord, again and again, through the written, preached, and spoken testimonies which point to God's glory. And mysteriously, the more we are strengthened in our faith and vision, the more we begin to also see God in the faces of those who walk through life with us and around us – especially the vulnerable.

The writer of Hebrews, in the book's opening chapter, says that in times past, God gave epiphanies of the divine image to certain faith ancestors. Historically, beginning with Noah, Nimrod, Abraham, various patriarchs and matriarchs, elders, judges, preachers, prophets, and law-givers, God would give glimpses of God's will at work through the Jewish people, in a variety of ways - through flood-proof arks of salvation and rainbow covenants, through miracles and Exoduses from slavery, through rituals of circumcision, and through the Mosaic Law and fastidious systems of animal sacrifices. But the author goes on to note that in these last times, looking back from the vantage point of the cross and an empty tomb, the Messiah has come through the Jewish people, as *a gift for all people*! God has chosen to reveal Himself, most clearly, through the One, *"…whom God appointed heir of all things, through whom also He made the worlds"* (Hebrews 1:2). Jesus has now been revealed, to young and old, black and white, wealthy and impoverished, as the image of the invisible God - merciful, yet holy; gentle, but at times exacting; wildly creative, yet economic; disciplined, yet quick to improvise; willing to suffer and die for creation, while being Lord over that same creation; One who is speaking, and calling others to take part in the task of spreading the vision of God, by bearing witness, with all our faculties and energies to the goodness of God. This call has marked the lives of those considered the best among us – The North African patriarchs, Tertullian, Clement of Alexandria, Origen of Alexandria, Augustine of Hippo; and those who furthered this African Christianity, like Frederick Douglass, Harriet Tubman, Mary McCloud Bethune, William J. Seymour, Rev. Vernon Johns, Mahalia Jackson, Dr. Martin L. King, Rev. Jessie L. Jackson, Bishop T.D. Jakes, Bishop Vashti Mckenzie, Dr. Tony Evans, Professors Cornel West, and Michael Eric Dyson; and other popular figures from the world of entertainment to politics like Jill Scott, Common, hoop genius Stephen Curry, and of course, First Lady, Michelle, and President Barak Obama. Our challenge as promoters and godly curators of the vision of the reign of God, is to keep our sights and focus on the Lord.

This is the closing message of the writer of Hebrews, beginning in chapter 12. After going to great lengths throughout the epistle, to explain how old visions of God have served their purposes for the Jewish people, the writer explains that God was expanding God's revelation and doing a new thing in Christ, for both Hebrew and Gentile:

> Therefore we also, since we are surrounded by so great a
> cloud of witnesses, let us lay aside every weight, and the sin
> which so easily ensnares us, and let us run with endurance
> the race that is set before us, *looking unto Jesus*, the author
> and finisher of our faith... (Italics mine, Hebrews 12:1-2a)

These words remain instructive for those of us who desire to be a part of something greater than ourselves – a part of a grateful and praising sea of black, white, Asian, and Hispanic, humanity; all caught up in a lively, compelling vision of faith, hope, and love, inspired by the presence, power, and personality of Jesus. Dietrich Bonhoeffer, the German pastor, and theologian, who died as a martyr - one who was one of the key leaders of Germany's Confessing Church Movement, and of a resistance movement which had plotted against the fulfillment of Hitler's vision of Germany - wrote a book entitled, *Christ the Center*. In it, he discusses how Christ, who is God's Word, is found in the church and in the sacraments; and how Christ is the center of Human Existence, History, and the relationship between God and Nature.[6] He says in a variety of ways that Christ, as God's word, personified, is both the center and the boundary of our existence, at every level. These claims mirror the biblical witness. For example, in the book of Revelation, chapter 22, Christ reveals himself to be Alpha and the Omega, the First and the Last of all that pertains to life and godliness.

Upon reflection, based on my limited experience, and on what I know

---

[6] Dietrich Bonhoeffer, *Christ the Center: A New Translation* (New York, NY: Harper & Row paperback edition, 1978), pp. 49-65

of God's word, I would have to concur with Jesus' self- description and Bonhoeffer's assessment and conclusions. Why? Because, at a personal level, I have found that there *ain't* nobody quite like Jesus, except the Father, the Spirit, and the church, when at its best! Also, through the powers of observation, I have noted that those who scoff at Jesus' teachings; and those who base their lives on something or someone other than God's revelation through Christ, lack a certain love ethic, and a sustaining hope that lasts beyond the cemetery. Only the resurrected, alive, and speaking Jesus can give a black teenager in Chicago, as well as a white senior in a nursing home in Appalachia, a lasting vision of hope, purpose and meaning beyond the ghetto, the cabin, the trailer park, and the grave. And the way we commonly "look" to this Jesus is by study, confession, praise and prayer; by filling our minds and hearts with the written testimonies of his story and glory - testimonies written by those who walked with him, talked with him, and died, not denying the veracity of their claims. Most powerfully, we look to Jesus, in the process of walking out what we have prayed and contemplated through the inspiration of the written and sung word. In other words, we see Him best, as we follow Him, as witnesses, and as servants of the Lord and humanity. As we silently gaze upon the accounts of healings, teachings and parables, miracles, acts of forgiveness; as we listen to Bible-based, Christ-centered teaching and preaching, with ears and eyes of faith, and hearts ready to obey; as we roll up our sleeves to place our hands in the dirt of helping to lift our sisters and brothers, Jesus shows up in our souls, imaginations, and actions, day after day, and year after year; and his showing up is no mere optical illusion.

As an eighteen-year-old, not long after I had just started making my epicurean excursions to Rush Street, *I saw Jesus, for myself!* On April 28, 1984, during a crisis moment in my life, hours after drinking brandy and smoking marijuana - with my heart pounding uncontrollably and my mind racing in a panic; with my soul in terror and turmoil, as I thought I was nearing death – I heard *a word* which seemed to come directly from heaven's throne! Through this experience, I was enabled to hear and envision a speaking, loving, and saving Lord. This word came through the preaching of the gospel of Jesus Christ, on a television program, about two o' clock in the morning, as I was gripped by drug-heightened fear and panic. The Lord spoke specific words to me, captured in John 14:27;

words about how God could give peace and calm my troubled heart; and the preacher continued to talk about how God could help anyone who was searching for tranquility, peace, love, forgiveness, and acceptance, through God's unconditional love in Christ. With heart pounding and fears raging, I cried out, "Lord help me to believe, what I am hearing!" After this desperate prayer, it was as if I was given the ability to believe what previously seemed unbelievable, unrealistic, and undesirable. For the first time, I *really heard* preaching about Jesus Christ and truly *saw* what was being conveyed about Christ. After catching this initial glimpse of Him, and after years of developing the practice of gazing upon His luminous majesty through contemplating the scriptures, I have found nothing else to be as compelling, soothing, and challenging as the person or call of Jesus Christ – no disco light, no club crowd, no throngs of people-watchers in beautiful cars, nothing! Indeed, when we open ourselves up to gazing upon the beauty of our Creator, as revealed in the sacred scriptures, the Lord becomes the light of the world!

Study Questions

1. As you review your life, can you track what you have spent most of your energies viewing and pursuing? What tends to draw your attention and gaze?

2. What visions have you had about your past and your future? What roles have these visions played in your present status?

3. What kind of places and events are you really attracted to? Concerts? Parties in nightclubs? City parks? Business Conferences? Art galleries? Sorority and Fraternity events? Academic endeavors – lectures, libraries, philosophical debates?

4. Read chapter 1, of Genesis. Write down how you envision the emerging creation – was it a fast process, or a slow process? What descriptive words come to your mind? What words would you use to describe the creative personality of God?

5. Read Hebrews, chapters 1 and 12. Write down traits about Jesus that the author describes. What do you find amazing and attractive about Christ? What do you find puzzling?

6. As you think about many of the sermons that you might have heard, jot down what kind of impressions you've been left with as you listened to them - good or bad.

7. The Bible claims that Yahweh became flesh, in Jesus Christ; and that Jesus is the expressed image of the invisible God. Read through one of the Gospels. If you had to describe your ideas in just a few words, how would you describe your overall picture of Jesus/God?

8. How have you responded to whatever epiphanies of God you have had? What are you doing with the vision of Jesus we have been allotted via the Scriptures?

2. Searching like the Magi

When they saw the star, they rejoiced with exceedingly great joy. And when they had come into the house, they saw the young Child with Mary His mother, and fell down and worshiped Him. And when they had opened their treasures, they presented gifts to Him: gold, frankincense, and myrrh. Then, being divinely warned in a dream that they should not return to Herod, they departed for their own country another way.

(Matthew 2:10-12)

When I was in High School, there was a popular dance song that was released by a group called, *Unlimited Touch*; the song was entitled, *Searching to Find the One*. It was a record, often mixed and blended with other dance songs, using a technique that was growing popular in certain urban Disc Jockey circles, that allowed for music to play continuously at parties without any breaks between records. This genre of musical magic, known as "mixing," took flight in the late 70s and early 80s, in many large cities located on the East Coast and in the Midwest. The mixing of soul records, European imports, and techno dance music by creative

DJs, eventually gave birth to the earliest forms of House Music[7] which were popularized on radio stations, and in dance clubs in northern cities like Chicago, Detroit, Philadelphia and New York. The popularity of this music reached its meteoric peak during the mid-to-late eighties, until the early nineties. Like countless songs from this category of music, *Searching to Find the One*, had an infectious and danceable beat that would make the most novice dancer want to move and groove to its strong, soulful, pulsating, rhythms. The lyrics of the song told a story. They depict a woman's search for a soulmate; her ultimate, and ideal man. The song says:

> *Gotta keep on, Gotta be strong when you're searching, searching to find the one. Searching to find someone that's strong, someone that'll really turn me on; And I've been searching like this for quite some time; And up till now no one has blown my mind...*

I believe these lyrics capture what many people are doing as they amble through life; they are searching to find the ideal person; the ideal experience; someone, or something, worthy of our deepest commitments. Nothing highlights this fact more than the ritual many of us initiate each new year. At the beginning of each year, with Hanukah, Christmas, and Kwanzaa behind us, and our New Year's resolutions before us, many of us are excited and spurred on to search out ways to improve our souls, bodies, money, and relationships. Each year we begin to search for *the better*, whatever meaning *the better* might hold for each of us. These impulses, which often push us to take steps to improve ourselves, seem to intensify with the anticipation of a coming new year. We are motivated to start new diets, initiate new saving plans, begin new exercise regimens, change our

---

[7] House Music is a genre of dance music which reached the zenith of its popularity in Chicago, in the early 80s to early 90s, and is experiencing a bit of a resurgence in certain places all over the world. In the late 70s, at a Chicago dance club called, "The Warehouse," Frankie Knuckles, a DJ who originally hailed from New York, began mixing a style of dance music which had disco, disco-soul, new wave, Electronic dance, Italian-Disco, Philly-Soul, and Gospel building blocks. The kind of music played at The Warehouse became affectionately known as "House Music." In the U.S., it remains popular among middle- aged black, Latino, and Italian adults in Chicago, Detroit, Atlanta, Philadelphia, New York, and Miami. Abroad, it is played in clubs in London, France, Germany, and in various places in Asia and Africa.

negative attitudes, and even search for new, meaningful, and satisfying relationships. Some of us embark on new adventures and we decide to enter the dating scene - so we start club-hopping, or we join an on-line dating site; or we begin attending certain churches where we think that there are a wide range of eligible bachelors and bachelorettes, in attendance. Others of us are not interested in searching for new relationships, but we are searching for ways to rid ourselves of old problematic ones; some use the start of a new year to begin to cut off all toxic relationships; the dysfunctional "love" connections and strained friendships that have kept us ensnared.

It is a common practice, in our American culture, to begin each new year strategizing how we are going to better run the race of life; and for some, each beginning of a new year, sends them into a searching frenzy. With these New Year's resolutions, we sometimes rush about our Januaries, into our Februaries, with our new plans and goals rolled up and tucked away under our arms, like a neat collection of blueprints for how we can better construct healthy souls. These efforts point to the all too human, and sometimes unconscious search for self-fulfillment, with a healthy dose of the need to secure the approval of others, tossed in for good measure.

Our New Year's resolutions often indicate that we are searching for ways to be better, to experience the better, and to be viewed as better. Over a twenty-year period, I can remember the many times, at the beginning of a new year, I told myself that I would get into shape to play basketball the way I did in my early twenties. I would diet, eating only soup and salad; I would get on the treadmill to burn off the calories; and once spring came, I would jog outside. But by the late spring, it always seemed an injury would occur; or some other task would take precedence; or the flu or a bad cold, would interrupt my new-found exercise and workout flow, and soon I would find myself, back where I had started, weight and stamina wise. By the time I reached my mid-forties, something shifted. When a new year would approach, I realized that something within me had changed. I had discovered something new – I had discovered peace, and self-acceptance, even though I was twenty-five pounds heavier than my twenty-year old self; I accepted that I was also a knee surgery and torn Achilles tendon away from my twenty-year old self. Consequently, I would never dunk a basketball, on a regulation height rim again this side of glory, and it was finally okay. Instead of making beginning- of- the- year resolutions to become healthier, I decided to live healthier year around. So, I gave up the relentless search for a radical, beginning- of- the- year change, and I gradually changed my entire diet, and incorporated a steady exercise routine, that I practice to this day.

Black folk in this country have had a particularly tough time learning how to accept themselves and how to receive the acceptance of others, because we have often been rejected, harassed, hunted and haunted by the dehumanizing effects of white supremacy and racism. As a consequence, internalized racism and a relentless sense of inferiority have become the perennial companions of black folk. Many of us have discovered that racism, in all its forms, can be a hard task master on the spirit and soul. For many African Americans, given our very difficult history in this country, when these annual efforts of searching for better relationships, and our better and best selves, are not centered in God, and or are not realized, they inadvertently, and ironically, become the very factors which deepen our levels of dissatisfaction, depression and self-rejection. An unfulfilled search can damage an already wounded soul.

I have learned and witnessed that a failure to find self-love and self-fulfillment, in God's agape' love, can lead black folk (all folk for that matter) through a wilderness of barren and dry deserts, as well as through thick concrete places of the soul, where we discover we have become hardened, confused, lost, unfulfilled, unaccomplished, and unsatisfied. When this happens, we become vulnerable to destructive elements; in a sense, we can feel exposed and left naked before the principalities and powers of evil. Exposure to these earthy, earthly, and sometimes cosmic creatures, who master in duplicity and subterfuge, can leave us in great psychological, and emotional danger. The devil and his minions know how to twist the knife of a disappointing failure into our unclothed souls. Many hope-filled romantic relationships which have started with much heavenly promise in January, end up in hellish jeopardy by June. The co-worker, the deacon, the fellow committee worker at church, with whom we took a risk at friendship, to whom we opened ourselves up to in February - by May, has already betrayed our fragile trust. Consequently, with our budding relationships quickly revealed to be on precarious foundations; or with diets-gone-bad and forsaken, and exercise routines forgotten; with no promotions offered to us at the job, after we worked for it, named it and claimed it; sometimes only six months into the year, we can come to the unsettling and disillusioning reality that we just might have to start over, scrapping former plans and hopes. We conclude that we will try harder to muster up and marshal our will power and energies, again and again, in attempts to discover a modicum of the self-love, unconditional acceptance, for which we began searching in earnest at the start of the year.

Youth are not immune to discovering this hard truth about the kind of disappointment one experiences when one has earnestly searched for and sought out fulfillment, acceptance, meaning and love, only to find all that the heart was seeking, was an illusion. In cities and suburbs all over this country, many young black, poorer white, and Hispanic teens, join their first gang or neighborhood clique, or prostitution ring, as they search out to fulfill an inner quest for connection, and unconditional love. Unfortunately, many shoot their first weapons, turn their first tricks, take their first drinks, or have their first hit of weed, or even rock cocaine, as they attempt to satisfy the hunger, thirst, and quest for meaning and adventure. Many young people are surrounded by a sea of other young searchers who are looking for satisfying revelations. But in far too many cases, the search turns bad, and many people are hurt in the process; their trust is severed; criminal record files grow larger; and addiction, death, and jail, become the tragic triplets --unwanted partners in a turbulent and sad life. This terrible trek downward happens outside of the narrow precincts of our inner cities, and large suburbs, as well. In smaller towns, and in rural America, far too many disaffected white and affluent black youth are unconsciously searching for a cause or an experience that is thrilling and fulfilling. In efforts to discover and corral *it,* whatever *it* is, they turn to materialism, nihilism, paganism, illicit drugs and promiscuous and dangerous sexual behavior. Without much parental guidance, village-wisdom, ecclesiastical input, or spiritual rooting, they quickly become lost. In the absence of the long-established institutions and structures of true community – the home, schools, churches, synagogues, mosques, community centers, places of employment, and a vibrant and exciting relationship with something (really, Someone) larger than the individual self – our thirst for authentic love and meaning remain unfilled, and our searching continues, until our dying days.

As humans, we demonstrate in our annual attempts to improve ourselves, and our continuing struggle to know love, and to realize, what my former seminary professor would call, "a sense of *somebodyness*"[8]; which we hope will heal our deepest pathologies and failures. This, anchoring of the soul, can only be found in our Creator; the only being who will challenge us to rise above our deepest and most sinful predilections and grant us a love that will comfort us when we don't achieve righteousness the way that we had hoped we would have. God is the one who offers us a love that will correct and corral us, even when we are off target and miss the mark. It is because we desire this kind of love, that we sometimes desperately cling to those persons - like a godly momma, uncle, deacon, prayer partner, lover or coach - who seem to offer a modicum of what the Greeks called, *agape. This, above all else is what we are searching for.* Unconsciously, we crave it all the time, and when pushed beyond the brink because of a agape love-deprivation, we will sometimes act foolishly, decadently, salaciously, reprehensibly, and desperately, in efforts to grasp at a facsimile of it. With this in mind, a critical question arises: How do we properly channel this strong impulse to search for self-fulfillment, and being loved unconditionally, so that in our searching we do not end up with singed hearts and embittered souls?

The Magi reveal something important to us about the journey of trying to locate the true subject and object of our inner longings and hopes, in Matthew, chapter 2. There is a message in the text for all of us who are searching for self-fulfillment, and the promise of agape love. In the text, we have a cadre of first century astrologers who were on a journey of divine revelation and self-discovery. For years, in other situations, the Magi had studied the celestial bodies - the planets and stars. They had practiced their skills and arts to satisfy their curiosity, and to discern great political and spiritual machinations that were happening in and beyond

---

[8] A term I first thought originated with the "I am somebody" statements of Rev. Jessie Jackson. I eventually discovered that the term had an earlier origin. My seminary Professor, Garth Baker-Fletcher, in lectures and in his book, *Somebodyness: Martin Luther King Jr. and the Theory of Human Dignity* (New York: Fortress, 1993), revealed an antecedent use. Through Dr. Baker-Fletcher, I learned that the term was used by King to the describe a human dignity that is not based on our social status; *somebodyness* represents the fundamental human dignity that is given to us by God. In speeches, King said that his sense of somebodyness was a gift from loving parents.

the borders of their country. Their reputations now preceded them. They were famous for their abilities to discern the sky and solve omens. Their latest search, orchestrated by Herod, centered on locating the greatest hope for the world --God's Messiah!

Who were these magi? They were part political, and part religious, advisors; they were part fortune teller and root worker – they were something akin to the West African "doctors" of magic, who solved enigmas, and riddles; who interpreted dreams and functioned as the arbiters of physical healing. Like the African healers, the Magi were an important part of the cultural and spiritual landscape of Mesopotamia, and in Northern, and Eastern Africa. More than anything, they were serious searchers; and in their research of the Hebrew Scriptures, as they gazed at the heavens, they had finally seen something that piqued their curiosity and fueled their imaginations beyond previous quests; there was a star in the Eastern Sky! They tell King Herod that they had seen a bright star. This was the fulfillment of prophetic declarations, astrological musings, and theological possibilities - the Messiah, the King, would be born soon! Unbeknownst to the Magi, King Herod is chomping at the bit to locate the one who was prophesied to be the ultimate divine-human ruler, that he might kill the Child, before the he can reach the height of his powers. After they make their long arduous trek in the light of the Eastern Star, they observe that it is positioned over Bethlehem. They search Bethlehem, until directly under the beautiful bright orb in the sky, they find a young family: Joseph, Mary, and a very young Jesus. The Magi's journey had been long and taxing, but they were propelled forward by hearts which hungered for a beneficial truth. Often, the same is true for us as we search for meaning, purpose, love, and God.

As the Magi anticipate their exciting encounter with the young King, they come into His presence bearing valuable gifts. They had prepared themselves for this moment. The Magi, out of honor and profound respect, show their submission to the royal one of Israel. They bring expensive gold, frankincense and myrrh. These oblations are a most appropriate response of gratitude and honor. Whenever we encounter love, grace, and mystery, embodied in a personal presence, it seems natural to the human soul to give the very best that we have, in return. This fact can be understood via the substance and symbolism we know is dramatized every time we hear of men falling on one knee, with ring in hand, to propose marriage to a woman in whom they have found their ideal embodiment of beauty, love, hope, and even a kind of salvation. In western culture, the proposing suitor is willing to offer a circular trinket made for his loved one's finger, because he is hopeful and grateful about the possibility of actualizing his ideal love. This notion of offering up that which we value most, as a token of our love and commitment, is what we do when we have been captivated by a presence or an idea which ignites the love/lust fires of our souls. Once we have found what/whom we were seeking – like finding a pearl of great price – nothing is too valuable to give up, in exchange for it.

This text opens the door to the rest of the gospel narrative about Jesus' extraordinary calling and ministry to save the created order through His dynamic power and compassionate presence and salvation mission. In some rudimentary way, the Magi had recognized that they had found that one person who would be able to redeem and rightly judge Israel, the Gentiles, and the entire world. For a few moments, through a simple act of worship, they impacted the young Christ, and were in turn impacted by His mysterious presence, even though he was just a child. What they offered would be recorded in history. This experience foretells of the way God was now making Godself available, to not only the Jews, but also to *searching* Gentiles, who were looking for God; and it also foretells of how we ought to respond, in heart-felt gratitude, when we have finally found (and been discovered by) the Messiah.

Consciously and unconsciously, we are all on a lifelong journey of searching for meaning, hope, recognition, satisfaction, and love. As you consider your journey, what does the trajectory of your life say about that for which you have been searching the most? As you reflect upon your most passionate pursuits and your most unfulfilling efforts, about what have you been the most tenacious? Self-improvement and self-discovery? Money? Health? Power? Sex and Sensuality? The testimony of the Magi, and of the great heroes and heroines of our faith is that the most exciting, daring, and ultimately satisfying search of all, involves pursuing the One whose ways are knowable, yet also thoroughly inexhaustible; whose love and wisdom are graspable, but also beyond full human comprehension.

The Magi, being warned by God of Herod's evil intentions for the young Messiah, left their encounter with the Lord, instructed by God to go home a different pathway. This is often what is the consequence of our searching and finding God; *God transforms us through our searching and our finding!* Once transformed, we will find that as we make our way home, and begin to rely on familiar pathways, God will move us to leave the familiar so that we might take an entirely different pathway home; one not considered or understood before. Thanks be to God!

Study Questions

1. Have you ever made and tried to keep a New Year's resolution? What kind of success have you had?

2. Have you ever failed to keep a promise that you made, or a goal that you had for yourself? When you failed to achieve, or succeed, did you brush yourself off, and quickly recommit to the effort? If not, why not? If you did, why did you?

3. As you think about your life up to this point, what have you been pursuing? The perfect relationship? A better career? A healthier body? Better mental health?

4. The Magi were in pursuit of the Messiah after King Herod secured their services. Do you think this was the only reason why they were searching for the Messiah?

5. When they finally locate the Child Messiah, they bring offerings to him. Why is it important to express gratitude when you finally find what you had been searching for? How important do you think such expressions of thanksgiving are to God? Should this be important to us?

3. Uniting with God: Our Mission at United

Jesus said to her, "Woman believe Me, the hour is coming when you will neither on this mountain, nor in Jerusalem, worship the Father…But the hour is coming, and now is, when the true worshipers will worship the Father in spirit and truth; for the Father is seeking such to worship Him. God is Spirit, and those who worship Him must worship in spirit and truth."

(Selected verses from John 4:21-24)

Not that I have already attained, or am already perfected; but I press on, that I may lay hold of that for which Christ Jesus has also laid hold of me….I press toward the goal for the prize of the upward call of God in Christ Jesus.

(Selected verses from Philippians 3:12-14)

*Note: A shorter version of this pastoral reflection was shared three Januarys ago in a Sunday's bulletin, with the hope of reminding our congregation, at the beginning of the year, about one of the important tenets contained in our congregation's Mission Statement, part of which says: *"The Mission of The United Christian Church of Detroit is to Unite People with God through our Worship…"*

As a boy, I remember attending worship with my mother and sisters; and as I did, I would imagine the Spirit of God, floating and hovering in the sanctuary, above the worshipers. From the church's balcony, I would look up to the wooden rafters of the sanctuary of the Park Manor Christian Church of Chicago, and as I would look down at the preaching preacher and the singing choir, I would imagine God's Spirit hovering over all of the liturgical happenings that were taking place. In whatever underdeveloped notion I had of God, I pictured and visualized God as being "up there" somewhere – even hovering above us, cloaked in God's perfection and invisibility. In moments like those, I felt that we were all united under the gaze of God.

When we have a strong inclination to unite with the Spirit of God, via worship that inspires, motivates, and offers gratitude, this inclination is what scholars call "the religious impulse." Since the dawn of human history, settled tribes and wandering nomads, field shepherds, farmers and city dwellers, despotic rulers and humble servants, have given themselves over to this impulse. In most of our known religions, men and women have sacrificed animals, sung, danced and preached, wept and meditated, because they were overwhelmed with a desire to worship and please their concept of God and the gods. One of the earliest places where this notion of uniting with God and the gods would become manifest, would be among those of various tribal communities as they gathered outdoors, amidst the earthiness of nature; under the sun, moon, and stars, *on the tops of hills and mountains*, with crudely, or elaborately, constructed altars and temples. In ancient and modern religions all over the globe, from Africa, to the Fertile Crescent, to the Americas, to Europe, to Asia, people have sought to observe their religious traditions in the high places.

It has been believed, especially in pagan religions, and in Greek Mythology, that the hills and mountains are the dwelling places of the gods. Hills and mountains were thought to be *the bridges and ladders between the heavens, where God, or the gods existed, and the muddy and green valley parts of the earth, where lesser beings lived.* Even in our Judeo-Christian heritage, as in the cases of Moses, and Mt. Sinai; and Jesus and the disciples on the Mt. of Transfiguration, there is a history of people communing with God in high places. Why is this the case, beyond the spatial element of a place which seems to hover between heaven and earth? It is in part because we seem to instinctively believe that God exists somewhere atop our mundane, and maddening existence down here. So, instead of looking down, when we pray in moments of desperation, with clenched fists, we tend to look and cry upward. We seem to possess an almost congenital inner knowing that directs us in our efforts to reach God by going upwards to God, because although periodically *God looks low,* we know that ultimately, *God sits high*! This *seeking God in the high places* kind of sensibility, reveals something about the psychology of human beings – that maybe we are innately aware of the existence of higher intelligences and levels of consciousness; and if/since this is so; if/since God/some higher power is our greatest and highest conception of reality, then it makes sense, in the physicality and psychology of who we are and how we perceive, to want to go to literal higher ground to connect with the highest being. Ancient and now abandoned temples, monuments, altars, mind altering mushrooms and poppies, leave a testifying witness to how human beings, for thousands of years, have worshipped God, or the gods, on elevated areas, with an elevated consciousness. These physical locations, when coupled with drug use, or deep meditation, have served as the psychological mirroring of our strong inner desire to reach and go up higher, in God-consciousness. In other words, I believe that at the heart of the matter, most seekers of God/ of some sort of higher consciousness, have had an innate sense that there is Someone/something above and beyond us that is transcendent; though, with this notion in our heads, we might also often feel and believe that God is immanent (present with us, and in us). But when push comes to shove, I think that those who remain open to God, still tend to believe and are convinced that God is also above and beyond us (enthroned in some notion of the highest heaven/paradise). Consequently, this sense of God being *up above us,* or higher than us (in holiness, in intelligence, in love, in power, and in immortality) causes us to keep reaching and building upward. This "god- impulse" has been manifested by many groups who have sought to worship God, in high hill and mountain spaces.

In John 4:21-24, Jesus challenges, and in many respects, upends a few aspects of this sort of theology and ideology. In a conversation with a Samaritan Woman, Jesus reveals that worshiping God in high places alone, is not the kind of worship that God considers as the most pleasing form of devotion. Jesus carefully explains to her, and us, that we have not been called to *go up* to God in order to sing and sacrifice on high hills and mountains, but instead we are challenged and coaxed by the Spirit to *grow inwardly*, in the Spirit of the Lord! This, Jesus says, begins to set forth the ingredients of true worship.

In Christ, God is calling all of us to go deeper in our faith and faithfulness. Those who worship, must worship in spirit and truth. To live lives that are filled with duplicity and deception. To sit in the highest balcony, in the tallest cathedral, with a soul that is truncated and dwarfed by selfishness, is to remain spiritually ensconced in a valley, and distant from the Lord. God is calling us to mature in our spiritual faithfulness, truthfulness, and spiritual perception, as we seek to fulfill the Lord's perfect will for us, our families, congregations, and communities.

This is what Paul intimates about our high calling in Christ, in Philippians 3:14. It is first a call that addresses our dedication to the Spirit of God. Paul wrote to the Christians in Philippi and encouraged them to always pursue their call to suffer and reign with Christ, as they lived and shared the gospel. Again, this upward call is inextricably tied to an inward journey. Ironically, Philippi was built on an elevated area where there were idolatrous temples and much idol worship. Paul explained to the Christians there that the high calling in Christ is not merely a calling to physical elevation, or a social status promotion, but it is a calling which includes deep suffering, along with high glory. God seeks and draws closer in intimacy to hearts that are obedient and open to God; such obedience requires self-denial and even draws persecution. From what is chronicled in the Holy writ, God is not as inclined to share God's secrets with a people, or persons, who are only striving to climb the ranks, and rungs, of our cultic rituals, for self-aggrandizing purposes. God wants us to learn from the love God shares with us, using that love as a catalyst to serve God, the community, and the stranger, even as such service causes pain and loss.

When a godly people are focused on the high religious impulse of worshiping God with our entire lives, as we acquaint ourselves with God's truth; as we live in that truth; as we also learn to be spirit-guided, spirit-empowered, spirit-encouraged, spirit-dependent, and spirit-inspired, then the sky is not even the limit of how high we can go up, and grow up, in spiritual maturity and Christ-likeness! The space between us and God is reduced, because God reduces it, when we seek to please God in Spirit and in truth. Consequently, we rise, not because we are standing in a physically, elevated place before God; or because we have been aided by hallucinogenic drugs; but we ascend because we have gone down deep with God. A well has been dug and shaped within us. Jesus says that it is only Spirit and truth worship that God desires of us. God desires us to worship not just with our mouths, songs, and with hand claps and stomping feet; God desires us to worship, not just on instruments of music, with an accompanying Pentecostal dance; but, God wants us to be passionate and authentic before God, when we leave our sanctuaries. When this kind of authenticity becomes the beat of our hearts, then the singing, shouting, dancing, praying, and the other liturgical staples we perform, have substance in God's sight. When our private and public worship become sincere liturgical acts of sacrificial living and giving meant to glorify God, eventually other people will be moved and become surprisingly curious about the One whom we are worshiping.

The Tower of Babel reveals what happens when a people are unified in trying to ascend to high places on their own terms. The narrator, in Genesis 11:4, says that the people of that region's climb upwards was not about exalting God, but they were actually engaging in self-worship, as they *sought to make a name for themselves*. In this ancient narrative, we are reminded again of how only God-centered, passionate and authentic worship, truly unites people over the long-haul. The builders of the tower are strangely unconcerned about God's desires, and God's perspective of their building project. They are busy with their construction plans, without consulting with their Creator. This project of self-worship ends in confusion and babbling. The writer says that the Spirit of God seems to descend to where the people are working and living in order to confuse the common language of the people. I believe that this was done not just to cease the development of the tower of self-worship, but also to save the people from the unattended results of their own self-destructive ambitions. The story of the Satan's limitless selfish ambition remains as a cautionary tale of how unlimited selfish ambition can lead to a fiendish, and an irrational chaos.

Our church's theme for the year, challenges us to unite with God through our passionate, and authentic worship of God. Jesus said to the

Samaritan Woman, and says to us, that God desires persons to worship God in spirit and truth. As our faith community worships God with spiritual passion and joy; coupled with an integrity rooted in the truth of God's word, then God will do something; God will touch the hearts of visitors and neighbors, so that they become inquisitive about God's work in, and through our congregation. This is how we unite people with God, through our corporate worship. This kind of God centered worship, is what will help us to climb "Jacob's ladder" together, not just as we ascend the stairs into the church house; not just as we step up into the pulpit and the choir loft; but also, as we step out of our sanctuaries to serve and help save a humanity which suffers in the valleys of sin and estrangement. If each of us will make serving and worshiping the Lord with integrity and honesty our primary goal, while also being passionately led by the wind and love-fire of the Spirit, then I believe that our members and guests will discover that we are ascending – not up to a literal hill top – but in the high calling of Christian ministry. As we worship God from our sanctuaries to our city streets, as we sing, shout and mentor; as we play drums and give groceries; as we dance, and as we demand justice for an impoverished community paying some of the highest car insurance premiums in the nation; I think that we will discover that "the plateau" upon which we now stand, is miles higher up from where we stood this same time, last year.

Study Questions

1. Do you think of God as being up there, somewhere? Is God the Man/Woman upstairs, for you? Is this the only way you conceptualize God' presence?
2. In John 4:21-24, why do you think Jesus challenges the Samaritan woman's assumption about how God was to be worshiped, only on a particular mountain?
3. What does Jesus teach her and us about true worship?
4. What is your understanding of spirit and truth worship? Can God enjoy the worship you offer, inside a sanctuary, as well as out in the park?
5. What does it mean to be authentic in the presence of God?
6. Paul teaches the believers in Philippians 3:14 that they have a high calling in Christ. Why do you think the Apostle describes their calling to fulfill their ministry, a "high calling?"
7. How are you engaged in answering the "high calling" God has on your life?

4. Vision: Next Level Ministry

Let love be without hypocrisy. Abhor what is evil, and cling to what is good...Do not be overcome by evil, but overcome evil with good.

(Romans 12:9,21)

Brethren, I do not count myself to have apprehended; but one thing I do, forgetting those things which are behind and reaching forward to those things which are ahead, I press toward the goal for the prize of the upward call of God in Christ Jesus.

(Philippians 3:13-14)

*NOTE: A shorter version of this pastoral reflection was originally shared in a Sunday's bulletin, on the day of my third pastoral anniversary (2015), held at the United Christian Church of Detroit. Prior to this three- year period of service, I had been the Interim Pastor of the congregation for a year. The purpose of this reflection was to give thanks to God and the congregation for their love; it was also to remind the congregation of our vision, as we worked toward fulfilling it; I discerned the need to call us together in love and unity, so that disunity would not thwart our work. As in the previous pastoral reflection, I employed Philippians 3:13-14, (Along with Romans 12:9, 21) to stir up our members' sense of a next level calling to fulfill our vision in the New Year. Unfortunately, with several new ministry initiatives beginning to flourish, we were also beginning to see evidences of disunity.

Wow! What a difference three years make! I praise God for allowing me to pastor one of the best churches on the west side of Detroit. We have not yet been perfected, but we are on an adventure with a good and glorious God; and as the older saints used to say, *"I wouldn't take nothing for my journey."* From prayer meetings, to praising God; from preaching to teaching; from vision planning, to fellowship dinners; from funerals to weddings; from counseling, to business meetings; through laughter and tears; through joyous days and sleepless nights, there have not been many dull moments over the last three years. I am privileged and blessed to serve as your Senior Pastor. I came here four years ago, not knowing any of you. For our first year, we planned and prayed together during my one-year tenure as your Interim Pastor. Since that time, I have gotten to know many of you very well; and with all of you, I have become acquainted on some level. My family and I have been blessed with a new spiritual family – our new home church family.

The covenantal commitment between a congregation, its pastor, and the pastor's family, is like a marriage. At the outset of most marriages there is an immediate zenith to the top of high and joyous emotions and experiences, but after the wedding cake is consumed and put away as a keepsake; after the honeymoon love and pleasures have been fully indulged, the real work of learning to be a couple, commences. In the process of becoming a unified partnership, there are highs and lows; elation and frustration; these are the vicissitudes of life and of marriage/ministry which can help make a union strong, if both parties are committed to being vessels of love, used by our Creator, to glorify Christ. I believe that United has made me a better and stronger black man, and stronger follower of Christ; and I hope that I have been used by the Master to help impart to you, through sermons, teachings, counsel, and friendship, the source of my strength.

If someone were to ask me, "Pastor Bryant, if you had it to do all over again, would you accept God's call to serve the United Christian Church of Detroit?" Without much hesitation, my answer would be a triune,

"Yes, I would…..Yes I would…..Yes I would!" You want to know why I would answer with such conviction? I would answer like this because I believe God called me to serve as your pastor for such a time as this in your history; and to borrow Pauline language, from Philippians 3:14, I believe it is an "upward call of God in Christ Jesus." After much prayer and listening, the way to Detroit was opened wide and decisively; and I am learning that whenever God opens a door of service, it is a high calling – a privilege not to be taken lightly. Secondly, I would answer again in the affirmative, not because the journey has always been easy; not because feathers have never been ruffled in the trenches of trying to exalt and give witness to Christ, and celebrate the best things God has deposited within African culture; not because things have gone *exactly* as I had envisioned, four years ago, but because God called me to serve a people I have grown to love; a people who have joined with me in God's upward call to exalt God, in the Cody Rouge neighborhood of Detroit. Together, in patience and in prayer, through much struggle, we are gradually *uniting with God, and going up to the next level!* This is our vision for this year, and overall, it is the main reason for which God has called you and me to be together this season. We have been linked together during this moment in time, to attempt to build up that which has been lacking in our fellowship and in our neighborhood. Like the Nehemiah of old, we have a great work in front of us, and we must not be distracted, detoured, or denied. We have been blessed to name, and then shore up our five main ministries/committees: Worship, Evangelism, Outreach, Fellowship, and Discipleship. To fulfill the call on us regarding our worship, we have met week after week, in regular services, special services, as we have praised, shouted, and preached ourselves into God's presence. To become evangelists, we have knocked on doors throughout the Cody Rouge neighborhood, sharing with our neighbors our testimonies of Jesus' goodness and the latest ministry events of our congregation. As part of our effort to disciple our youth, we have started a year-round mentoring ministry for those, ages 8 – 18, called *The Daughters of Imani*, and *The Young Lions*. Through comprehensive Black History programs and Kwanzaa celebrations, we have learned, taught, and remembered the good things God has done to liberate and celebrate our people. Through dinners and community movie nights, we have had great koinonia. And when our neighbors have needed food help, or when

our women's fellowship group has identified families and individuals with various needs, our outreach efforts have been noteworthy.

On behalf of the entire Bryant family, I thank you for the years you have blessed us in ways that have revealed the love of God; and I thank you for the years we have struggled together to live into a Nehemiah-like vision of erecting the kind of ministry which impacts our hurting neighborhood community. We have enjoyed three years of moderate, to rapid, numeric and spiritual growth; three years of service, patience and prayer. I realize that with these blessings, the devil comes to deceive and divide us so that we will end up cursing our own efforts. The last couple of months have challenged us to examine whether we have formed church cliques that keep newer members out; we have even had to ease tensions, after some very volatile disagreements among a few of our leaders. Sometimes these are simply the difficult growing pains of a growing congregation. I believe the forces of evil see the soul-winning, life-transforming, and community-changing potential of our church. I think it is time for us to pray, forgive, roll up our sleeves, and not be intimidated. Often, until God says it is time to move to new pastures, and vineyards, our challenge is to bloom where God has planted us. So, for now, let's make sure we are agents of love, and let's bloom where God has planted us! Let us till the ground that is beneath our feet. God gets the glory out of light, shining in spiritual darkness and distress.

In Romans 12, Paul taught the believers in Rome to make sure love was always at the center of their works, and that the quality of their love should be without hypocrisy. A love that is practiced across the board, without nepotism and favoritism, is a love without hypocrisy. This is a pure love that is a force with which to be reckoned. God is exalted as we love everyone in our church fellowship. We cannot just choose to love and extend grace and compassion, to those who make up our subgroup of friends and family members in the congregation. Paul said that the power of God becomes palpable when we work to love without hypocrisy, as we overcome evil with good. It is through the gift of being placed in a context where we must learn to love all of our co-laborers, and patiently endure any misunderstandings that might arise along the way, that we develop a deepening of our character and a closer walk with the Lord. We cannot run from every situation we find displeasing. We must wait until we are released by God to move to something new. Sometimes God's release, if it comes, only comes after years of faithfully toiling to bring to pass God's vision right where we are. God is a God who honors commitment and a spiritual stick-to-itiveness. So United, in my best Al Green voice, *"Let's stay together...."*

I remember a time in my life when many of my high school friends and I started wishing we were enrolled in a school that was different from the one we attended. After a couple of years of being students at Lindblom Technical High School, some of us longed to leave. One of the problems we had was that our school, like most, had some tough cliques to break into. If you were not on good terms with some of the more popular cliques, our school could be a difficult place to navigate, socially. I had the privilege of playing high school basketball during the early 80s. Lindblom was a large school, better known for the academic and college preparation of its students than for having great basketball teams. It had just recently become a football power-house and had only achieved spotty success on the basketball court. During the years I was on the team, as a role player, playing out of position, we were mediocre at best. To make matters worse, our team had cliques. There was a point in my high school career when I talked to my parents about wanting to transfer out of Lindblom. Along with several of my friends, I wanted to attend a different high school; one which seemed to offer *better* – a better and newer building; better teachers (my grades weren't great, and I sometimes blamed the teaching staff, instead of my terrible, nearly non-existent study habits); better coaches; better equipment; a better winning tradition – *a better team!* In a nutshell, I had lost sight of the real reason why I was enrolled in one of the top academic schools in the city. Instead of looking at my situation through proper lenses, I wanted to be a part of an environment which seemed to be headed toward athletic victory and not defeat; I wanted to be part of a fun social environment, without major cliques, and I wanted to be a part of a winning team, without any obvious signs of disunity. But, in all our longing, we were forgetting the great college preparatory vision that the school offered to those who focused on their academic work.

In our immaturity, many of us were impatiently wrestling with a basic human desire given to us by God. God has made us to desire to achieve success, and to be in a successful environment. God wants us to rise up to new levels, instead of sinking into old patterns of frustration and defeat. God wants us to enjoy life and enjoy it in abundance, according to what Jesus says in John 10:10. My friends and I wanted to prosper socially and athletically. But, in my myopia, I had lost sight of my main reason for being a student. Sometimes the problem with desiring to reach new levels can be that our ideas about what it means to live and achieve success, are about as adolescent and immature as that of the 17 year-old, I was. Sometimes, God does not want us to run away to what we think is a better school, or a better marriage, or a better house of worship, because God's conceptualization of what it means to be successful can be at odds with our notions of success. In God's equation, winning and achieving often mean learning to let one's light, one's gifts and talents shine, wherever one is surrounded by those who need to see it. Sometimes true victory with God means deciding to stand our ground where we are and learning to love anyhow; it means learning to add your gifts, talents, and anointing, to the mix of ministry right where we are. Such efforts, with the help of the Spirit, can help change and overcome an environment of mediocrity, defeat, and even evil. God's vision can become our new reality, if we will be yielded vessels. This is not to say that God wants us to perpetually settle for a context of mediocrity, defeat, and evil. There are times when the school, the marriage, the church, are bad grounds for continued planting. Especially when the environment has become abusive and extremely toxic, and you have a sense that you have done all that God sent you to do in that environment and situation. When this is the case, as we cry out to God, God will move us to a different school, and maybe a new relationship, and ministry environment; one in which we can flourish and help others to flourish. But, I have observed that the way churches build strong ministry, is by members committing to love each other through the thick and the thin. God can take us up to the next level if a church's members will commit to the work of Christ together, through the good and the bad.

Until God directs us to another pasture, looking for new ones should not be our first reaction, when trouble arises. I believe God has planted our congregation and our ministry in the Cody Rouge part of Detroit, for such a time as this! We have a high calling placed upon us as a prophetic mantle. We can go up to next levels of spiritual growth together right where we are, if we will love without hypocrisy, and be willing to overcome evil with good. We have had a good three years together. I believe that God, God's angels, God's word and laws, God's presence, provisions, grace, protection, reassurance and love, all form the foundations of an unstoppable Kingdom. As we put our hand to the ministry plow together, I am godly glad, and hallelujah happy, that holiness wins out over sinfulness; truth wins over lies; and that love will outlast hate! But, here's the tough thing: To see these graces manifested, God often places God's children in daunting difficulties, with spiritual darkness showing up all around; from squabbles in the choir, to fisticuffs in the fellowship hall; from bitter wrangling and arguments in the church board meeting, to a lack of commitment in the pews; from a beleaguered neighborhood, to folks in the community who are indifferent, or even hostile to faith. God then moves in us and through us to rise-up to a higher state of spiritual consciousness in Christ, so that we will have word-based perspective to overcome the disappointments and the evil, with God's good. In certain seasons of our lives, this means not seeking a quick out, as we look for greener grass. After all, greener grass can only be grown, if we take proper care to fertilize what has the potential for growth. Most of us know that the most natural fertilizer consists of some stuff we do not normally want to deal with – feces! Every now and then, to help us to grow, feces-like situations show up in our church dealings and interchanges.

So, with three years down, as your pastor, and more to come I hope; my word to us is: *Stand together and let us go up to the next level of ministry engagement!* Stand together in the choir; stand together on the Usher's Board; stand together as church officers; stand together through the next tough board meeting; or the next disagreement in the committee meeting. Paul instructs us in Romans 12:9 and 21:

Let love be without hypocrisy. Abhor what is evil, and cling to what is good…Do not be overcome by evil, but overcome evil with good.

This has been the legacy of the victorious children of God, from Joseph to Jesus; from Martin to Mandela. If we will remain faithful, God will reward us immensely. Until God shows us a different path, let us remain faithful to God, right where we are; doing the last thing, God has told us to do!

5. What Jesus are you Following?

Now Jesus and His disciples went out to the towns of
Caesarea Philippi; and on the road, He asked His disciples,
saying to them, "Who do men say that I am?" So, they
answered, "John the Baptist; but some say, Elijah; and
others, one of the prophets" He said to them, "But who
do you say that I am?" Peter answered and said to Him,
"You are the Christ."

(Mark 8:27-29)

In the first of three autobiographies, Frederick Douglass (Apparently,
Douglass' life was so full, he had enough experiences and stories for three
lifetimes!), the noted abolitionist, orator, and writer, wrote powerfully
about the difference between the Christianity that is not much more
than a mere religion, and the Christianity that is a dynamic expression
of a relationship with God, through which persons find themselves on
a love journey with the living Christ. After differentiating between the
perverted religion of the slave owners, and the life-changing relationship
with the risen Christ, rooted in a love for God and neighbor, Douglass
explicitly touches on the main reason why many African Americans made
a choice to follow Jesus. According to Douglass, the enslaved Africans were
choosing to follow a Jesus who is different from the Jesus who was being
claimed and practiced by the slaveholders who subjugated and defrauded
them. In a section entitled, *Slaveholding Religion and the Christianity of
Christ*, Douglass asserts that, like himself, other 16th and 17th Century
African Americans could discern and distinguish the life-transforming

Jesus who comes to forgive, love and liberate us, from the phony and false Christianity revealed in the hypocrisy and hatred of their oppressors. He notes that though many slaveholders in the south claimed to be strong Christians, many practiced a religion which, in the words of Douglass, was only:

> ... a mere covering for the most horrid crimes, - a justifier of the most appalling barbarity, - a sanctifier of the most hateful frauds, - and a dark shelter under which the darkest, foulest...deeds of the slaveholders find the strongest protection. [9]

Douglass goes on to describe a truer form of Christianity; one rooted in divine love, forgiveness, and amazing grace; a relationship with God which motivates persons to live a life of kindness, fairness and holiness; a relationship which causes us to walk in peace with others, because we have found peace in knowing that Christ has become our inner peace, no matter one's color. He said about the authentic relationship with Christ versus a religion which merely uses Jesus' name as a ruse for evil works:

> ...between the Christianity of this land, and the Christianity of Christ, I recognize the widest possible difference – so wide, that to receive the one as good, pure, and holy is of necessity to reject the other as bad, corrupt and wicked.[10]

Though thankfully, many persons are not enslaved in chains that lock up the body today, many have remained enslaved in a concept of religion which is filled with ritual, hypocrisy, self-righteousness, and materialism. Sometimes twisted forms of Christianity have even become covers for a life lived in rebellion to God. Historically, we have seen strange versions of Christ proclaimed by the Reverend Ikes, and Johnnie Colemans of the

---

[9] Frederick Douglass, *Slaveholding Religion and the Christianity of Christ*, in *Afro-American Religious History: A Documentary Witness*, ed. Milton C. Sernett (Durham: Duke University Press, 1985), p. 101
[10] Ibid p. 104

world; men and women who have suggested, among other things, that the collection and displaying of material wealth is an outward sign of an inner godliness. Worst, we have had the Jim Joneses, Charles Mansons, David Koreshes, and similar shadowy religious figures in human history, to rise and fall, century after century, after having proclaimed themselves to be Messianic figures who offered perverted utopian visions, only to eventually manifest very dark, demonic and violent impulses. Beyond these extreme heretics and false Christs, the Christian church has routinely had many religious leaders to stand week after week in pulpits, proclaiming a Christ who is only concerned with baptizing their own group's political and social interests. In the thirty years or more, that I have intently listened to and engaged in the preaching of the gospel, I have heard a tendency of many Christians to hug and hallelujah a Christ who has been co-opted and forced to ride on the backs of our special interests sacred cows, or donkeys and elephants. From the political Left, I have heard the preaching of a Christ who is not so much concerned about people's personal sins, but has only come to overturn the governmental, financial, and political, status quo, abrogating our systemic sins of capitalism, classism, imperialism, racism, sexism, and heterosexism, so that all forms of perceived oppression are dismantled in this life. From the political Right, I have heard about a Christ preached who is only concerned about people's personal sins: a Christ who rails against all forms of sex outside of heterosexual marriage, along with pornography, abortion, a lack of patriotism, sloth, cussing, and drug use. There are many images of Christ floating about in our culture and in the church. And some of these images are not tethered at all to the Christ proclaimed by the Apostles and the early church. With so many diverse opinions and messages about Christ around, how can we know that what we claim to know about the Lord is true? How can we know that the One we worship in our liturgical gatherings is really the Lord? How do we come to know the authentic Christ? Is there any way to know whether the Christ we are celebrating on Sundays is a mere self-projection of who we want Christ to be? In our text, in Mark 8, the disciples were about to be confronted with a question, which is at the core of today's meditation. Jesus asked them, "Who do you say that I am?" This is a question of epistemology.

When Jesus asks this question, the twelve were standing just outside of the Gentile occupied region of Caesarea, Philippi. They were standing at the very edge of a cornucopia of idolatry. The Gentile city of Caesarea was built at the foot of Mt. Hermon, and adjacent to an area which included a spring, and a cave. In the very walls of the foundation of the mount and the cave were placed carved statues and images dedicated to the Greek god, Pan. Pan was the primary deity worshiped in Philippi. Pan was the half-goat, half-man god of the pasture land, shepherds, music, and sexuality. He was also the god believed to create "panic" in his enemies. This was the theological and topographical backdrop of Jesus' question about his identity. It was almost as if Jesus was saying to the disciples, "In light of us standing in the shadow of pagan images; and given that I have been hinting at my own divinity through an elucidation and reinterpretation of the central meaning of the Mosaic law, supplemented by inimitable miracles and healings, are people getting it? Are you getting it? Who do people say that I am?" The answers come back: "Some say that you are Elijah.' 'Others believe that you are John the Baptist, or Jeremiah, risen from the dead." Jesus then turns the question directly toward the disciples, "But who do you say, that I am?"

This is life's main religious and spiritual question. Never has a human being who did the kind of works Jesus did, asked this direct probing question. It is a question which caused these disciples to reflect on the nature of God's divinity, and our humanity. What is our assessment of Jesus' person and work? And, what is Jesus' assessment of us? These two questions are tied together. Our assessment of Jesus not only potentially reveals something powerful about Jesus and God, but it also discloses something about who we really are. In other words, if we know the truth about God, God ensures that we will know the truth about ourselves; likewise, if we don't *get* God at all, neither will we *get* ourselves. Because we are made in God's image, we are tethered to that image.

Simon's answer to Jesus' question, and Jesus' response to Simon's answer, illustrate the dual nature of an authentic spiritual revelation; once we discover something about God, simultaneously, we discover something about ourselves. After the disciples expressed what they had heard about Jesus, Simon comes to the fore; he seems pushed by an answer that suddenly surfaces in his heart and soul: *"Thou Art the Christ!"* By making this statement, Simon - a man, standing before another man - makes an astounding claim. Simon claims that he was standing in the presence of the ultimate human being – one smeared with the very presence of God, like no one else. He claims that this young man standing before him was the chosen *Christos*; the anointed one; the Messiah; the personification of all that is good. By uttering this revelation, Simon acknowledges that he was standing in close proximity to the one whose birthdate was not the date of his origin, or the start of his history. This is a fascinating moment in time, and Jesus acknowledges this. Jesus' response sheds light on just how remarkable this moment was: *"Simon, flesh and blood has not revealed this to you; but my Father in heaven has revealed it!"* Simon had been given insight that the ancients could only have dreamt to receive. In just a quick flash, after a few years of observation, Simon saw that the hope of Israel – the hope of the world, was all wrapped up in a friend who was sticking with him, closer than a brother. Jesus then tells Simon something that would redefine Simon's self-understanding. Jesus tells him, *"And now you are Peter (Petros – a piece of rock), and upon this rock (larger rock of revelation and confession), I will build my church, and the gates of hades will not prevail against it!"* Simon is given a new name by the Lord; a name which would characterize how this flash of revelation into Jesus' identity would function in establishing God's church; and this revelation of Christ would also reshape, and redefine, Simon's identity and character. Simon, the fisherman; the impetuous, temperamental, disciple, would become the strong, stable, out-front leader of God's early church; emerging as the key disciple after Jesus' resurrection, and the coming of the promise of the Holy Spirit, on the Day of Pentecost. This is the dual nature of divine revelation. When we realize something new and authentic about Jesus, we are also given new insight about ourselves. Abraham, Jacob, Moses, Miriam, Isaiah, Paul, Augustine, Jarena Lee, Julia Foote, William J. Seymore, momma, grand momma, and great-great granddaddy, are all witnesses. Once we have confessed Jesus as the Son of God, the Christ, and our Lord; once we have made our faith commitment to Christ, the Holy Spirit comes to aid us in the area of epistemology; and the written text of the Spirit is the Gospels. In other words, the way we come to know the authentic Christ, begins with humbling ourselves before God and confessing our sinfulness, as we prayerfully study the Gospels and the New Testament. Through prayer, confession and meditation in the word, we are given a diverse, and comprehensive picture of who Jesus is. In the scriptures we are not only allowed to hear again and again, Jesus' teachings on life and godliness, but we are also able to observe how Jesus operated in various settings and circumstances. It is our prayerful, open, study of the scriptures, that the Spirit uses to clarify and sharpen what we know of God's glorious Son.

Allowing the Spirit and the word, to arbitrate within our souls a powerful relationship with God, is very different from the practice of merely attending church and doing churchy things to get the religious monkeys off our backs. Jesus is a living Savior, who still speaks, through the Spirit and the New Testament, and desires to be linked up with us, in a revolutionary relationship that changes who we are, and how we live our lives. When we follow the Jesus of the biblical texts, the chains of a weak, anemic, special interest-based, Pollyannaish, religiosity will fall away; and the liberating love of God, empowers us to live lives of love and holiness, so that our friends at the job, classmates at school, along with our neighbors and enemies on the block, are positively impacted by our connection with the Lord. Does such a connection mean that we will never stumble over our feet and sin, if we know the Christ revealed in the Gospels and the New Testament Epistles? No, not at all. But it does mean that with our sinful predilections, our stumbling becomes more the disdained exception, than the embraced rule; it means we are not comfortable with living according to this world's system; it means that our intentions, inclinations, and actions, indicate that we desire to live Holy lives; lives dedicated to God, as we serve and advocate for our neighbors. This is what God has been calling His disciples to do since time immemorial.

Study Questions

1. Who is Jesus to you? Prophet of Islam? Enlightened Sage? Son of God? Messiah?
2. Why do you think the disciples were willing to die for their testimony of Jesus' Sonship, and resurrection?
3. How does confessing faith in Christ, as God's Son, help to transform Peter's life?
4. What does Peter's name-change say about the dual nature of divine revelation?
5. How do you know that you have had an encounter with the Spirit of Jesus Christ, and not fallen subject to your own emotional and imaginary whims?
6. What role do the words and teachings of Christ, along with the testimonies of the Apostles, play in confirming whether or not you have met the biblical/real Jesus?

Part 2

Black History Month and Lent

6. The Purpose of the Black Church

Texts: The Souls of Black Folk and selected verses from *Matthew 13*

I recently heard the lecture[11] of a scholar, preacher, and pastor, named Jonathan L. Walton. He is *Professor of Christian Morals, and the Pusey Minister* at Harvard University's Memorial Church. In his lecture, Walton was discussing some of the beliefs that W.E.B. Dubois held about the black church; convictions reflected in a certain section of Dubois' famous book, The *Souls of Black Folk.* There is a chapter in the book dedicated to the religious and spiritual practices of African Americans. What Walton notes about this chapter is that Dubois had a somewhat tainted view of what the purpose of the church was and is. Walton explicates that Dubois seemed to interpret many common black church practices through the white supremacist lenses of his European American academic colleagues. According to Walton, Dubois, like most of his associates, seemed to imply that there were many backward aspects of the black church (especially the working-class black church), like the dancing and the shouting – the spiritual exercises in worship (this is what Dubois called "the Frenzy") - these were deemed primitive and uncouth activities. Dubois, according to Walton, also tended to disparage the fact that many blacks enjoyed and practiced church for reasons which exceeded what he considered the one valid reason for religious gatherings -- to receive moral instruction. He seemed to not appreciate that many black folks found spiritual help

---

[11] Walton's lecture, entitled, *The Du Boisian Dilemna: Sacrificing the Faith in Order to Save the Race.* Chicago Theological Seminary, at the 7th Annual C. Shelby Rooks' Lecture Series. Published on Youtube, October 24, 2013. Accessed, February 2015.

and healing as they also assembled to socialize, enjoy community dinners, exercise gifts and talents, initiate fundraisers, court a potential mate, etc. Walton intimates that because of the prevailing academic views of the time, Dubois seemed to believe that these other reasons for black religion were not as noble, or even necessary. For him, the church should exist fundamentally to instruct African American citizens as to how they could function better with principles, morals, and civility in civil (and uncivil) society. Church, for Dubois, and many of his white academic and scientific counterparts, was not necessarily meant to stir one up emotionally, but to tame our primitive emotions.

In the light of Walton's lecture, as I read and re-read Matthew 13 in preparation for a sermon I would be preaching in our congregation for Black History Month, I was left with a few questions about Dubois' and my own views of the black church. These were the three primary questions, with their several linking sub-questions*: 1) **What is the main purpose of the black church, or any other church for that matter?** 2) **Was Dubois right, in any way?** Should the church only concern itself with matters of moral instruction? Or does the planted word of God bring up more fruit than just the fruit of instructing people in matters of morality and ethics? 3)**Does Matthew 13 have anything to say about the purpose of the church, as it seeks to help manifest the Reign of God, on earth?**

As I thought about these questions, I reluctantly concluded that Dubois, having been greatly influenced by a racist society, had to some degree misunderstood the broader value of the black church as being a holistic social and spiritual center, where black folks could be fully themselves. Therefore, he had distilled the purposes of the black church down to one main variable – that the church and religion in general are only for moral and civic instruction. Concomitant with this idea is the subtle, and not-so subtle notion that black folks need to be tamed of their exotic and wild sexual and emotional passions.

I think that as brilliant as Dubois was in several academic disciplines, he was maybe a bit ignorant of the full scope of American church history. For most blacks (and for many whites, especially poorer, Southern whites), the church has always been about more than moral instruction. As important as morality and ethics are, the church has been a broad space and place of social connection, emotional release; prayer, praise and even entertainment; a place which has offered a broad and profound psychological and social catharsis. From New England to Mississippi, the American church has been an amalgam of preaching, politics, ethics, social entertainment, education, and mission work. As a part of its ethos and agenda, the black church has included enthusiastic expressions of worship, socializing, testifying, expressing and identifying talent, courting a potential mate, helping black folk learn how to manage their marriages and their money (the moralizing aspects which Dubois championed are also included). Dubois, by purportedly desiring to reduce and narrow the powerful, broad, multi-faceted, village aspect of the black church, did not seem to fully realize just how much his anti-religious, and anti-African views were being shaped by the views of his white counterparts. Walton cites the ideas of Biologist and white supremacist propogandist, Jean Louis Agassiz; and the ideas of one of Dubois' most admired teachers, paleontologist, Nathaniel Southgate Shaler, as key influences on Dubois. In the lecture, Walton explicates their racist views in painful detail, in efforts to illustrate and establish how people close to Dubois; some, his most admired professors in fact, believed and taught doctrines associated with now-debunked evolutionary theories (apparently, Harvard was a major purveyor of the now debunked idea that humans of different races, were really beings of different species; and that blacks were of a lower species). Walton brings this historical and contextual information to light to illustrate how much Dubois' social and intellectual environment had shaped and "colored" his evaluation of the complex and beneficial spiritual and social aspects of the black church. Thus, he saw no benefit in the shouting, dancing, praises, and trances, exhibited in worship. He did not comprehend that when black folk were exhibiting "the frenzy," something powerful, and needed was happening in the souls of black folk; and it was happening, not because of being racially inferior, but because of a manifested, African-influenced, grace-centered, deep spirituality; an expression which did what no group psychology session could do to keep African Americans sane, and filled with the substance of hope, in insane surroundings.

We can all fall victim to this trap of seeing ourselves through the eyes of adversarial others, if we are not careful, prayerful, and humble. In his work, without thinking critically about his own views in relation to the black church, Dubois explains that this difficult juggling act is something that blacks must do, in a society that is majority other. It seems that as he consciously and unconsciously wrestled with his own demons, he wrote astutely about how blacks in America are cursed with a double consciousness – dual perspectives of the black self in a predominantly white society. Because he too, lived within this dual prism, I think that Dubois, at times, suffered from an analytical and cultural imbalance, as he saw the black church, uncritically, through the eyes of white critics, enemies, and oppressors, who also happened to be Dubois' fellow scholars and colleagues.

Perhaps, in saying that moral instruction is the sole critical purpose of the church, Dubois went too far. But, this does not mean that the church is *not* to be about making sure that moral imperatives take effect in the human soul. In all fairness to Dubois, maybe even with his faulty analysis, there is something to salvage of an aspect of his perspective. Could it be that Dubois was *partly right* to point out that the church *has to be* the place where persons learn how "good people" are to live; the place where African Americans and all people learn how to be transformed by the gracious love of God, as revealed through the person and teachings of the Christ? Though not the entire picture, I do think there is something of value to consider here. According to the Gospels and the Epistles, God has placed a moral imperative on the shoulders of the faithful – we are to love and live in a particular way; we are to live holy lives in a corrupt society, in light of the reign of God. The church is to live rooted in a kingdom/kindom culture, opposite of an alien value system. Along with the important social, political, psychic healing role that the church has played in black communities, on a variety of levels, Matthew 13, clearly depicts Jesus as the one who has come *to sow the Word of God into our hearts so that we will live lives that are very different from the world.*

Hearing the word of the love of God, revealed in Christ; learning the word; practicing the word; praying according to the word; obeying the word; spreading the word is our primary reason for being. It is through the word of God, especially the New Testament witness, that we learn the workings of the reign of God, and of its critical mandates. It is by virtue of this word that we learn how to love, forgive sins, confess our own sins, as we testify about the goodness, mercy, and salvation of God, through

Jesus Christ. It is through the help and power of the Spirit, with our Bibles and hearts open, that the Lord transforms our minds, and defines/redefines for us who we are, and who God desires us to become. Along with worship, this issue of revolutionizing our moral and spiritual center, through meditating on the written, preached, and taught word, should be one of our most central concerns as the black church (or any church). It is as Jesus said to the Pharisees about another matter, in Luke 11:42, "These you ought to have done, without neglecting the others!" I think in such statements Jesus points to a particular imperative, while recognizing that the kingdom should also influence and transform our lives on a variety of broad levels.

So, I do believe that our central purpose as the church is to open ourselves up to having frequent encounters with the word of God, which helps us to live new lives; but when we do, *we will also* be moved to grow into a village of love, fellowship, praise, dancing, preaching, and shouting that helps to provide fire to our energies, as we seek to address and meet whatever other important social, emotional, and material needs our communities might have – needs that are broader than just that of providing a venue for moral instruction. This is where I believe Dubois could not appreciate the full role and scope of the black church; and it was in his missing of the inherent power of these important outgrowths which come from our welcome and embrace of a new moral center, vouchsafed to us by the workings of the word, that he missed the holistic satisfaction the black church has given its practitioners. Dubois seemed to assume that with, and within the singing, dancing, social connections and activities, there was no good, and needed, transformation taking place within the hearts and minds of black folks. Often, celebration, joy, dancing and good fellowship, can be the greatest re-enforcers of what has been taught during a religious discourse; sometimes these other adjoining phenomena can also be instructive, and more effective in communicating theology or ethics, than just a lecture or sermon. If I am reading Dubois right, and if Walton's observations are right, it seems Dubois failed to adequately understand that the word which instructs our moral center, also liberates us to celebrate, create, socialize, entertain, and protest on so many levels, as we enjoy God and one another, resisting evil, in our worship, play, and work. There is value in shouting, dancing, social events, meetings and fundraisers (okay, maybe he was right about the ubiquitous church fundraiser, in black churches).

In our text, in Matthew 13, the apostle tells us that one day, Jesus told a large audience via a parable, that the Sower (God) goes out to sow (plant) the word in our hearts, in efforts to begin the process of creating the conditions for the spread of the Kingdom of God. He also says that the planted seed would effectuate broad change throughout the culture, on every level. God's Village, the Beloved Community, would spread and impact various levels of living and loving throughout our society. It is the word of God's unconditional love, liberation, and uncompromising strivings toward justice, mercy and holiness, coupled with our faith, that transforms us into Dr. King's, *Transformed, Nonconformist*[12] – these are folk who have been changed to do some changing; folk who have been loved to do some loving; made up of people who enjoy working and playing together; persons who desire to evangelize, entertain and eat together; who cry and laugh together, in a way that is different from what moves secular society! Because, unlike what Walton describes to be the conviction of Dubois, I strongly believe that a truly transformed moral center, gained from moral instruction, spills over into countless areas of our social existence, including our emotions and our entertainment. Consequently, the black church has always been about more than just offering religious instructions for the attainment of civility, or righteousness; it has also been a holistic experience; it has been about praising the Lord, shouting away pain, networking and leveraging for community strength; it has been about standing and marching against oppression, and developing and sharing our artistic and business talents and gifts; it has been about opening black-owned credit unions and funeral homes, while birthing schools, sororities and fraternities; it has been the ground-zero of our earliest, organized fashion and talent shows; the black church has been about fundraising; fellowshipping, courting, and witnessing; these are just a few of the important functions of the church, in the black community.

Jesus taught us how the word is a like a seed that when planted, will grow up to transform and bless the world. He said the birds will nest in its

---

[12] The title of a sermon published in Martin Luther King Jr.'s book, *Strength to Love*. The biblical text, Romans 12:2.

branches. The Kingdom of God is planted in human hearts through divine speech and vision, and collectively grows into an organism that changes its surrounding community, at every level. Ideally, the church is to be the center of the village – especially in urban centers, where the pathologies and demons seem to be legion, and the positive resources and exorcisms seem few. I thank God for the church's profound impact, on every level of black life; it has been so much more than a place for a certain notion of moral instruction. The church has been the black extended family, rooted in the word of God.

Study Questions

1. What do you believe is the purpose of the church? Do you think that predominantly black churches have a different purpose/function than other churches?

2. In what ways do you think your views about race have been influenced by the broader American culture?

3. How do you characterize churches that exhibit a very emotional and lively, praise and worship atmosphere? Do you see any value in shouting in church? What about in social dinners, and dances; fashion and talent shows?

4. What do you think of Dubois' struggle to see holistic value in the church? Does this change your admiration for Dubois, in any way?

5. Matthew 13, offers us several parables that Jesus teaches about the kingdom of God. As you read through the parables, do you detect that God places any limitations on the potential scope and influence of God's kingdom on earth?

6. In your observations, when and where have you seen the word of God have a broad effect on our culture and society?

7. Do you recognize areas of your life that you are not so keen in allowing the seed of the word of God to influence and transform? If so, why?

8. How has our society benefited from the contributions of the black church?

7. Can I get a Witness?
The Evangelistic Work
of the Black Church

O Lord, You induced me, and I was persuaded; You are stronger than I, and have prevailed. I am in derision daily; Everyone mocks me. For when I spoke, I cried out; I shouted, "Violence and plunder!" Because the word of the Lord was made to me a reproach and a derision daily. Then I said, "I will not make mention of Him…But His word was in my heart like a burning fire, shut up in my bones…

(Jeremiah 20:7-9)

For I am not ashamed of the gospel of Christ, for it is the power of God to salvation for everyone who believes, for the Jew first and also for the Greek.

(Romans 1:16)

Now an angel of the Lord spoke to Philip, saying, "Arise and go toward the south along the road…So he arose and went. And behold, a man of Ethiopia, a eunuch of great authority under Candace the queen of the Ethiopians, who had charge of all her treasury, and had come to Jerusalem to worship, was returning. And sitting in his

chariot, he was reading Isaiah the prophet. Then the Spirit
said to Philip, "Go near and overtake this chariot."

(Acts 8:26-40)

I still remember the joy, excitement, and anxiety we felt, when two friends
and I decided to occupy a busy intersection at Ashland and 87th Streets,
on the Southwest side of Chicago. We were there to share our faith in the
public square. It was a beautiful summer's day. We were all in our early
twenties, and willing to take youthful risks. The three of us had decided
that we would each take three of the four corners of the intersection; we
would stand at three of the four stops, with our Bible tracks in hand. We
had agreed that as we interacted with the public, we would say, "hello,"
and identify who we were; and then we would ask for a brief moment of
their time so that we could share quick testimonies of what Jesus meant to
us; and finally, we would share our church affiliation, leaving with them
a gospel pamphlet for their consideration. The three of us were members
of the same in-home Bible study class, which met in a friend's home. It
was led by Pastor Arthur Guice,[13] a skilled expositor of God's word who,
theologically, had a Word of Faith background. Though he did not fully
subscribe to what has now come to be known as the Prosperity Gospel,
he was firmly rooted in a theology which taught that to overcome life's
obstacles we must learn to demonstrate the faith and authority God has
given to God's children, as we learn to wield God's word in faith. He
was about four to six years older than most of us and remains a pastoral
colleague and friend to this day. I was asked by him to teach the class (from
my own theological perspective), whenever he could not teach. It was a
glorious period in the faith development of our college-aged group. Our
knowledge of the Bible skyrocketed. Through much prayer, and fasting, we
also had some powerful group encounters in the Spirit. Eventually, many of
us felt compelled to tell as many others as we could about the good news of
what Jesus had done in our lives, and about the radical difference that the
word of God had made in our hearts. When several of us decided to go on

---

[13] Guice is the Pastor of the Spirit of Liberty Church of God, in Markham Illinois, and has
also served as the Cook County Coordinator for a national prayer organization called, *Cry
Out America!*

our evangelistic excursion to the abovementioned intersection, it was our first organized foray into offering our public witness. It seemed we could not help but to tell others about our faith in Christ, because God's word had become like fire, shut up in our young bones!

In a sermon which I recently preached during the month of February, we considered how important it is for African American Christians to not be ashamed of the power and liberation God has given to us through the gospel of Jesus Christ, which is primarily about the glorious cross and resurrection events, but also includes a recognition of the gifts God has deposited in black people, in the form of our faith, intellect, overcoming joy, rich history and deep spiritual heritage. Historically, as our ancestors engaged in worship, preaching, and hearing the word, they drank deeply from the wells of such texts as Jeremiah 20:7-9, and Romans 1:16. As we were attracted to the imagery of "fire being shut up" in our bones; as we heard about how we should *not be ashamed of the good news* of Jesus Christ, because it was the root of our love-power; as we contemplated what God had done for Africans in diaspora, we were won over by the power of God revealed in our experience, and expressed in these evangelistic texts and metaphors. Consequently, many African Americans were converted to Jesus by fiery, Great Awakening, revival preachers; so much so that, we in turn, led others to Christ in exponential numbers during the eighteenth and nineteenth centuries. This is well-chronicled by Dr. Carter G. Woodson in his seminal work, *The History of the Negro Church.* Woodson notes how the Spirit used the good news of Jesus Christ, shared primarily through Baptists and Methodists missionaries, many of whom presented a passionate and exciting version of the gospel message (which was a welcomed contrast to the quaint gospel presentations of the Anglican and Catholic missionaries), which convicted, inspired, and offered a new birth experience to displaced Africans. History reminds us that because of this powerful, testifying, witness, shared by both white and black preachers, many enslaved Africans received the loving and liberating Jesus as their own Savior and Lord; and again, these Africans shared countless conversion testimonies with other Africans. Our African American ancestors, who converted in large numbers during both Great Awakenings, became Baptist and Methodist believers in large numbers. They adopted and adapted the fiery truths of the Christian faith and retrofit them to their own African expressions of praise, preaching, and worship. They applied their faith in the liberating Christ to their struggles for freedom in America; and as they preached and testified, in fields, towns, and the backwoods, about the One True God, revealed through Jesus, their message was received by other Africans who were new to America, who could identify with a Jesus who was the embodiment of a suffering love; a love that gave them an inner freedom and the promise of freedom on earth and in Heaven. To these suffering people, Jesus was the revelation of a God who was paradoxically both the Suffering Servant (who ends up whipped and hung on a tree) and the Lord of an existential freedom, which culminates in the defeats of the devil and death, and rewards eternal life wherein God dries every tear.

Today's meditation centers on how this spiritual fire -- the gospel of Jesus Christ - was unleashed during the Great Awakenings of America. As America was flooded with the spirit of revivalism, African Americans heard about a power which comforted their souls and promised to liberate their bodies one day. During this period, black folk, became *evangelical* in the purest sense of the term. Enslaved field workers, elderly grandmothers and grandfathers, even freed men and women, went about living the gospel and sharing about the joys of serving Jesus beyond the dark veil of the forced earthly servitude they had to endure. And like those early good news sharers, today's African Americans who have been comforted and liberated by this same Lord, have a similar call and responsibility to share the news of their salvation in Christ with others. God desires for us to look out and listen for opportunities to share Jesus with those we encounter along life's pathways; sharing with those who may be yearning to know the God who loves them so much that God was willing to take on the form and limitations of humanity, in efforts to save them. Many persons, walking through the confusing spiritual wasteland of our postmodern society, are eager to hear the message about a God who was willing to suffer and die, while also displaying the power to rise up above that which frightens us the most – the fear of death, along with the condemnation of sin.

African American Christians have always leaned on the Bible, its stories, its characters, as guides for how and why we should share our faith. Biblically speaking, we see this evangelistic impulse at work in the life of a first century, North African disciple named John Mark. This is the same John Mark who concludes the Gospel which bears his name, with the commission to "Go into all the world and preach the gospel to very creature..." Long before there were thousands of books on ways to systematically, and effectively evangelize communities, the gifts of African memory and oral tradition reveal that John Mark, who had hailed from the city of Cyrene, in North Africa, made sharing the good news of Christ his main vocation. According to many Africans, and a few American scholars like Thomas C. Oden,[14] after John Mark's encounter with Christ, and after having walked with the Apostles, he was commissioned by the early church to go back to Africa to establish Christian communities by passionately telling the story of the One who lived, died, and rose again. Without a ten-step program for reaching seekers, John Mark simply relied on the Spirit and went back to Africa, trumpeting what he had seen in and heard from Jesus Christ. This is the stripped-down essence of evangelism. Evangelism is about meeting people where they are and sharing with them the faith stories of what Christ, and the reign of God, means to us. John Mark was so effective that many Africans have believed that he is one of the key reasons why the Christian faith spread throughout Northern Africa.

In the book of Acts, we also see the power of *telling the gospel story* through the actions of Philip, the disciple, who plays a central role in the narrative about the Ethiopian Eunuch's conversion. The Ethiopian Eunuch was a man of high rank in Ethiopia's kingdom. He lived a life of spiritual and political dedication and sexual chastity; in fact, he had either been born with a physical condition which prevented him from pursuing and fulfilling his sexual interests, or he had been castrated, either accidently or intentionally, with the result being that his total allegiance would be to matters, political, administrative and spiritual. He was a dedicated servant to *the Candace* (a title for female rulers, in Eastern Africa, kind of like *Pharaoh/Emperor* was for the highest male rulers), and yet, he was also a man who had a much greater allegiance - he was dedicated to the God he

---

[14] Thomas C. Oden is the author of one of the definitive works on John Mark's impact on the church in Africa. In his book, *The African Memory of Mark: Reassessing Early Church Tradition (InterVarsity Press, 2011)*, he argues persuasively, that the long -held African practice of attributing its Christian origins to the evangelistic church planting work of John Mark, is a more reliable practice and source, than previously thought by skeptical European researchers. Through years of researching the broad, and consistent, anecdotal evidences rooted in an extremely powerful oral tradition, Oden has concluded that there seems to be a certain veracity to these African claims.

had learned about through his exposure to Judaism. Though the Eunuch was a man of political power and influence; though he was educated, dedicated, and connected; though he already had faith in Yahweh, in Acts 8, he is depicted as one who was not satisfied with his spiritual station. He was hungry to grow in his faith; and he grew hungrier as he studied and grappled with the content of the Word of God. When we are introduced to him, the Eunuch is wrestling with a biblical text. Heretofore, the eunuch knew about various teachings found in the Law and the Prophets, but he was puzzled by a particular scriptural description of a mysterious figure, in the book of Isaiah. These factors indicate that a person can have high rank socially, politically, but still lack important revelatory knowledge about life and God – still lack new levels of spiritual knowledge that God desires to impart to God's children. The disciple, Philip, is used by the Lord to bring greater illumination to the Eunuch's spiritual comprehension; this encounter would be a life changing experience for both men.

Philip is directed by God to meet with this powerful African, while the African was in spiritual and theological reflection, reading Isaiah 53, as he sat in his chariot. Philip takes the lead and introduces himself to the man (who had many questions about the text, about which he was deliberating) and witnesses to him about how Jesus was the mysterious Suffering Servant/Messiah, who was led as a sheep to the slaughter for the sins of humanity. After expressing a desire to be baptized right then and there, the Ethiopian Eunuch becomes the first Gentile convert to Christianity recorded in the book of Acts! All his sins are washed away! He is saved by the gospel of Jesus Christ! He receives "blessed assurance." His relationship with God, and his understanding of God's love, go up to new levels. And church tradition tells us that the Eunuch becomes an evangelist to Ethiopia. As a consequence of his witness, a powerful, Nubian, branch of Christianity takes root in the world.

In the light of these examples, have you ever taken any time out of your schedule to witness to your home town folk, like John Mark purportedly did? What about former classmates? What about those who currently traverse through the hallowed halls of your life? Have you ever discerned who is your "Ethiopian Eunuch?" Or like the Eunuch, have you ever sensed that after your baptism, it was your call and mission to help transform your community by your witness? Our faith should not be the kind that is only relegated to the people and walls of the church. But, if we actually know that God has done wonderful things for us, such gratitude and thanksgiving should motivate us to look for opportunities to share what we know about Christ with others. We should have an urge to share our faith with all who might be questioning what life means: what life as a black person, in a sometimes racist society means; what life means for a single white mother, living on governmental assistance; what life means for a wealthy stockbroker, who is contemplating putting a gun to his head because of a shaky marriage; what life means for an athletic young teen who has just lost her good pitching arm, in a car accident. It is important for today's Christian to explain what the Bible means when it espouses that the greatest virtues in life are faith, hope, and love; what the scriptures suggest for us today when they speak of God's miracles at work through yielded vessels; how do miracles happen today in societies which clamors for empirical proof? It is important for Christians to be able to discuss the meaning of salvation and the purpose for God's church, in a world running over the brim with anti-religious claims about life!

Have you ever talked to someone about your faith? Have you ever led anyone to Christ? Evangelism is one the most important reasons why Christians of all colors and cultures are not immediately transitioned to heaven upon making their initial confessions of faith. We are on the planet, to bear witness to the gospel of Jesus Christ. It is through our relationship with Christ, as the Holy Spirit and Word of God guides and comforts us, that we are able to enjoy a revolutionary, soul-changing, intimate connection with God. It is a connection so good that we just can't keep it to ourselves!

This has been the legacy of faithful believers of African descent, since the days of the Great Awakenings. Therefore, since we have found such a priceless pearl; since we have been given fire shut up in our bones; since we have the gospel which is the power of God for Jews and Gentiles, it is only fitting to want to share that joy with others. Can I get a witness?

Important Observations of Philip's Evangelism

1. When it came to sharing his faith, Philip was prayerfully open and yielded to the Spirit's leading.

2. With a heart intent on sharing Jesus, Philip was obedient to the Spirit's commands about when and who to approach with the gospel message.

3. Philip knew enough about Christ's salvific work, to answer the African's questions. He knew enough about Jesus to share what he knew with others.

4. Philip was willing to help the Eunuch to act on his faith, immediately.

5. After this encounter, Philip was ushered away by the Spirit to his next assignment.

6. As you reflect on what Philip did, how can your observations help you share your witness in the world?

7. As you leave out of the comfort of your home, are you looking for opportunities to bring Jesus up in your conversations?

8. Black History and Lent: Lent is More than Fasting from Food

When you reap your harvest in your field, and forget a sheaf in the field, you shall not go back to get it; it shall be for the stranger, the fatherless, and the widow, that the Lord your God may bless you in all the work of your hands.

(Deuteronomy 24:19)

"So, which of these three do you think was neighbor to him who fell among the thieves?" And he said, "He who showed mercy on him." Then Jesus said to him, "Go and do likewise."

(Luke 10:36-37)

As we near the beginning of Lent, and as we celebrate Black History month, our focus is on two biblical texts: The First Testament text in Deuteronomy 24, which emphasizes the holy moral principle of sanctifying a portion of one's own personal harvest blessings for the purpose of blessing and nourishing the poor and the stranger; and the New Testament text, in Luke's Gospel, chapter 10, through which Jesus teaches us about our responsibility to aid the wounded and hurting neighbor. Through both pericopes, in essence, we hear the shouted command of God for us to *"Go and do likewise!"*

In Luke, Jesus' command for us to imitate the altruistic Samaritan, goes right along with the command of Yahweh, in the Mosaic Law, in Deuteronomy, to bless those who would benefit from the overflow of our harvests; both texts point us in the direction of what I believe is God's desire for God's people, especially during Lent. Along with denying ourselves of our favorite food and drink items, for the purpose of drawing closer to God, we should also concern ourselves with helping those in our society who have been bloodied and burdened; we should see ourselves as set apart/sanctified for those who need help to satisfy their hunger for bread for the body and the soul. This is the Lenten call on the church to deny ourselves and do good works for the well-being of our neighbors; and the need for the church to answer this call is very critical in the urban church setting.

The black church, when attentive to God's Kingdom Agenda, has been given the grace to stand sentry over the lives of its black denizens, as an agent of healing and advocacy; mercy and pardon; charity and sustenance. Historically, the outgrowth of the church's posture in black society has spread outwardly and positively affected and helped heal black life on many, many levels – spiritual, physical, social, economic, and political. As we move through Lent, toward the commemoration of the Passion of Christ, it would behoove the church to intentionally enter into a season of prayer in efforts to discern ways in which the church could better model the self-emptying nature of our God, by engaging in particular ministry acts which help meet the needs of people in the community. Forty days of sanctification is not just a process through which we are being set apart *from*, but it is also a process through which we are being set apart *for*.

Even a cursory look at the historical record will show that the black church has been the primary institution which birthed needed social service agencies, socio-political organizations, and businesses for black constituents who had been left starving and wounded on the margins of society. When we were unable to glean blessings and provisions from other lending institutions; when we could not get loans, discerning black Christians started credit unions in churches; some of which grew into solid banking institutions. When we could not get insurance companies to service our needs, black Christians formed insurance companies in the corners of church offices. When the hue and cry of black folk ascended to the steps of city halls, state houses and even the Whitehouse, it was lawyers raised up in the church, along with organizations birthed in the church, like the SCLC, SNCC, and the NAACP, which ensured that those earnest and desperate cries would be heard. When African Americans were left injured on the margins, in sharecropping fields and in ghettos, needing rental assistance, food, and safe places to be educated, to socialize, to be politically informed, and to have legal representation, the black church, led by black preachers, bankers, cooks, social workers, and lawyers, was the central hub of advocacy, charity and a healing outreach. Although governmental assistance is now one of the main safety net structures which helps American citizens who are in need (thanks to initiatives started under the administrations of Presidents Franklin D. Roosevelt and Lyndon B. Johnson), today's church, especially in our urban centers, continues to demonstrate the kind of mission outreach to oppressed people, which sounds similar in spirit to what Moses wrote about in Deuteronomy 24, and Jesus taught about in Luke 10. The black sector of the church, particular those congregations with a social agenda and consciousness, continues to be one of the main sources that God uses to help many in neglected urban communities. Therefore, as we look forward to the coming of holy week, we must not forget in our quest for a deeper walk with God, that the God, after whom we seek, seeks for those who are not only willing to fast in conventional ways -- fasting by giving up a certain delicacy or beverage for a period; God is not only seeking those who will worship behind the safety of stained glass windows, as we shout praises to the Lord, for all that Jesus endured, on our behalf; but God is also seeking for those who are willing to intentionally share this self-sacrificial love through myriad good works; good works which are rooted in divine compassion and visions of liberation.

The discerning reader will note that in the upshot of our text in Luke 10, Jesus never directly answered the lawyer's original question about what constituted someone *being a neighbor to* the lawyer. But in the telling of the parable of the Good Samaritan, Jesus inverts the lawyer's question, and commands him to be a neighbor *to, and an advocate for,* someone else! Jesus upends the man's focus.

As we seek to draw closer to God during Lent, as we engage in the intensification of our spiritual disciplines, we should not only commit to meditation in the word and fasting, while selfishly ignoring God's command to look for opportunities to hear and respond to our brothers and sisters' cries for help. Through our sanctified imaginations, I can imagine and hear the Spirit saying to us:

> "Church, you must learn from your text in Deuteronomy 24, wherein the community of Israel is commanded to intentionally share its harvest with those who were on the fringes, and you must continue to learn from the Samaritan's example, because this is one of the key ways God spreads love!! And what better way to share My love, than to bless others in tangible ways? So, why not be transformed by My word, and *go and do likewise?*"

What could this new approach to Lent mean for us and others? Could it mean that we must remember and reenact what has been one of the key roles of the church, particularly the black church, for years? Could it mean that we must say, "goodbye" to multifarious versions of a prosperity ideology which is only interested in building bigger barns for self-aggrandizing purposes? And say, "hello" to a 40- day period of preparation which might help us to create biblically-based, social justice and charitable ministries? Our Lenten fasting must lead to more than personal breakthroughs *for us four, and no more.* Lent is about reexamining our total lives, in the context of the ministry and message of Jesus. The Spirit has been given to us to help us to fulfill our callings and assignments to help a hurting world. The Kingdom of God challenges us to engage in a faith that is Holy-Spirited guided, pietistic and progressive; a spirituality rooted in the biblical tradition and in moral imperatives which cause us to live holy, as we reach beyond ourselves to touch the pain and problems of our neighbors; a moral burden that calls us to personal and private righteousness, as we offer up to God and neighbor acts of public service. We are saved to do some saving; loved to do some loving; liberated to do some liberating; delivered, so that others might be set free!

When at its best, this has been how the black church has operated in our society. Historically, the black church has always been about more than fasting and praying to break bad personal habits, and sinful strongholds, as important as this is. Therefore, in this Lenten season we do not want to just trumpet the importance of participating in some new variation of another *Daniel Fast*, while forgetting the call to fast from our self-centeredness. As we consider the history and work of the NAACP, the National Urban League, the UNCF, Operation PUSH, and many black sorority and fraternity organizations, it is a testimony to the power of God that many of these organizations can trace their roots back to church sanctuaries and basements, and to founding members, who were also members of black churches, and who believed that our Lenten religious beliefs and practices, should open us up to, and prepare us for, multi-faceted resurrections in our communities.

Laying hands on the sick for the purpose of healing, is a wonderful thing, and is needed; but so is laying our hands on some of the pathologies in our neighborhoods, so that a once oppressed people might enjoy a modicum of the abundant life. I believe in praying down demonic strongholds in our personal lives, as well as praying and working for change to happen in the political arena, where principalities and powers can use policy makers to inflict harm, like what seems to have been the case in the terrible events which led to the water crisis, in Flint, Michigan.

God, through the Mosaic law, continues to teach us to leave our gleanings for our neighbors. Jesus continues to speak to us, through the parable of the Good Samaritan; He keeps saying to us that our best spiritual practices, must go beyond public pronouncements of orthodox theological positions; we must see hunger and hurt for what it is, and then draw closer to those who lie wounded in the road of life's injustices.

Study Questions

1. What is the main purpose of Lent, in your estimation?
2. Should focusing on one's personal piety be the main thrust of the season?
3. What are some powerful ways that you can open yourself up to practices which foster spiritual growth, beyond the traditional Lenten practices of fasting and prayer?
4. There are some trends which indicate that an increasing number of Christians are beginning to view Lent through a different understanding of Lent; many are beginning to emphasize the need to commit to engaging in charitable and justice-based social ministry, during Lent. What do you think about this perspective?
5. How can your congregation move beyond fasting rituals, to new forms of self-denial and community engagement, during Lent? How has the African arm of the church been an example to the world in helping to turn an inner faith into community action?

9. Lent: Learning How to Tackle Our Giants

Selected Verses from 1 Samuel 17

I, like many, have had to face many scary giants in life. I have had to deal with demons and fears from without and within. I remember a time in my mid-teens when I was afraid to be me, because I had a terrible self-image. I can remember other times in my life when I had to deal with haters and instigators who inexplicably seemed to want to destroy my reputation and character. At other times, I have had to grapple with my own moral weaknesses and sinful proclivities. A few years ago, I can remember receiving an invitation to preach at one of the premier African American churches in the country – I only slept three hours that night, because of various giants floating around in my restless mind. And there have been yet other times when I have had to contend with racist giants -- strangers who have yelled out derogatory racial epithets from passing cars, as well as white co-workers who have jokingly called me names such as "Mr. James Brown," in the work place setting. As I move beyond my forties, and into my early fifties, the prospect of losing more and more of my youthful energy, coupled with the growing awareness of my mortality, all loom as intimidating giants; especially, when I lose sight of the presence and promises of God over my life. I know I am not alone in my experience of having to had to fight giants. Lent is a wonderful time to learn how to slay our giants, with the help of the Lord.

David became a timeless and legendary hero, for the ancient and modern world, all because he was willing to boldly face his giant, in the name and courage of the Lord. Because of what he and God did in 1 Samuel 17, David's name was shouted out in song by all the women of Israel and feared by all of Israel's enemies; and his name is still used today whenever and wherever a less esteemed contestant must face an imposing adversary who seems to have the overwhelming advantage. We often hear sports announcers, political pundits, military strategists, and even experts in business and industry, who describe how some small "David" sports team, or politician, or army, and even some start-up business rose up to defeat a "Goliath" team, political opponent, army, or company. Believers employ the names *David* and *Goliath* as metaphors to describe how the little person can rise above the shadows of any threatening, brutish, giant, and can experience victory, if he/she will only face the threat or threats with God and courage.

Young David was *chosen by God* to become the second King of Israel; and the heroic act of killing a trained soldier, nearly ten feet tall, would become what God would use to catapult David into the monarchy of Israel. David's family and his society had pegged young David in one hole; while God and the prophet Samuel had other plans for David! Samuel prophesies over Jessie's youngest son, that he would be the next king of Israel, and God would use the defeat of a giant to move David toward his coronation. In the genius of God's mind, God knew that David's willingness to face Goliath, in the power of God, would end in the giant's defeat. Once defeated, the song books, epic-poetry, and the record of history, would cause David's reputation to *blow up*. God would use David's courage, faith, and previous experience as a fearless shepherd, to propel and elevate him to the palace courts. But don't forget, in order for the prophesies over his life to be fulfilled; in order for David's destiny to become reality, David would have to conquer a big giant. One of the lessons we can learn this Lent, is learning how to better war against our big giants, so that once on the other side of our resurrection celebrations, we are legitimately walking in resurrection power!

It is important to remember that all of us are living in an inner and outer world filled with giants. We might not be in a contest with the champion of the ancient Philistines, but many people are facing all kinds of imposing and threatening obstacles. Some of the giants we face are external, while some are internal. Many youths have to deal with external giants such as, bullying from peers, senseless violence in the streets, low expectations among teachers; as well as internal giants like, fear, selfishness, pride, boredom, an out-of-control sexual lust, and a lack of concern or empathy for others. Couple these with a huge giant which stands against the forward progress of all black folks; a giant in the form of a country and culture too steeped in a history and climate of racism and classism, and one can be left wondering, *"Lord, how am I to win against such formidable forces of evil?"* Racism is one of the biggest giants ever unleashed against America! After years of silence, churches are beginning to face and confront this giant. This is why many churches in the Disciples of Christ (my denomination), the United Church of Christ, and the Evangelical Lutheran Church, have laid aside a certain Sunday during the year, as a day to praise God for the coming day when the giant of racism will be decapitated by the sword of God's Spirit of truth and love. Beyond annual days, our denomination has a unit of our church called our Pro-Reconciliation Anti-Racism ministry. The task of this ministry is to help inform and remind the church that racism is a sin that must be repented of. The sin of racism and any kind of ethnic/racial- based ideology of supremacy is definitely a sin to be renounced, during the season of Lent.

Whatever our giants are, whether they be internal, or external, personal or systemic, the good news is that God is fully aware that we are living in a sinful world, filled with big, threatening and even dangerous problems; and God is not only aware of our exposure, but God has equipped us with all that we will ever need to win many of the confrontations we will face in the form of troubling situations which seem inspired by demonic powers marshalled to crush our hopes. We just have to be willing to face the giants assigned to us, with courage, in the name of the Lord. But, in order to utilize the name of Jesus effectively, we must spend time getting to know the person, the ways, the teachings, and the authority behind that name; and then we must be willing to repent of all attitudes and proclivities that are the antithesis of what the name of Christ represents. The Lenten season is a time to hone in on how we can better cooperate with the will of God, in the name of the Lord, so that our giants are defeated.

I have found the forty-day period leading up the commemoration of the cross event and the celebration of the resurrection, to be a time to recommit my heart, mind, will, and actions to the purposes of the Kingdom. It is a wonderful time to learn more about our God, our weaknesses, our strengths, our gifts and our weapons for spiritual warfare. When one rededicates one's heart to the spiritual disciplines of prayer, fasting, giving, being charitable, the roar of our giants seem to grow, more faint. And though our giants might temporarily loom large, their exaggerated size only makes them better targets for God and us to knock down! Amazingly, we serve a God who promises that even such gargantuan giants as poverty, serious illness, and even death, will in time yield to the superior instruments of war God has created for our overcoming them. Love wins over hate; abundance will smother poverty; healing will cause illness to flee; and life will swallow and destroy death. When you begin to feel weak during your Lenten journey, you, plus God, make an unassailable combination!

Study Questions

1. How can the story of David and Goliath, inspire you to conquer your sins, and bad habits?
2. What was the source of David's courage?
3. How did David's past victories, over predators, while a shepherd, prepare him to fight Goliath?
4. How can we fight racism, and win?
5. What is the value of Lent, in helping you to be more intentional in resisting immorality and giving in to your moral weaknesses?
6. Fasting can help us to become more aware of spiritual realities. How can fasting help you become more aware of the power of God?

10. Lent: Making Room in Our Hearts

Now in the morning, having risen a long while before daylight, He went out and departed to a solitary place, and there He prayed. And Simon and those who were with Him searched for Him. When they found Him, they said to Him, "Everyone is looking for You." But He said to them, "Let us go into the next towns, that I may preach there also, because for this purpose I have come forth."

(Mark 1:35-38)

The Reverend Wyatt T. Walker, gospel preacher, fearless Civil Rights icon and activist, and friend of Dr. King, was also (unbeknownst to me) a brilliant song writer. He wrote a hymn entitled, *Is There Any Room in Your Heart for Jesus?* The song asks a very important question of every singing *saint* and spiritually disconnected *ain't;* one which gets to the heart of a sermon series that I recently preached at United Christian Church, titled, *Be Still, But Not Stagnant!* In the sermon series and in the song, the question is raised about whether our hearts are too crowded to allow the Spirit of Christ to do the inner work of transforming us into new creations. Through Walker's words, which reference how Jesus was born into a world which seemed to have no room for him in Bethlehem, we are challenged to examine our own hearts so that we might discern whether we are intentionally or unintentionally crowding out Jesus today. I think this question about the possibility of crowding out the Lord, is a central one for all 21st Century saints; and it is an issue I believe the Lord wants us to grapple with as we consider what it means to put into practice what I call, *the art of being still.* When we structure and manage our schedules to include quality quiet time with the Lord, we are making room in our hearts for Jesus. Whenever we regularly spend time in private worship, private prayer, private Bible study, with a posture of silent anticipation, we are making room in our hearts for the Lord. What is the effect of this discipline? When we make room for the Lord in our hearts and souls, we are providing the necessary spiritual space for the Lord to forgive, heal, and empower us, as the Lord speaks peace to our souls and gives us new direction. When we set aside twenty, thirty, and sixty minutes a day, for quiet reflection, eventually in the process of communing with God, it has been my experience (and countless others) that God will give us new and important instructions related to our current, or next, God- assignment. Quiet- time, leads to victory time. Meditation can lead to better marriages, parenting, work performance, and community organizing. In principle, this is what happened in the opening chapter of Mark's Gospel. Though John Mark had a penchant for writing about how God's kingdom was often on the verge of breaking through our realm, *immediately*; though Mark frequently describes how Jesus immediately did this and that act, Mark also makes it clear that before the occurrence of these sudden and amazing miracles, Jesus would spend large swaths of time cultivating his relationship with God in quiet stillness and prayerful solitude. Before God would do something dramatic, immediately, Jesus had spent time in the slow-moving activity of gradually, and consistently, fellowshipping with his Father.

In the opening chapter, after doing a wonderful and powerful exorcism, and several dynamic healing acts, Mark makes sure to record how Jesus would get up, early in the morning, and leave for a distant grove, meadow, or hilly area, where he could be alone with God; talking, listening, and discerning his next move. This practice of making room in his heart for the Spirit to speak to him and through him, was obviously something Jesus did quite often. In fact, in verse 36, the text says that Simon Peter and the other disciples knew exactly where to find him praying that morning, when they felt compelled to tell him what they felt was urgent news. Interestingly enough, when they find Jesus in his familiar spot, they begin telling him the urgent demands that people wanted to make on his time, focus and energy: "Everyone is looking for You," they exclaim. Jesus is at the apex of his ministerial fame in this particular location. But, it was right after spending time with his Father in solitude, that Jesus answers Peter's urgency in a curious way. Jesus responds to Peter and the others by sharing with them that He is clear that it is time for them to leave town. Though ministry was going well where they were, it was time to go! Though everyone in the area was anticipating Jesus addressing their pressing and urgent needs, Jesus is fully persuaded, by verse 38, that it was time to, "go into the next towns," that he might preach in an increasingly expansive geographical and social setting. He understood that it was for the purpose of preaching the good news of the kingdom to a much wider audience, beyond the provincial boundaries of any one town, that he had been sent by God. I submit that it was precisely on the heels of his practicing *the art of being still*, that Jesus is granted the laser-like focus to distinguish between the demands of others, and the will of the Spirit. Obviously, his sense of God's will and God's timing was clarified; this clarification dictated his next ministry move. Jesus knew the next towns to which they must immediately travel. In your life, are you taking the needed time to connect with God, especially when you're beginning to sense an uneasiness in your spirit – the source of which, you can't quite put your finger on?

Fundamentally, as we make room in our hearts, we become changed on the inside, for the better; and once we are changed, we are ready to become change agents! When the Lord has said something powerful to us, within us, in the time of solitude and silent reflection, the Holy Spirit will then move through us and motivate us to share that powerful insight with others. *God calls us to stillness, not stagnancy.* There are certain seasons when the intensity of the need for these disciplines seems to increase for weeks, and months, at a time. There are many times when we must open ourselves up to that which is deep in God, in order that God might speak to that which is deep in us. But there are certain times when a heightened urgency to connect with God's will surfaces. As the psalmist said, "Deep calls to the deep." It is in these moments of stillness that we can allow ourselves the space to hear God whispering to us the need to forgive, confess sins, speak up, be quiet, pursue a new path, revisit an old situation, disconnect a relationship, go back to school, begin a new project, write a book, witness to a neighbor, bless someone with money, start a business, or amazingly, answer the call to preach!

Most of the heroes and heroines of the biblical record, spent a good portion of their lives resting, wrestling, and dancing with God in deserts, in wildernesses, and even in prisons. But, if one searches the scriptures, from Genesis to Revelation, whenever God led one of God's prophets, prophetesses, priests, kings, and Apostles to a place of solitude, it was almost always in order that that person would be rejuvenated, reinvigorated, or redirected, for the purposes of engaging in more effective expressions of prophetic, liberating, and Christ-inspired ministry to, for, and with others.

Through penetrating lyrics, Wyatt T. Walker asks us:

> Is there any room in your heart for Jesus? He is dying to be born there today.
> Is there are place or a space in your heart, So the Lord of Lords can enter today?

If we would only regularly make room for Christ's Spirit to speak to us, like Jesus made room for his Father to speak to him, we would soon discover that God will meet us in that sacred space and tell us things about God, ourselves, and the world; things that will encourage us to run forward in the power of God. Once we are empowered by a new knowledge of the Lord, ourselves, and our situation, as we serve to be change agents for Christ, we will find out something powerful that the writer of Isaiah 40 said: we will discover that we are......*running and not getting weary; that we are walking and not fainting.*

Study Questions

1. How are you consciously making room in your heart for Jesus? Is it by your church attendance, alone?

2. Do you have a time dedicated to scripture reading and journaling your thoughts afterwards?

3. Do you ever sing to the Lord in private? How about humming, if singing is not what you normally do?

4. One of my favorite practices, since college, is to regularly go on prayer walks, in solitude. Where do you have dedicated space for prayer?

5. In Mark's Gospel, we have clear indications that before important decisions, Jesus would steal away to be alone with His Father. If Jesus, the Son of God, had to seek solitude to discern God's movement in his life, what does that mean for us?

11. Lent: An Encounter with The Well, on top of a Well

Now Jacob's well was there. Jesus therefore, being wearied from His journey, sat thus by the well. It was about the sixth hour. A woman of Samaria came to draw water. Jesus said to her, "Give Me a drink…Then the woman of Samaria said to Him, "How is it that You, being a Jew, ask a drink from me, a Samaritan woman? For Jews have no dealings with Samaritans"

(John 4:6,7 and 9)

There is a popular, but derogatory term that many of our young people are using to describe a young lady who seems needful of a lot of attention, money, intimacy, or sex – such a young woman is called, "thirsty." Often such a descriptor is meant to be an insult; one that seems to carry with it misogynistic and sexual undertones. Rarely, if ever, is this phrase used to describe a young man who also seems to desperately go after much of the same things as his female counterpart is pursuing. The fascinating thing about our human frailty and vulnerability is that any one of us can, at certain points in our lives, find one's self thirsty for something or someone. This thirst is a universal fact, and, if not properly managed and quenched, can become the bane of our existence. Most importantly, it is the way that we try to quench our thirsts that can lead us to the doorways of satisfaction and joy, or to the threshold of misery, addiction and shame.

A Samaritan woman has to grapple with her thirst issues in John 4, when she encounters the long-awaited Messiah near, what was at the time, a popular landmark, known as *Jacob's Well*. As a Samaritan, she was a woman who had been segregated from the broader Jewish religious and social culture (The Jews considered Samaritans as a half-breed people; part Jewish, part Gentile; maybe equivalent to how some mulattos were and are viewed in our society by racists). She was a double minority – she was a woman, living in a patriarchal society; and she was despised ethnically, and considered a second-class citizen by most Jews. Undoubtedly, there must have been some psychological damage done to these people who were considered so repulsive that many of the Jews, in their sense of religious superiority, frequently elected to walk extra miles to avoid encountering the Samaritans. This, at best, pointed to a lingering bitterness that many Jews had against Samaritans because of the Jews' perception of the Samaritan's past idolatrous practices; and at worst, it pointed to raw, naked, ethnic, and religious bigotry.

As we reflect on the purpose of Lent, it can, and must include learning to shed negative emotions, like bitterness and unforgiveness. Like the woman at the well, black folk, especially black women, have had many reasons to be very hesitant to warm up to those whom they believe are racist, sexist, and have ulterior motives for engaging them in conversation. In the Samaritan woman's case, after an initial icy response to Jesus' request; a response indicative of her shock that a male Jew would talk to her, she eventually softens her tone and releases her guard, to engage Jesus in conversation.

To have to endure centuries of being judged harshly and discriminated against severely, primarily because of one's ethnicity and gender, is a terrible thing. Such experiences leave scars, which can fester into sores of bitterness. Racism, sexism, and segregation can form triplet demons which antagonize and terrorize, and create an atmosphere of mutual hatred. These are the demons Rosa Parks faced, as she rode in the front seats of that historic Montgomery Bus, when a hate-filled white man demanded that she get up and yield her seat to him. He was filled with the sad and fallacious belief in white male supremacy, while she was afflicted with a fatigue, weariness, and empowered by a supernatural boldness, which gave her the courage and kinetic energy to remain seated for justice, equality, and a God-given freedom. Eventually, she and many others, who became the foundation stones of the movement, talked and wrote about the importance of shedding our corresponding hatred of whites, for what they had done to black people, so that we might drink deeply, without poison, from a nourishing and satisfying well of love, that only God can provide.

Not only was the woman in our text of an ethnicity and culture which had been shunned by her Jewish neighbors, but to add to the shadow on her reputation, she was also one who had been in numerous failed romantic relationships. She had been married five times, and the sixth man she was with is described by Jesus, in verse 18, as someone who was *not her* husband. She seems to have resorted to settling for either someone who wouldn't marry her or couldn't marry her (he might have been already married to someone else!). As we take a long look at ourselves during Lent, we cannot solely point to outside factors which may increase our thirsts for love and acceptance, sometimes there is a deep hole within; often there is something lacking – some vacuous space within each of us that ideal social circumstances alone can never adequately satisfy.

As we read the small bit of biographical information about this woman, provided by John, we might surmise that she made some poor romantic choices in her life. What of her past marriages? It is quite possible that she had lost several husbands to the cold imposition of an untimely death. But all five? It is doubtful. And even if so, a woman with her kind of poor luck, would have also left a cloud of suspicion hanging over her reputation. Through speculation and conjecture, we might conclude that she was a woman who was just "unlucky" at best, or deeply flawed morally, at worst. Because of her misfortune and her negative reputation, this woman had probably lived a very difficult life; one, I imagine, replete with tragedy, and or, possible romantic improprieties and scandals, all which would have resulted in a definite lack of emotional fulfillment – increasing her inner thirstiness. It is safe to conclude that life had left her thirsty for a lasting love. As you reflect on your life, have there been circumstances which have caused you to have an insatiable thirst for better, or more? For this woman to be involved in this many broken relationships, and failed marriages, was frowned upon by both men and women, in her cultural context. Maybe she had been considered by the other Samaritans as "cursed," "whorish," "loose," or "sluttish," depending on the particularities of her many relationships. She might have often suffered the indignity of having been *slut-shamed* by the people of her town.

Unfortunately, and with deep regret, I can remember my friends and I, using some painful pejoratives, as we described certain girls when we were in our pre-teens. We sometimes used hurtful words to foolishly label girls in our school who had reputations for being very sexually active – whether the rumors were true or not. The strange and shocking thing about this memory is how early we had bought into a social double standard. Because, unlike how we were quick to categorize girls a certain way, to us, our male classmates who were known to pursue and succeed in multiple sexual encounters, had reached Olympian heights in our minds, and were envied and held on pedestals of glory. These "whorish" guys were the ones we wanted to be like, in many ways. Growing up, our heroes, were movie characters who had a way with the ladies, like the black, private detective, John Shaft (most famously played by actor, Richard Roundtree), and the British agent, James Bond (most famously played by actor, Sean Connery); they were not only athletic, violent, and experts in killing bad criminals and evil spies, but they were cool and suave, and able to easily bed countless women, from the opening credits, to the ending ones. None of us viewed their casual sex-capades as being wrong, undesirable, or immoral. In fact, to impress our friends, many of us often told lies about the number of "conquests" we had enjoyed, in attempts to project an enviable posture, power and position over the other boys. Most of us had a record of zero "reaching home-plate" experiences, at ages thirteen and fourteen. It is sufficient to acknowledge that there was a stark double standard among us, rooted in patriarchy and a not-so-subtle misogyny.

This encounter that the Samaritan woman had with Jesus, reveals a very different perspective. Jesus was not your typical man. Jesus does not shun her, but engages her in holy conversation, no matter what the prevailing social norms were at the time. When Jesus met her, the meeting took place during a time in history when multiple marriages, divorces, and *shacking*, were not widely accepted; such is not necessarily the case today in our "liberated," postmodern, Western culture, of the new millennium (though there remains in some sectors of our culture and society – especially among more senior women and men, who traverse in certain socio-religious circles – a disapproval of the kind of life's choices which seem to mirror the Samaritan woman's). These post-modern voices trumpet the notion that above all else, we must keep trying to make ourselves at home in the triplet cities of personal satisfaction, carnal pleasures, and a moral relativism, which all shout from the roof-top of the culture, the virtues of a selective non-judgmentalism. The predominant message in our society is that we must do what makes us feel good, and that no one should try to impose their Victorian era beliefs on us. Despite our faults and failings; in spite of our hubris and self-deception, Jesus still desires to meet us, in our *Samarias*, because Jesus is about the business of quenching our most pressing thirsts. The Samaritan Woman's life experiences had negatively impacted her sense of self and her self-understanding, in terms of what it meant to be truly satisfied via a love relationship, characterized by a holy covenant, longevity, and unconditional love. In the text, while alone, at noon, possibly when she wouldn't be harassed by the women from town who would give her "side-eyed" looks and acerbic remarks, God has a love-showdown with her! And he has life-giving water! This is a high noon moment. She is confronted by the One who promises to satisfy her deepest thirsts — especially her thirsts for acceptance, forgiveness and a covenantal love.

As their conversation unfolds, Jesus tells her that God is looking for persons who will worship God beyond locations like Mt. Gerizim or in the city of Jerusalem; beyond the limits of time, space, size and race; beyond cultural traditions and a flawed provincial theology. God desires to be linked up with persons from all races and cultures, who will worship God in spirit and truth. But with this, she must have wondered, "What is spirit and truth worship?" As she and Jesus engage in theological conversation, this issue of what makes for true worship is one of the first things Jesus teaches her. Jesus hints that spirit and truth worship is a fountain of life. Spirit and truth worship is the kind of worship that bubbles up and overflows from the heart of a person who has been touched by God's love, forgiveness and acceptance. It is worship that is honest and sincere, and without fakery and a negative fear. It is biblical-based worship. It is the kind of worship which originates from deep within a heart of gratitude and flows out and through a person who desires to express love back to God, to the exaltation, and glory of God. This kind of worshiper is then imbued and graced with the power of the Spirit's presence and love. Spirit and truth worship is the kind of worship where people lay down the garments of pretense and come clean before God, because God has disclosed God's self to them in a way that is life-altering. Practically, with spirit and truth worship, there is an earnest desire to enthusiastically bless God with our voices, our music, our instruments, our preaching; through praises and singing, as well as through service, and the sanctified commitments we make. For Spirit and truth worship to occur, one must be open to being filled with the Spirit; and one must be vulnerable and available, as one submits to the teachings of the Messiah, in the context of community.

After Jesus reveals Himself to her, and after he, through divine revelation, touches and addresses those vulnerable and painful aspects of her life, he promises to soothe and satiate her heart's core desires, by giving her "living water." She leaves the well and the water pot behind, after hearing His soothing, liquid-like words of grace which pour over her soul; words which reveal God's desire to be in an intimate, freeing, relationship with her! By the power of His word, she forgets her original purpose for going to Jacob's well. Filled with awe and wonder, and a sense of acceptance, she runs into the city, transformed by the encounter. She is not a whore, but instead, she is one who has been touched by the holy. She has a new purpose, and a new word to share. She becomes a holy herald of good news! After hearing and receiving Jesus' penetrating words of intimacy, insight, and theological clarity, she testifies everywhere that she has seen and had conversation with a man who told her everything she needed to know about her life. She becomes a preacher, in the truest sense; an evangelist of the first order! God had shown up at the doorstep of her heart, with pure water; and God had entered in, and won her over. God revealed to her that God knew her, and still loved her, completely! She had to tell as many as she could, about The Well she met- a well, who had been sitting on top of Jacob's well.

This is not how she had thought of God, previously. This is a new revelation, which revealed to her that God was deeply concerned about her; and had come to quench her deepest longings. Through this thirst quenching encounter she is on the new pathway to become her truest self. Given what the Lord has declared to her, it makes sense that she would become so excited that she would leave her water pot behind. She had forgotten her prior mission – that of quenching her physical thirsts. This blessing of living water had given her a new mission. She runs into the surrounding towns, villages, and hamlets, serving God by offering her witness; earnestly crying out, "Come meet a man, who told me all that I ever did! Could this be the Messiah?"

The Samaritan Woman gives us a picture of a woman who is unlike the women, commanded to be quiet in the Pauline Epistles. She is not one who should only be seen, but not heard in the gatherings of the faithful, if it included men. This is a woman who had found her voice, located in the voice of One who has connected with her, as only God can. From that moment on, she is determined to help quench the thirsts of other women and men, who were living their lives in silent desperation. This scenario of the Lord confronting and comforting thirsty souls, continues to play out over, and over again. Throughout history, God has shown up in the lives of people who had reputations that were less than stellar, and less than satisfying. God makes it God's business to cross the pathways of millions of very thirsty men and women, each day; often in the very places where people are seeking to quench thirsts which seem unquenchable. Today, our modern-day Jacob's wells are located in business boardrooms, single's bars, athletic clubs, cruise ships, freaky parties, drug houses, and even churches. Often because someone is/has been praying and interceding for us, God confronts us, and speaks into our souls, drawing out those issues that have drained us and left us dry. If we will keep listening to the Messiah's voice, we will discover that there is only One who has the insight, power and the compassion to clarify for us, both our unconscious religious longings and unknown existential purposes. After the encounter, we will simply know that His name is *Jesus.* With such knowledge, we can come out on the other side of our meetings with the Lord, having forgotten about those many water pots, and cisterns, which at one point, seemed so important, but which were never meant to quench the eternal thirsts of our souls. This discovery and the announcement of a thirst-quenching well; a living well, deeper than any other well, has made up the substance of the testimonies of preaching women like Jarena Lee, Julia Foote, Brenda Little, Prathia Hall, Ella Pearson Mitchell, Jacqueline McCullough, Claudette Copeland, Cynthia Hale, Stephanie Crowder, Vashti McKenzie, Suzan Johnson Cook, Gina Stewart, Yvonne Delk, Carolyn Ann Knight, and my mother, Barbara Elaine Bryant, to name a few. I praise God for a Jesus who still quenches thirsty hearts and souls! I praise God for all of God's preaching women and men!

Study Questions

1. Does your history indicate that you have "thirsts" in your life which have caused you to search for excitement, accolades, affirmation, and meaningful relationships, in ways that are less than healthy?

2. What does Jesus' encounter with this woman reveal to us about Jesus? About the Samaritan woman?

3. Do you think Jesus, in his humanity, was ever thirsty for excitement, accolades, affirmation and meaningful relationships? Can you recount any Gospel stories which indicate this?

4. How can encounters with Jesus satisfy our deepest longings?

5. When we have unmet needs, we can end up "eating" and "drinking" from bad buffets and "poisoned" wells to satisfy us.

6. What role does church have in helping to satiate the appetites, and quench the thirsts, of those who have been eating from bad "buffets," and drinking from "poisoned" wells?

7. What do you think our youth are most thirsty for? How can Christ and the church satisfy that thirst?

8. What do you think our middle-aged adults are most thirsty for in life? What about our seniors? How can Christ and the church satisfy these thirsts?

Part 3

Holy Week and Easter through Pentecost

12. Hosanna in Tough Times

And some of the Pharisees called to Him from the crowd, "Teacher, rebuke thy disciples." But He answered and said to them, "I tell you that if these should keep silent, the stones would immediately cry out. Now as He drew near, he saw the city, and wept over it...

(Luke 19:39-40)
Also Psalm 100

God wants us to grow in every facet of our lives, especially in how we offer up praises to God in both the privacy of our hearts and in the public gatherings of our worship services. As the older preachers would say to their audiences, "Y'all don't want God to make the rocks cry out, in your place!" We, who are God's children, are at our best, in every way, when from an authentic place, we raise our hearts and voices to praise our Divine Daddy, in worship. Praise and worship blesses God, and us. It blesses God in the same way we feel blessed when a child we are raising, and have doted on, says, "Thank You" from a place of gratitude and love. Praise blesses us in that our praises confirm that we are spiritually awake, because it is simply the right thing to do to express appreciation to a person, or persons, who have shown us great love and have blessed us with great gifts. The manner in which we praise and worship the Lord, indicates how much we truly recognize, or are failing to recognize, that even through the vicissitudes of life, God is a good Father/Parent. The writer of Psalm 100 is someone who was obviously a serious worshiper of Yahweh. The Psalmist knew it was right to give God thanks and praise; and wrote about what should be our method and motive for worship:

> Make a joyful shout to the LORD, all you lands! Serve the LORD with gladness; Come before His presence with singing. Know that the LORD, He is God; It is He who has made us, and not we ourselves; We are His people and the sheep of His pasture. Enter into His gates with thanksgiving, And into His courts with praise. Be thankful to Him and bless His name. For the LORD is good; His mercy is everlasting, And His truth endures to all generations.

The Psalmist notes that our praises should include joyful shouts of acclamation, and heart-felt singing to God. This expression of worship is not a dry, contemplative exercise. It is loud, boisterous, bombastic, and emotional; it is also to be melodic and harmonious. The writer says that we are to come before God's presence with shouts and singing. Why are we to worship in this manner? Because God is greater than the musical artists we cheer, or the sports franchises we love. Beyonce' and Jay Z, did not save one soul; the Bulls, Bears, Lions, Warriors and Lakers, cannot make us whole. According to the Psalmist, our knowledge of God's greatness should elicit a vigorous, liturgical response. Our shouting and melodic praise is to be predicated on us knowing that Yahweh is God, and *we are not*! Though we might often think we are the center of the universe, actually the Creator is. The God of Abraham, Isaac, and Jacob, is the one who has made us. The God revealed to us in Christ, is the one who has given us life and everything good pertaining to it. God has allotted us a world of experiences; some we deem good, and some we consider bad. God has given us a plethora of dynamic relationships -- some good, and others bad. But the good and the bad together make up this tapestry of experiences we call "life." God has shared life with us. Therefore, it is on this basis alone that we should conclude that God is worthy of our sincere praises. None of us likes to experience the bad; and all of us like to experience life's joys and pleasantries, but without God we would have *no experiences*. Without God's creative hand, waving over a lifeless nothingness, we would not have had the chance to become. And this inner urge to become, is the heat of life. Our vocal praise is our clumsy way of saying to God, "Thank you for the chance to become all that you have originally envisioned me to be!"

In the light of our blessings and in the shadows of our struggles, as we walk with God, and grow in God's word, there should be a deepening of our love for Christ and a greater emotional connection to and with the One who has been better to us than we have been to ourselves. Though the way each one of us praises God is somewhat different (some love singing hymns, others love clapping, some rock from side to side, others stand and raise their hands, some bow at the altar silently as they offer up whispering *thankyous),* however we worship, there should be a growing eagerness within us to come to offer up to the Lord our best praises, singing, musical creativity, musicianship, preaching, giving, and general participation, even as we go through those strange wilderness moments when we feel temporarily estranged from God's blessings and goodness! Because of God's steadfast love and sovereign power, it would behoove us to learn how to shout Hosannas, even in what we deem to be tough times. Because as we continue to consistently vocalize our gratitude to the Lord, even when it seems as though we only have a few, meager reasons to praise God, our God takes notice of those who are willing to offer to God a sacrifice of praise.

In Luke 19, Luke recalls an important event found in all four canonical gospels. The gathered crowds begin to sing and shout, "Hosannah!" to Christ as he humbly rides into Jerusalem, as he nears the end of his earthly ministry. The Pharisees attempt to stop this praise procession. These men are religious killjoys – they are cloud bearing preachers; deacons of depression and devilment; elders of evil reports. Despite of the vehement protestations of these jealous religious leaders, the adoring and thankful crowds could not help but to give thanks for all of the wonderful things Jesus had done for them. They knew that someone special was in their midst. But unfortunately, for some in the region, this posture of praise was only a temporary perspective. In just a few days, as Jesus would begin to accomplish God's greatest work, located on Calvary. Soon, throngs of people in the public square would be shouting out an entirely different sentiment, filled with different words and intentions. Soon, Jesus would hear the deafening and devilish din of, "Crucify Him! Crucify Him!" At that terrible moment, the shouts of the public would not be rooted in the good theology of offering up a sacrifice of praise, even on what looked like, a bad Friday; but instead these new cries and shouts would be the result of the sudden shifting winds of public opinion, which had hastily, and wrongly concluded that Jesus was not worthy of thanks and praise. And, without enlightenment from the Spirit, this sudden shift, makes sense, in a limited way. On that frightening Friday, after the trumped-up charges and the beating by the Roman soldiers, Jesus seemed powerless, hopeless, and helpless. He seemed not be the Christ, but a criminal – he appeared to be a loser, not a winner. Even today, many persons will quickly conclude that if a young, unarmed black man, is shot in the back, numerous times by a police officer, he must have done something to deserve such a violent execution. Many are too quick to give the powers of the state carte blanche to render the ultimate judgement, just by virtue of a uniform and a badge. This kind of thinking is nothing new. I would wager that many people, in Jesus' day thought that if the Sanhedrin and the Roman authorities had concluded that Jesus was worthy of a scourging and then death, then he must have been someone evil. When we think like sheep, not guided by the Good Shepherd, we are easily swayed by popular opinions; and we can become quick to condemn those we suspect are guilty, with no proof to buttress our positions. And we all love victors. We hate to be identified with losers. The fascinating thing is that sometimes we are unable to discern the difference between who's really winning, and who's really losing. Because of the people's sad spiritual state, Jesus could foresee what was to come. This is why he wept over Jerusalem before his crucifixion. He could see, that many could not/would not see who He really was, in any consistent way; consequently, they would not be able to see the true extent of God's love for them.

There is a lesson in these events. God is looking for a people who will grow in their understanding of praise and worship; those who will praise the Lord passionately and with joy, not only when it is Palm Sunday, but when the earth seems covered in the darkness of a Crucifixion Friday – when the forces of good, *seem* to be outnumbered and outfoxed. The question which looms large before us in such times is, "Is this God, the God who seems unable or unwilling to do anything right now; is this God worthy of my praise?"

I remember a particularly difficult season in my life, during which I was asking God to reveal some important information to me that seemed hidden by dark clouds. What I was searching for was critical information that I felt I needed to guide my future steps in ministry for the next several years. I was praying fervently, because, at that time, I had reached a ministerial dead-end. My family and I were greatly frustrated and perplexed by what seemed to be a fortified stronghold of spiritual stagnation and a devilish disunity, which had seized the congregation we were serving. After six years, it seemed as if many of the congregation's key leaders were not willing to enact the necessary changes that would help the congregation become more of what God intended it to be – a center of help and hope for those who lived in the neighborhood around the church. Also, it seemed as if church officers were not being held accountable for divisive behavior. Leaders were fighting with other leaders. Many seemed unwilling to consistently give their time, talent and treasure, to the work of our congregation's ministry and vision. Our leaders' less than stellar example, was having a trickle-down effect on the congregation. More than a few seemed to be operating out of a "Do what I say, not what I do" philosophy. In addition to this, though we were experiencing some modest growth, our giving was not that great among many officers and members. So, as a response, there was a stealth decision made by four or five of our congregation's leaders, to cut my salary, nearly 50%, with only six weeks' notice. They hoped that this move would put the congregation on better financial footing. This was done, without consulting with other key leaders and the congregation. Such a radical move was also done with more enthusiasm and energy than the energy that went into supporting a Stewardship initiative which I had created, and shared with the Elders, one year prior called, *GPS* – **Giving**, and **Pledging** for the **Sustainability** of our church's ministry. Just twelve months earlier, many of these same leaders who were quick to offer up my already modest salary as the key sacrifice for the financial health of our congregation, talked very negatively about the possible results that could come from a one-month, Bible-based, stewardship initiative, which emphasized the importance of ministry and tithing in order to support the work we believed God was calling us to do.

It was also during this same season that I was asking God to strengthen and deliver us from other spiritual attacks that were coming against my family and me (my wife and I had recently experienced the deaths of close family members – her parents, and my mother; we were also in two serious car accidents, which totaled one of our cars; I was held-up at gun point, and tied up in a bank robbery; my emotional and physical health were being tested; and our financial situation was real sketchy, especially with two sons in college, who weren't on full scholarships). We were living in a very small parsonage, with most of our belongings from a large home we once owned in a previous city, kept in storage, with an expensive monthly charge attached. During this period, the trials of life seemed to be incessantly flooding and swamping our lives. Infighting in our congregation seemed to be getting worse and not better, and I was beginning to wonder would things ever change; new members were joining in modest numbers, but those who had joined were not yet committed to stewardship, discipleship, or even regular attendance. During this season of our lives, I felt as though the prospect of brighter days ahead were just the pitiful pipe dreams of a confused preacher. One evening, during this tough season, I fell asleep and had a dream. In the dream, I was standing before a crowd that was gathered beneath a second or third story window. The people were assembled in a parking lot below; they were waiting to hear a sermon. As I approached the window to preach to those below, I realized that I did not have a prepared manuscript, or a particular text in mind. Somehow this preaching assignment had caught me off guard. As, I approached the podium, which was positioned right in front of the third-story window overlooking the parking lot where the listeners were gathered, I heard myself saying, "Our text will come from Psalm 100!" In the dream, even though I could not remember the theological details or the content of this Psalm, I had an intuitive sense that it *was always an appropriate Psalm from which to preach.* I woke up suddenly. It was morning. I grabbed my Bible to review Psalm 100. As I read through this Psalm of thanksgiving, it was if the Lord was directing me to give God vocal and vibrant praises of thanksgiving, even as I awaited answers, strength, and help. I started to realize anew that whether it was a season of darkness or light; joy or sadness; peace or anxiety; clarity or a lack thereof; giving God thanks and praise is always wise and efficacious!

God invites us to be the kind of worshipers who do not base our joyous praise on ever-changing circumstances. After hearing tough news, pray, and then praise God! You do not have to wait to be whipped into a praise frenzy by a Hammond organ, a powerful preacher, or a gifted soloist. This call on our lives to praise God through the tough times, is not always easy; it is not our first nature to do so. I have not mastered all aspects of this spiritual discipline, especially when multiple weights are suddenly piled on my soul. But, I am learning that after a week of frustration and failure, it is best to pray and sing shouts of gratitude to God, if for nothing else than the good news that the week is finally over! I am learning that when my projects and godly efforts are haunted by devils, hellions, or just misguided folk, who think they are doing God's work, I must patiently stay the course, and praise the Lord because it blesses God, and me. I will reap the tremendous fruit of a maturing character.

When temptations weaken your intestinal fortitude, in that very moment, as an initially clumsy act of your will, proclaim out-loud, your love for God, and then note how quickly that temptations weaken in strength. In fact, the funny thing is, as we praise God, especially in tough times, God gives us a great gift in return; God gives us joy! It is as Nehemiah declares: *The joy of the Lord is our strength!* It would be a tragedy, not to access this divine strength, and to have a rock crying out in our places.

Study Questions

1. Are you growing in your praise and worship? How do you know if you are?

2. Do you regularly go to the house of prayer, to offer up to God the sacrifice of praise no matter what you have been through during the week? No matter how you feel?

3. Have you ever experienced joy welling up in your soul, after you started singing a hymn? Or after joining in with the choir, or a gospel artist on tape, disc, or flash drive sticks?

4. Why not start practicing the discipline of worshiping and praising God this week, in the privacy of your home? You do not need musical accompaniment.

5. As a part of your preparation for worship routine, why not begin reading, or singing, Psalm 100 to God, a few times in succession? By the fourth reading/singing, you might very well feel the presence of God.

13. Learning to Stand Apart from the Crowd

And a very great multitude spread their clothes on the road; others cut down branches from the trees and spread them on the road. Then the multitudes who went before and those who followed cried out, saying: "Hosanna to the Son of David! Blessed is He who comes in the name of the LORD! Hosanna in the highest!

(Matthew 21:8-9)

I am grateful to God for the arrival of Holy Week! Holy Week reminds non-Christians, and all observant Christians, that Christians believe that God went to extraordinary lengths to redeem and rescue humankind from a terrible destiny – a destiny of us forever being separated from God's glorious presence. I thank God for giving us the most wonderful Savior! In today's text, Jesus' coming as the Savior of the world, is briefly celebrated by the crowds. For the first time, in the gospel narratives, a large swath of the Jerusalem populace seems to briefly understand and celebrate who Jesus is, and why Jesus came. As the Lord makes his processional to His divine destiny on Calvary's hill, and to a three day stay in a borrowed tomb, the crowds are shouting praises of jubilation as they cry out for salvation! The crowds seem to recognize him as the fulfillment of Zechariah's prophecy about the Messianic figure, who would come humbly riding into town on a Donkey, to fulfill God's divine purposes (see Zechariah 9). They seem to discern that this is that powerful moment of fulfilled history and prophecy, as he courageously goes forth on his mission of revealing God's love and redemption work, through giving his back to the whip and hard wood of the cross; and his wrists and ankles to sharp nails of a crucifixion, along with his furrowed brow to a crown of thorns. They seem to finally get it, *but do they?*

Somewhere in this question lies a simple, yet paradoxically complex truth: *It has been, and is still possible for the same population to celebrate the Lord one week, and the next, cry out for his crucifixion!* This is especially true if our spirituality and theology are only tethered to the prevailing opinion of *the unmoored crowd*! Is your faith primarily based on what the crowd says is good, true, and right? Are your politics based solely on what your family has always believed? Have most of your life's choices been based on pleasing others? Is your walk with God primarily dependent on how those who live around you are living their lives?

God is a God who calls each one of us to find our unique niche' in the world. Even though we might live in a city with millions, no other person has our unique fingerprint pattern. No one has our exact DNA coding. No one thinks, feels, or perceives exactly as another person does, when faced with a plethora of similar choices and circumstances. Therefore, because each individual is unique in this way, there are times when we must learn to stand alone, with God! Perhaps, we might be pressed to do so today. Though *no man (person) is an island*, as John Donne said so eloquently in his poem, *Meditation XVII*, there are those certain moments in our lives and in history when we must stand apart from the crowd. There are times when *the crowds* are operating against God's will; there are moments when a crowd mentality results in an increase in immorality, hopelessness and violence. The crowd mentality has, at various points in ancient and modern history, temporarily crowded out God's preferred agenda for the world. Within the last three centuries, *the crowd* was known to scream out for the severe beating and lynching of black men who had often been falsely accused of various crimes, especially sexual assaulting and raping white women. The crowds in Germany, sent many Jews to death camps. For many young people today, *the crowd* is a throng of temptation and peer pressure to behave without moral and spiritual restraints; for many youth, *the crowd* can push them to engage in promiscuous, misdirected, selfish, and violent behavior.

I remember having a friend in elementary school, who had become one of my young basketball playing buddies one summer. He was friends with one of my best friends, Benjamin. Over the next couple of months, I got to know Desmond, through Ben. I was just starting to learn how to play the sport, while both Desmond and Ben, were a couple of years older, and already advanced in their basketball skill level. Desmond had a smooth left-hand jump shot, and nice ball-handling skills. Benjamin was a gifted basketball talent at a very young age. I on the other hand, was very raw. Just starting out, having primarily played baseball my preteen years, I was tall and gangly, but learning basketball quickly. Desmond, like Ben and I, was from a middle-class, two parent family; and though Desmond and I were not best friends, he was friends with Ben, and therefore, I trusted him. He had an easy-going personality; a great sense of humor, and occasionally, he gave me a few pointers on how to improve my game. Unfortunately, about a year later, something had drastically shifted in Desmond's personality. The next spring, Ben and I saw Desmond walking with a different group of guys; they were not athletes; he was with a shady crowd – a group of guys who we knew were always up to trouble. As we approached them, from a distance, all of them started running toward us, yelling, "Let's get them!" At first, we thought they were kidding around, because we knew all of them to some degree, especially Desmond; and we had never had any trouble out of any of them. But, as they got closer, we began to sense that they were not kidding around. Without a second thought, we took off running. They chased us for a couple of blocks, threatening to jump us, once they caught up with us. I still remember, that as we ran, Desmond was yelling out threats too, even at Ben, with whom he had had a real close friendship. As we ran, we ran as if we were trying out in the Olympic trials, and it seemed as if they were gaining on us. By God's grace, by only about twenty feet, we made it to my parents' door. Once safely inside the house, we sat in my basement bewildered – wondering, "What was that all about? and why was Desmond with them?" And then, it dawned on us. *"Desmond had decided to join up with a different crowd – some gangbangers."* Some of the gang members in the neighborhood, as an initiation rite, had evidently coaxed him to break ties with his old friendships in a way that was clear, impactful, and severe. From that day on, our young lives clearly headed in different directions. Over the next few years, Ben and

I became more skilled in basketball (By the time I was about 15, I had developed a reputation as a player with great potential, who might develop into one of the better players in the neighborhood). Though Ben and I, attended different schools, we both made our high school teams; other athletes became our main *crowd*. Curiously, over the years, I would see Desmond around the neighborhood, and his total demeanor and dress, had become that of a young thug. I was no longer intimidated by him. I had grown taller and stronger. I could see that he had permed his hair, and he walked with what we used to describe as a kind of "pimp walk"; and was always smoking and hanging with guys who were neighborhood gangsters, hustlers, and criminals. We didn't really speak or greet, since that incident in our early teens. I was not holding a grudge against him, it was just that we each knew, without speaking, that we now lived many miles apart, existentially and socially.

The masses, the crowds, can delay, deter, and even destroy us, if we let them. In the case of far too many older persons, *the crowd* of our youth obsessed society shouts out to them, in various ways, that their witness and worth is no longer valued, because they are over the hill – too old to make any meaningful difference in the world. There are crowds which persuade some men to mistreat and denigrate women. There are crowds which persuade some women to always be suspicious of all men. The *crowd* of this world's system still cries out against the authority of Jesus, and sometimes foments suspicion toward those who have decided to follow Him. At the same time, there is a strong push which comes from those who run with the popular masses to ensure that Quinten Anderson's, Imperial Self[15], is glorified, and seated on the throne of our egos. Conversely, the message of the New Testament is that often we cannot follow the crowd of this world's system, if we are going to follow God. If we claim to be a disciple, then we must always follow our Christ. He is the One, who loves us completely, and unconditionally, showing us the heart of God.

Jesus climbed off that donkey, amidst the adulation and palms of the crowd, and yet only a week later he heard them yelling, "Crucify him!"

---

[15] A term that literary critic and cultural historian, Quentin Anderson originally used to name how American writers like Emerson, and William James, seemed to exalt individual experience over communal experience and tradition in literary themes and content. This author, and others, have now coined the phrase to denote the narcissistic self.

Despite such spiritual instability amongst the throngs of citizens, he was not deterred in his quest to save them and us. He kept standing through the harsh judgements against him; and against the brutal scourging, designed to break him; he kept marching toward victory, even under the heavy weight of the crucible of the cross. *Why?* Because Jesus, looking down the long corridor of time, could see Ben, Desmond, and I, and everyone else, who would reach the ages 14, 34, 54, and beyond. Jesus could see beyond our faults and identify our needs.

Study Questions

1. On this first "Palm Celebration" of Jesus' triumphal entry into Jerusalem, what was the tone of the crowd, and why?
2. What were the people in the crowd shouting out? Why?
3. Why did the people cut down palm branches and lay them in the pathway of Jesus and the colt?
4. From another Gospel account, we know that not everyone was celebrating Jesus' entry into Jerusalem. Some of the religious leaders were non-approving of what the crowds were doing and saying? Why were they trying to change the opinion of the crowd?
5. In a week's time, how could the crowd-sentiment about Jesus, go from celebration to condemnation?
6. As you reflect on your own life, how does majority opinion, affect your views on faith, church, family, and yourself?
7. How do you think our youth are being influenced negatively and positively by their peers?
8. How have crowds been moved to act like mobs in the past?
9. How can the church help to provide a climate of positive peer pressure?

14. The Empathy of God

For we do not have a High Priest who cannot sympathize with our weaknesses, but was in all pointes tempted as we are, yet without sin. Let us therefore come boldly to the throne of grace, that we may obtain mercy and find grace to help in time of need.

(Hebrews 4:15-16)

God seems to have placed something unusually strong down in the human heart, in the seat of our emotions. That something is called *sympathy*. Sympathy enables us to imagine what it must be like to experience misfortune; it gives us the ability to feel sorry for others. Sympathy pulls at the edges of our hearts and pushes us to pity the plight of someone who has fallen and cannot seem to get up. We praise God for the gift of being able to be sympathetic, because it is the doorway to love. But there is a force that runs stronger and deeper than sympathy. That force is *empathy*. Many say that empathy runs more deeply in our hearts than sympathy because to be empathetic means more than feeling sorry for someone else's plight while we remain perched atop some lofty position, far removed from pain or suffering; instead *empathy comes to us through the vista of having had a similar kind of pain and suffering as others have.* When one feels empathy, one is motivated to walk alongside the person who has been knocked to their knees with pain, because one has already been in that same position and posture, but by God's grace was able to climb up to a new place or endure the trauma. Having empathy means we have already walked in that other person's shoes to a degree; or because of a Holy Spirit-guided inner knowing, we are allowed to deeply imagine and feel the suffering of others. Good Friday, Jesus' cross experience, reveals to us the very empathy of God for us. Through Jesus' intercession in Gethsemane, and his death on Calvary, Jesus became the ultimate High Priest who comes, not only *bearing* a sacrifice for our sins, but as the one who *is* the sacrifice for our sins. It is through the lens of the cross experience that we see the empathy of God the clearest.

In a recent episode of the PBS documentary about the powerful, presidential family, *The Roosevelts*, the story of how President Franklin D. Roosevelt's personality was changed by his terrible bout with Polio was told. Evidently, before he became president, and before being stricken with Polio, he was a very athletic, strikingly vibrant and handsome man. Roosevelt, by many accounts, was also a lady's man; a playboy - wealthy, smart, and successful at almost anything he attempted to do. But with all of these attributes going for him, according to historians, he seemed to lack something very important in the cracks and crevices of his personality - empathy. It seemed before his debilitating illness, his life revolved around himself. According to those telling his story, it was only after Franklin was stricken with a very painful and paralyzing form of Polio, which robbed him of his ability to walk, that he became deeply concerned about people who suffered from diseases, poverty, and depression. Why might have this been true? Because, through his own profound sufferings, Roosevelt had experienced the awkward insoles; the worn and weak leather; the crooked and uneven heels; and painfully restrictive upper, of someone else's shoes which hurt to wear; he experienced the pain of others, because of his own pain. It seemed as though Roosevelt's difficult infirmity helped him to become a better leader; it helped him become a president who was concerned about others who were suffering profoundly, physically, economically, and socially, both nationally and even internationally.

In Hebrews 4:15-16, we have a description of our High Priest; one that sums up the results of his suffering in Gethsemane and on Calvary. He was exposed to immense suffering and temptation, and therefore can relate to the extremity of the human condition. The writer, who was writing to new Christians who were very familiar with the Hebraic system of temple worship -- including the process of offering up various oblations; preparations made for animal and grain offerings by the priests in the temple -- describes the role of the Messiah, as the truest High Priest. Toward the end of chapter 4, through chapter 5, and beyond, the writer describes in detail the work of our High Priest; he prays on our behalf and can completely empathize with our plight! He is not the ordinary religious priest of old, who would only sacrifice animals, or burn incense for the sins of the people. Jesus, himself, sacrificed the joys of being in eternity, in perfect bliss and creative power, with the Father and the Spirit. Jesus knows what it is like to be human; Jesus knows what it is like to be weak and tired; Jesus knows what it is like to be persecuted and humiliated; Jesus knows what it is like to be tempted and tested by evil; Jesus knows what it is like to endure accusations, fear, temptation, and even a very painful death. Jesus even knows what it is like to fall under God's judgment; what it is like to suffer under the burning scrutiny of a God who must deal with our sins. I believe this is one of the key reasons why Jesus cries out as an estranged malefactor on the cross: "My God, my God, why have you forsaken me?" Jesus knows what it is like to suffer at profoundly deep levels, on our behalf, and yet he remained sinless. Also, Jesus reveals the suffering of God.

On Calvary's wooden intersection of death, pain, and shame, Jesus experienced what humankind experiences when we perceive (rightly or wrongly) that we are guilty and are under the judgment of God; and he experienced what God experiences while loving and dealing with a broken and sinful creation, which often ridicules and blasphemes the very God who created it. On that Friday, the one to whom the angels had sung, from eternity's past, experienced the totality of both God's sufferings and humanity's sufferings – God's sufferings as a loving Creator who yearns to help and redeem a creation that has been sabotaged; and humanity's sufferings because of the judgment of being estranged from God, goodness, and all blessings, because of the nefarious effects of humanity's collective sin. In this way, Jesus is profoundly our High Priest, representing both God and humanity in our sufferings. And since God was in Christ, reconciling the world to God's Self, God doesn't just *sympathize* with us, but God *empathizes* with us as we face whatever we might be going through today.

Any pain, discontent, shame, guilt, sickness, trouble, violence, that we might face, God, in Christ, has endured something like it. The agony of the scourging, the ridicule, the crown of thorns and the nails, only amplified the suffering that God, in Christ, was already enduring internally, because of the Fall of humanity. But the great news is this – God, in God's empathy, worked out a plan of salvation that would yield much fruit. Through the pain of rejection, physical abuse, and misplaced hate, would come forgiveness, healing, love, resurrection, and salvation. God's suffering is ultimately redemptive in nature. A way has been made, through the precious blood of our High Priest. We should be grateful and go boldly to the throne of grace to obtain mercy and grace, from God, in troubling times. God, through Jesus Christ, knows about troubling times. God feels where we are, probably more than we are able to believe it right now! But, the testimony of the New Testament is true – you and I are loved, felt and understood! God knows, and cares.

15. Easter Sunday

So when this corruptible has put on incorruption, and this mortal has put on immortality, then shall be brought to pass the saying that is written:

"Death is swallowed up in victory" "O Death, where is your sting? O Hades, where is your victory?"

(1 Corinthians 15:54-55)

One of the mightiest American preaching oaks recently fell on Easter Sunday. The Reverend Dr. Gardner C. Taylor, affectionately known as *The Dean of Black Preachers,* died at the age of 96, on Resurrection Sunday, 2016. According to scholar, Jared E. Alcantara, who wrote the book, *Crossover Preaching: Intercultural, Improvisational, Homiletics in Conversation with Gardner C. Taylor,* for many astute preachers, black, white, Hispanic, the late pastor Emeritus of the Concord Baptist Church of Brooklyn, New York, was considered one of the greatest and most eloquent gospel proclaimers the nation had ever seen. Taylor's love for the gospel; his command of the English language; his ability to connect the struggle of today's oppressed peoples to the struggles of the Children of Israel, and the New Testament Church; his many insightful allusions to historic facts and classic literature; his understated humor; and most importantly, his commitment to exalting Jesus Christ as Lord, all came together to make Dr. Taylor, an inspiration to countless worshipers and preachers. Having listened to many of Dr. Taylor's classic sermons via cassettes and video and having heard many of Dr. Martin Luther King's greatest sermons, using the same media, it is easy for me to hear the unmistakable Taylor influence on King (Many of King's biographers note King's admiration of Taylor, and the great influence that Taylor had on King's sermonic delivery). They were great friends, whom the Lord used to start the Progressive Baptist denomination, as God yoked them together to fight for the civil rights of African Americans.

Taylor's Easter Sunday death prompted me to consider again a haunting Easter sermon of his which discusses the awful and intrusive work of death, against the backdrop of God's gift of life.[16] In his sermon, as he builds homiletically, he confesses that there is something about death that has a sad and an absurd quality to it. He notes that it does not seem logical or fair that women and men, girls and boys, would be granted all of the wonderful gifts that are attendant with life — love, relationships, friendships, growth, understanding, excitement, danger, fear, anxiety, peace, and joy — and then have it all come to either an abrupt, or a slow and tortuous end. At one point during the sermon, Taylor, very poignantly, paints a picture for the listener of a family enjoying a wonderful gathering. But unfortunately, over the course of time, each member of the family, is called away, one by one, inexorably, to a distant shore, seemingly never to cross paths again. Gardner said:

> See that family all laughing and gay, with little children playing happily around their mother and father. What a sight of joy and peace! But one day a dark cloud will settle over that happy family. Laughter will be silenced, and smiles will be frozen. Death will enter and there will be one less of that happy circle and then another. For our dearest loves are doomed to wither at the hand of cruel time. Is this all for which we can hope?[17]

Death comes with this terrible quality; death intrudes upon and

---

[16] Dr. Taylor's sermon is entitled, "A Strange Question in a Cemetery." It was originally delivered April 5, 1970; I first heard it, about seven years ago on cassette tape; and later, I read it in a book of Taylor's sermons, entitled *The Words of Gardner Taylor: Volume 1: NBC Radio Sermons 1959-1970, Compiled by Edward L. Taylor,* published by Judson Press.

[17] Taylor, Edward L., *The Words of Gardner Taylor, Volume 1: NBC Radio Sermons 1959-1970*: Judson Press, Valley Vorge, PA, pp. 148-149)

silences our laughter and experiences; and it makes things awful for us on this side of the eternal stream; it is the approaching and relentless winter to our spring time joy; it is separation and pain; it is the fear of the unknown multiplied to torment us. Using similar musings, tropes, and metaphors, preachers like Dr. Taylor, have suggested that death has a very absurd quality to it; and they are right. It does not take powerful abilities of observation to discern that there is something about death which seems woefully out of place; from the little girl who dies of a terminal disease; to the young man shot down in the streets; to the old woman who dies of loneliness and a broken heart; death strikes a discordant note. It is a terrible blue note splattered across the pages of the melody of our lives; it behaves like it should not be a part of the human experience -- an experience, normally, filled with sound, movement, sights, and feelings, bright colors, the beauty of nature, the storms of life, the wonders of the human imagination, and the elation of love. Death presents us with the penultimate case of cognitive dissonance (second to meeting God). I would have to concur with Dr. Taylor -- death seems woefully out of place; even here, on a less than perfect planet; and yet, it is here as a part of life.

According to our Judeo-Christian heritage, ever since Adam and Eve sinned, death has been a partner with life. Life and death come together – one embraced and celebrated, the other, despised and rejected emotionally. But it is at this point, that Jesus steps in and travels through this puzzling territory. As we think about the amazing life of Christ, we can see that in him, life and death come together. Although he reveals through his resurrection, that they are not equal partners in terms of power and endurance, life, death, and life again, come together in Jesus. According to the testimony of many men and women, some who would lose their earthly lives for their testimony and witness, God did something to death, through Jesus Christ. After reconciling the world to God, via the cross; and after seemingly succumbing to death, forever. In the short span of three days, Jesus shook off the clutches of death, got up from the pull of its gripping gravity, *and killed death!* In essence, Jesus took and shook, and wrested death of its horror, until death yielded up its power *to greater powers* – chiefly, the powers of divine love and everlasting life! I thank God, that we are reminded every spring, at the end of Holy Week, that death doesn't have the last word. The cold, icy, wintry, absurdity of death has been swallowed up by the powerful warmth and heat of new life! In Christ, we live, to live again!

The empty tomb of Jesus Christ reveals that ultimately, God's love and will cannot be thwarted! Death is not God; only God is God! This was the concluding theme of Dr. Taylor's powerful preachments in his Easter message, and the same can be said for many-a-preachers' Easter sermon. As believers in life beyond the grave, Christians have faith that Gardner C. Taylor, along with the Apostle Paul, Dr. King, Harriet Tubman, Julia Foote, Frederick Douglass, and countless others who are wearing robes of pure light, can now hug and laugh together with joy, because they know the answer to the question, which Paul raises, in 1 Corinthians 15:55 -- *"Oh Grave, where is your victory? O death, where is thy sting?"* As they wait for us to complete our courses, and join in the fun, these now-gone saints can answer the inquiry into death's victory and sting, like this: **"Death is not here. It is not with us, because we are with God!!!"**

Study Questions

1. What does the resurrection of Jesus Christ mean to you?
2. What is eternal life?
3. For those who will experience eternal life, what will make it so incredible?
4. In the resurrection, do you think we will we recognize our loved ones?
5. What are two aspects of your vision of heaven that will make it paradise to you?

16. Resurrection Hope

Texts: Selected Portions of Ezekiel 37 and Luke 24

Have you ever felt like your dreams had become shattered? Have you ever entrusted your personal secrets and most treasured plans to someone you loved, only to have them to betray your confidence and trust? When we are deeply disappointed by events, people, and even in ourselves, we can lose hope in the overall goodness of life. In fact, if we really lose our grip entirely, we can even misplace hope in God! But I am exceedingly glad that even when our hopes dim and become overcast, God is still shining brightly; and God is easily able to get a ray of light through to us, if we will keep hoping against hope!

Hope is a precious commodity in life. Hope is that mysterious phenomenon of believing that something or someone good is just around life's corner. Losing this precious spiritual resource can be a terrible experience. As I have traveled through this experience we call life, I have had many hopes to become diminished. I am not alone in this experience. One only has to survey the conditions and pathologies attendant in our urban communities to easily see the negative effect that a people's loss of hope can have on our economy, law enforcement, criminal justice system, families, schools and religious institutions. And yet, the strange thing about life is that no matter where one lives – in the inner city, on rural hills, or in the sprawling suburbs -- there will come a time when we all will be faced with the temptation to give up our most cherished hopes. The shattering of our hopes, and the giving up of our hopes, can be a disturbingly painful experience.

Again, I have had some hopes and dreams shattered, and I have had to give up some hopes that were not God's reality for my life. Having served in several urban communities rife with pain, abject poverty, addiction, violence, joblessness; undeniably unstable communities characterized by transient residents and single parent households; also, having served in congregations that have struggled to remember their main reasons for being congregations, has at times been a disheartening endeavor. Most pastors begin their pastorates with both, realistic and unrealistic hopes and plans for the vibrancy of the churches and communities they serve. I have been no different than most. I have seen rapid spiritual and numeric growth in congregations I have served; I have also witnessed squandered possibilities and the effects of deeply entrenched sin, which have repeatedly stifled growth. In my most recent ministry context, I can remember the start of my tenure of serving a once-vibrant Detroit congregation; a congregation whose "glory days" were twenty-five years in its past. The congregation, filled with many great parishioners, had fallen on tough times, for a variety of reasons -- some internal, like a church divided by a sordid past, filled with accusations of abusive church leadership; some other factors attributable to external realities, like major sociological shifts in the city, and in American culture. As I reflect upon those first few years, serving this congregation, I can remember how much I prayed and retreated with our congregation's leaders in efforts to discern God's will for us; I was filled with excitement and enthusiasm about our potential; I can also remember how much I prayed and retreated with God, privately. Initially, in short order, it seemed as if God answered our desires, adding scores of new members to our membership, and giving us a new vision for ministry that was grounded in the gospel imperative to share the good news story of Jesus, while also celebrating what God has done, and can do, in the lives of African Americans spiritually and culturally. This vision was also rooted in the powerful story of how Nehemiah and the people of God, took on God's project to rebuild the dilapidated walls of Jerusalem. But, after what seemed to be numeric and spiritual growth and progress, just shy of six years into our ministry together, it seemed the great stones and bricks we had erected in efforts to re-establish a vibrant ministry for our community, had been dismantled by forces, within and beyond our reach. Even as we continued to study and pray, the banes of a steady infighting, inaction, lethargy, and a general malaise, like a multi-headed Hydra, would continue to rear its ugly head. The prayers and the planning retreats continued, but many opportunities to establish a vibrant faith village, were lost to time. As we struggled to be the community God was calling us to be; and as it seemed we were only losing ground, I grieved in my soul, for the congregation; for the community; for my family; and for myself. I also hurt inside because I felt our back-biting ways were grieving the Spirit. Jesus' parable about the wisdom of not pouring new wine, into old wineskins (old mindsets), seemed to describe our congregation and community. Trying to pour new wine, into old wineskins just was not working; and many of the "new wineskins" which joined us, did not manifest a mind to grow spiritually, through Bible study, service, the exercising of their gifts and giving to ministry, financially. In fact, upon reflection, even the "new wineskins" were functioning like old ones.

Along with other members, I prayed, and searched the scriptures and my heart: Where did we miss it? How can I be a more faithful and effective servant and pastor? My wife and I (and even our children), continuously searched out our faith for breakthrough answers or an open door to other ministerial possibilities. As I look in retrospect, I must confess there were times when my hopes were shattered, because the distance between who we were, when contrasted with who we could be, was enormous, and the gap seemed to be growing wider each month and year. But, I thank God, that I can testify that during seasons such as these, God will ensure that Christ, family, faithful colleagues and golden-hearted members, will become a network of mutual support – a remnant community of resurrection hope! God will use others to demonstrate signs of God's presence, during the toughest times.

Many who lose hope become skeptical, cynical, and turn inwards in unhealthy ways, becoming bitter and angry. God doesn't desire for us to become mean-spirited and hard-bitten by life -- a people immobilized by hopelessness, and purposelessness. In both Ezekiel 37 and Luke 24, God is revealed as the One who restores, rebuilds, and revives our hopes, again and again. This is seen very clearly in what the Lord prophesies through Ezekiel, in a vision of dry bones, during and after Israel's exile in Babylon. In the vision, God places Ezekiel down in a valley of dry bones. The dry and divided bones symbolized the mindset and attitude of the Jews, who had been decimated spiritually by the Babylonian captivity, and its unwanted consequences. In the vision, the bones represented the best of the best of a once mighty Israel, which has become anything but mighty. God instructs the prophet to tour the bones in the valley, and then asks the prophet a question of hope: *Can these bones live again?* This is a question related to faith and hope in God and in the community of Israel. God questions the prophet, in order that the prophet himself, might do a self-assessment, related to faith. Does the prophet have any faith and hope for a people who have lost faith and hope? Ezekiel's answer to the question of whether dry bones can live again, is a good answer – "God, you know!"

In this passage of scripture, God is revealed as a God who specializes in resurrecting dead bodies, dreams, and hopes. This attribute of God is something about which Ezekiel and God's people will soon come to know intimately. God instructs Ezekiel to speak to the dry bones of Israel, and the winds of the Spirit. Afterwards, the dry bones come together; flesh and sinew cover the bones; the breath of life re-enters into the thousands of slain warriors, and they become a living army, symbolizing Israel's restored hope and purpose.

This God who resurrects, restores and expands our hopes, in the book of Ezekiel, is also revealed in Luke's account of an unusual post-resurrection appearance of Jesus, while two disciples are travelling on a road to the small town of Emmaus. Cleopas, and a disciple who is not given a name in the text, have just left Jerusalem. The crucifixion events have shattered their hopes that Jesus was the Messiah who would redeem and restore Israel (see Luke 24:21). From their seemingly hopeless vantage point, Jesus died brutally and publicly, as a mysterious, wonder-working prophet – possibly a false prophet who was executed by Roman powers, because He dared to challenge the religious and political establishment of that day. They have heard the fantastic rumor that He has been resurrected, but they are too overwhelmed by the ugly events of the last few hours, to give much credence to any of the many variations of that rumor; all the talk seemed nothing more than the work of wishful thinking, and a neurotic fanaticism. But, on the road, a cloaked stranger approaches them. Through this encounter with the scripture-quoting, prophecy-explaining, bread-breaking stranger, their eyes are opened to see that the stranger was Jesus! He was alive again! In an ironic twist, as soon as their *eyes of perception are opened*, he *disappears* from their sight. Their later testimony is that when he talked with them, their hearts burned with conviction. Maybe, God was trying to teach them to depend on the still small voice of God, more than the physical presentation of God. The rumor that the women and Peter had spread about an empty tomb, was no mere rumor, it was the truth! Jesus was alive again! Death – not just Rome; not just Israel's national enemies -- had been defeated! New life had transcended and trumped everything. The resurrection had completely swallowed up their despair, depression, and hopelessness. These disciples' once shattered hopes in a Messiah who would save Israel from her earthly enemies, had been reassembled, re-established, widened and stretched so that they would have new hopes founded in a Lord who could save anyone, anywhere, from the penalty of sin, and the finality of death! Sisters and brothers, the good news for us is that God walked with these disciples through the entire process of their journey; all the way from Jerusalem to Emmaus and then back to Jerusalem again; all the way from hope, to hopelessness, to even greater hopes! The One True God, revealed in Christ, is willing to make a similar journey with you, when life seems to cause your hopes to dry up like a raisin in the sun. God is willing to walk and talk with us through the experience of shock, deep disappointment, anger, skepticism, and recovery. I thank God for being our dry bones, resurrection strength, for the sometimes arduous and hope-snatching journey! Despite great disappointments, there travels with us a Jesus who is still in the resurrection and restoration business. I believe this, and I am learning to believe it increasingly more with each passing year.

Study Questions

1. What dry bone situations in your life need resurrecting? A strained relationship? A financial dilemma? A dream deferred?
2. How have you processed those seasons in your life, when God has disappointed you?
3. What do you think was the purpose for God telling the prophet Ezekiel to prophesy over the dead bones of Israel?
4. When going through seasons when it has seemed as though Jesus is not alive, and dry bones will only become drier, how can we snap out of our "deadness?"
5. In the cases of Israel and the two disappointed disciples, God proved to be the God who resurrects hope. Can you recall a time when God proved to you that God still resurrects that which seems to be dead and hopeless?

17. Revive us Again

Texts: Nehemiah 8 and Acts 2

As was noted in a previous reflection dealing with the themes of death and resurrection, there is something about death that is intrusive and absurd. It does not seem logical or fair that we would be granted all of the blessings that come with life and then have it all come to a slow or an abrupt end, as our bodies fail us because of genetic defects; or a terminal illness comes knocking on the doors of our lives; an accident or crime happens; someone runs a stop sign or uses a gun; someone is not watching carefully where they are standing; or simply, because old age runs its course and consequently, we are left breathless, literally.

As we think about death, I think it is noteworthy for us to remember that death doesn't just come in the form of strangely still bodies, and mouths that have been silenced; accompanied by funeral dirges and eulogies. There are other deaths. Death should not *only* be understood as the cessation of our conscious physical experiences. Death can creep in, subtly silencing our witness and our joy, our hope and our dreams, and our passions and our loves. This kind of death occurs without the obvious outward signs. A life lived missing God's purposes for that life, is a life lived in death's shadow. Living sinfully, without repentance, is a death, most terrible. At various points along life's journey, the spiritual traveler is threatened by unseen forces with a deadening of the spirit; we are lured into a kind of death, if we make choices to wallow in selfishness, sin, and evil. A deathly fatigue of the heart can set in when sin becomes the chosen norm; the kind of fatigue that will leave us weakened, deceived, depressed, and vulnerable to more of Satan's lies. When we yield to a sinful temptation, over and over without seeking to change; when we hold envy, unforgiveness and bitterness in our souls; or when a marriage, relationship, or dream dies, we can begin to question whether our connection with God was ever authentic. We can begin to think, "Maybe what I have believed about God being my Help and Deliverer is not true for me, or anyone, after all." "Maybe I have miscalculated my values and should utterly jettison my religion!" When we have these kinds of questions and musings, we need something (or Someone) to shake us out of our malaise before we completely succumb. We need a force to propel us out of our emotional pits, canyons, and graveyards; we need a reviving of our souls that will empower us to rise-up from the dead-end ruts of despair and unbelief!

Nehemiah 8 and Acts 2, are two very powerful texts that testify about how God is a God who is in the reviving and resurrection business. God can revive our hearts, homes, and communities. God can resurrect our dead hopes and stillborn dreams. In Nehemiah 8, God revived the national hopes, and spiritual vibrancy, of a ragtag group of Jews who had returned from Babylonian captivity. These post-captive Jews, were a people who had originally gone into captivity, decades prior, because of their years of sinful rebellion against the laws and will of God. According to the interpretative tradition of their own prophets and scholars, God had judged and punished the Jews through the Babylonians. But, the same God who had punished, was the same God who would revive! God would raise up the Persians to the highest seat of power in that region; the strength of the Babylonians would weaken. Nehemiah, a cup bearer for one of the Kings of Persia, would lead the people on a comprehensive reconstruction and reviving agenda; and by the time we come to chapter 8 of Nehemiah, God had resurrected them! They had rebuilt the city walls, and houses, and restored their religious devotion to God. They were now a brand new, praising community, devoted to anchoring their laws, economy, families and society, in a strict fidelity to Yahweh, through a renewed commitment to observing the Mosaic Law.

In Acts 2, another awesome God-led revival happens. With Holy Spirit-fire, and brand-new tongues, God revived the hearts of 120 disciples, who were struggling to know up from down. Roughly, a couple of months earlier, many of the disciples had forsaken their Lord, when He endured the injustice and inhumanity of the cross. The disciples had come through the worst of their fears, back-sliding, and denials. But now they awaited the fulfillment of a mysterious promise. God took these sometimes fearful, and uncertain disciples – disciples who were hiding out and questioning their own sanity -- God revived them by Jesus' resurrection appearances, as they wondered what was the nature of this promise of the coming Holy Spirit. But on the Day of Pentecost, wonder turned into fiery experience. They poured out of their group hiding place, ablaze; and as they did, that upper room became a launching pad of evangelistic passion, signs and wonders, healings, and many charitable works designed to help the poor and widows.

In both biblical narratives, the themes of resurrection and revival permeate the pages of biblical history. When we fully submit to the presence of the Spirit of God, there is always a revival brewing just beneath the surface of our lives, awaiting God's people's recognition of it. For the people of God, who have been crying out for relief. There is still hope, and help. And to God, we can always appeal:

> *Revive us again; Fill each heart with Thy love; May each soul be rekindled with fire from above. Hallelujah! Thine the glory! Hallelujah! Amen. Hallelujah! Thine the glory! Revive us again!*

18. Love Builds a Community

Text: Acts 2:38-47

More than thirty years ago there was a popular comedy show which ruled network television. It was a show about a group of friends who found love, sanity, acceptance, enjoyable fellowship, and myriad comedic situations, at a local Boston pub named *Cheers*. In Chicago, while growing up, there was a similar bar located not too far from my parents' home. It was called *Reese's* bar. Though I never attended, I remember that it always was busy and well attended, for many years. The show *Cheers* portrayed a similar social setting. During the opening credits, the theme song for the show named after the fictional pub, would say something to the effect that the pub was special because it is the place where, among other things, *"...everyone knows your name."* I believe that like the musical, lyrical, and dramatic theme intimated by this iconic show, more than anything, our hearts cry out for a sense of social and spiritual safety lived out in an atmosphere where everybody knows who we are, and still accepts us "beyond all of our faults and virtues" in the words of Howard Thurman.

As Christians, we have been blessed to find the joy of deep fellowship/koinonia (The Greek word for Christian fellowship) through our profound relationship with the Father, Son and Spirit, along with the saints. The public gathering of the church provides an invaluable context for further developing precious relationships among fellow and sister sojourners. In Acts 2, the newly birthed church, was flowing and overflowing in a palpable, fiery, love that affected all. After the Spirit baptized those first few believers (the 120), Pentecost's holy, love-fire, spread beyond the upper room, out to neighborhoods throughout Jerusalem. The Christian community that emerged, was one characterized by baptisms, group study, shared meals, unselfish charity, and miraculous works! Luke writes in Acts 2:44, that these new believers had *"all things in common, and sold their possessions and goods, and divided the proceeds for anyone who had financial or material need."* It is evident that the Holy Spirit filled the church with a holy love; a love that was unselfish and contagious.

We were created to be social beings. A mutually shared love is what builds up any social system. The English poet, John Donne, once said that *no person is an island.* I suspect that even the most introverted among us has something, somewhere on the inside of us that yearns to find a place where we can know and be known, without fear and persecution – a place where we can love and be loved, without selfishness and greed rearing their repugnant heads. The great African American mystic and theologian, Howard Thurman, said that *to feel at home everywhere, one must find a home somewhere.* Have you found that sense of belonging in God and among God's people, somewhere?

There are many insidious forces that can ruin our koinonia and shared love. The chief among them are greed, pride, and haughtiness. We must be on guard to not allow these divisive and nefarious devils to sink our love-unity and collective joy. Greed can show up in the form of an insatiable lust – a lust for power, sex, and illegal or legal drugs. Pride can delude us into thinking we are better than others, or that we know more, or that we are simply more important than anyone else. Haughtiness, which is a sibling of pride, can cause us to exalt ourselves over others in our families and communities, so that we will always appear to be on top. But, the devils of greed, pride and haughtiness must be exorcised, if the church is going to be a place of joy and social safety. The church should be the place where we are to learn to love our neighbors and tame our addictions; the church is the place, where together, under the preaching and teaching of the gospel of God's King and kin/kingdom, we are to learn that there are no *big I's* and *little you's.* The Father, Son and Spirit are the sublime sources of, and the mysterious power behind, our wonderful fellowship. God is the main attraction, and we shine the best when we seek to glorify God, as we love on our saintly (and not so saintly) siblings.

Church should be the place where we are beginning to know our

God, neighbor, and selves; and the place where we know and are known, without ridicule, scorn and scoffing. Church should also be the place where we learn about what our responsibilities are that we might live holy lives and make our families and communities better. Church is the place where we learn Christian ethics and morality, as is explicated in God's word, especially the New Testament. Church is where we should be on a collective journey, with other travelers, as we learn of our possibilities and limits; as we explore God's dreams for us, our communities, and our world. Ideally the church is the preeminent place of love and forgiveness, where God and others, *know our names*, and yet, choose to love us, anyhow!

Study Questions

1. Have you ever been a part of a job/school/religious organization that was such a healthy environment in which to work/play/study/worship, that you wanted to be a part of it for as long as you could?

2. Have you ever been a part of an institution that was so unhealthy, chaotic, cut-throat, poorly managed, and divided, that you could hardly wait to get another job/graduate/transfer/or join a new social or religious organization?

3. After Peter's sermon, and beyond the heavenly fire and cloven tongues, how did the Holy Spirit move these citizens in Jerusalem to become a community of love, in Jesus' name? What role did the Apostles play in helping to build up a sense of Christ's love, throughout the church?

4. When leaders of an organization are filled with the spirit of God's love, that essence will often permeate the rest of the group. What have the best church/community leaders done to make sure that a spirit of love, charity, and humility, infused the community they served?

5. How did Jesus build up the lives of those first disciples, as he walked, talked, and served with them?

6. Luke writes that the faith community had all things in common, as they studied, prayed, and worked together. What would it take for your church/school/work environment to become a place of profound love, righteousness, repentance, and acceptance?

19. Love Lifted Us!

Text: 1 Corinthians 13

As I was sorting through the contents of a drawer in our house in Indianapolis, I found two file folders with at least thirty manuscripts of sermons that I had preached more than two decades ago. Out of this collection, there was one sermon, that arrested my attention more than the others. It was a sermon I preached in 1993 entitled, *"The Glue that Holds Us Together."* The sermon was preached in a congregation that was trying to locate and live into its unity in God. The congregation was interracial but was increasingly becoming more African American in its demographic makeup, just like the suburban neighborhood in which it was located. At the time, the congregation was already over 78% African American, and some of our members were worrying that the demographic trend would soon make the congregation entirely black. There was a palpable fear among some of the congregants (especially among some of the black members), who had prided themselves in being a part of an interracial congregation. Given these, and other fears, I felt led by the Spirit to preach a series of sermons which would attempt to address and comfort anxieties, and hopefully re-shift our congregation's focus. I started a sermon series about our unity in the Spirit by emphasizing the criticality of congregations being Christ-centered, mi*nistry-minded, and seeking to operate in love.* My approach was to first, have us to consider 1 Corinthians 13, the famous "love chapter," in which Paul discusses the indispensable and undefeatable quality of God's agapé love. I felt led to discuss how our human-centered attempts to control that which is not entirely under our control (e.g. changes in our culture and society; and trying to entirely control the racial demographics of our congregation), is a losing proposition. I shared with them that while we should be prayerful and also take some practical steps in efforts to aim toward continuing a great legacy of demonstrating a multi-racial witness to the Indianapolis, Indiana, community, ultimately, God will be the One who oversees who is drawn and added to our fellowship; and that more than anything, God desires for congregations to be about the call to *deeply love whomever comes to our congregation for solace and service opportunities.* I reminded them that more than trying to feverishly tally up some external showing of racial equilibrium, God wants God's children to be excited about sharing unconditional love to …*red, yellow, black and white, because we are all precious in God's sight.* During the message, in no uncertain terms, I said that the challenge and charge to offer agape' to everyone who comes to visit our fellowship, **would exhibit the godly glue that would draw and hold new members, and it would be the divine adhesive that would ultimately anchor our ministry!**

Today, under very different circumstances, I sense the same Spirit leading me to revisit this message with you, the worshiping congregant (and the reader). Though the original message was preached over two decades ago and was intended for a congregation that was wrestling with different dynamics, several points from this message are relevant for us today. After rediscovering the sermon from that old folder, I became convinced that a second iteration of this message might be useful to remind our African American congregation/follower, located in the city of Detroit, that any persistent spiritual disunity threatens to tear apart any congregation; even a congregation that is entirely of one race. But, with this, there is a corresponding truth: No matter what the internal problems are in a congregation, or family; no matter what the specific points of division are, God's agape' love is what can work in our hearts and social systems, to hold together members, families, committees, fellowship groups, boards, and ministry teams!

Paul intimately knew of this divine glue about which he wrote. Not long after his conversion experience, Paul had seen how the love of God, fueled by the fires of the Spirit, had knit Jewish and Gentile believers together. Over the years, Paul had seen how a congregation like the one located in Corinth, could get carried away by the issues of immorality and a misunderstanding of the diversity of charismatic gifts which were coveted by the members, to the point of pride, distraction, and the near total splintering of the faith community. This is why Paul is compelled to respond to the Corinthians, via apostolic letter. His prose and poetry, in chapters 12-14, serve as one of the greatest reminders of the practicality, theology, and the indefatigability of God's agape' love.

Using a sermon (based on Paul's text), that I wrote 25 years ago, I offer a similar reminder to our congregation today. *We must allow the Spirit of God's agape' love to have its way in our fellowships; it is the glue that holds us together.* This is the central point of our sermonic text today. If we are going to get the victory over divisive issues related to inter-church power struggles; related to our immorality, envy, jealousy, legalism, and unforgiveness, then we must give up our hateful ways, and give in to God's most powerful force in the universe – agape' love. As Paul wrote in the opening verses of our text that speaking in tongues, being charitable, prophesying, and appearing to live a life of austere self-denial, if done without the core motive of loving others, will be an empty act, ultimately, not respected by God, Who is love. We don't want to be found guilty of being experts in dead religious rituals that are done without the main spiritual ingredient – a love that turns haters into lovers of God and the common good. Christians, and churches that are unwilling to operate love will not last.

Throughout God's holy writ, especially in the New Testament, God commands us to love friends, neighbors, and even enemies – political enemies; cultural and ethnic enemies; and those who express hostility against our faith communities. While we might find it easy to love most of our friends and neighbors, we cannot love our enemies unless we have help from the Spirit of God. It is unnatural to want the best for those who act as though they want the worst for us. It is virtually impossible, in our own strength, to express love to persons who have tried to set us up for a fall; or who have tried to break up our marriages; or who have exhibited racist or misogynistic tendencies. Yet, we are challenged and charged to love, even those who seem unlovable. This love is not rooted in emotion, but it is a strong, prayerful desire to see persons, as God sees them. To prayerfully see godly potential and purposes, even in the hater, is the goal. Such a perspective frees us from the tentacles of hate and bitterness.

Prayer is such an important practice for those who want the strength to love those who are a challenge for us to love. Without prayer, it would be too tall a task, under certain circumstances, to express the virtuous qualities of love described in 1 Corinthians 13, to everyone of God's creatures. Real love is otherworldly, and according to Paul, real love/God's love, consists of, and rejects, the following:

> Long suffering
> Kindness
> Not envious
> Not arrogant
> Not rude
> Not selfish
> Not easily provoked
> Thinks good thoughts
> Refuses to rejoice in evil, but rejoices in the truth
> It bears all things, believes all things, and hopes all things
> God's kind of love, endures all things, and it never fails.

From where did Paul get this understanding of love? Paul got his definition of love from becoming very familiar with the person, teachings, stories, and power of Jesus Christ. In addition to this, the Holy Spirit is the very spirit of Christ living on the inside of us. Hence, Paul knew that when we face haters and instigators; truce-breakers and religious fakers, we need a love that comes from beyond our human psyches and ability to conjure up good will. The Holy Spirit can cause Christ's love, to love *through* us. *This is a miracle.* Which brings us to the heart of our text. As we read this text in 1 Corinthians, we should be praying, *"Lord, I need you to do a miracle in me! Indwelling Spirit, help me to be a conduit, of your love! Help me to make manifest the qualities listed in this text that you have revealed are aspects of true love; also help me to reject those qualities that you list as being the antithesis of your love."*

God's agape' helps knit folks together who have significant differences and tend to always gravitate toward conflict. If allowed, through the power of the Holy Spirit, this love works in us and through us, way down in the cracks and crevices of the messy places of our relationships at home, in church, at work, and in the broader socio-political, faith village. If we let this kind of love breathe, we will find that it is the substance that holds our relationships, institutions, and the whole of society together.

Study Questions

1. Why do you think it is difficult for us to love some people?
2. Have you ever wondered how God can love everybody; even those who oppose God?
3. When marriages and ministries fall apart, how can love rescue us?
4. As you read through the text, note those characteristics which are your growing edges. Write them down.
5. How have you been a conduit of love in your congregation?
6. Can you discern any ways you've interacted in your family, or congregation, during the last month, that were less than loving? What have you done to set things right?
7. When you have experienced unconditional love, if you have experienced it, how did it impact your life?

20. Mother's Day

And a man of the house of Levi went and took as wife
a daughter of Levi. So the woman conceived and bore a
son. And when she saw that he was a beautiful child, she
hid him three months. But when she could no longer hide
him, she took an ark of the bulrushes for him, daubed it
with asphalt and pitch, put the child in it, and laid it in
the reeds by the river's bank.

(Text: Exodus 2:1-3)

Langston Hughes penned a powerful poem, entitled, *The Negro Mother*.
In this poem, he extolls the strength and the steadfastness of the African
American mother. He portrays the black mother as a woman, long
burdened because of racial injustice and oppression, but existentially free
and powerful enough to rise above life's difficulties to ensure that her
children – both biological and those entrusted to her through a kind of
social surrogacy - become the recipients of a legacy of strength and power.
There is a line in the poem that gives voice to this ideal mother figure – a
woman of towering strength:

Three hundred years in the deepest South; but God put
a song and a prayer in my mouth. God put a dream like
steel in my soul. Now, through my children, I'm reaching
the goal.

Over the years, God has indeed put steel in the souls of black women.

Black women have had to overcome sexual assaults, at the hands of their racial oppressors. They have had to deal with the absence of black men who were moved to new plantations; or the abandonment of black men who just wanted to be free of familial responsibilities -- men who thought themselves incapable of taking on the economic and emotional responsibility of protecting and providing for a family. Without argument, black women have been given a special strength by God to deal with terrible adversities, as they have birthed, nurtured, and protected black children.

In Exodus 2, the writer, (traditionally thought to be Moses) recounts the story of his mother's heroism, as she rebelled against the unholy fiat of the Pharaoh. Beginning in chapter 1, Pharaoh, because of his fear of the strength and the population boom of the Hebrews, ordered that every male Hebrew child, two years old and under, be put to death. After the shrewd resistance of the Hebrew midwives is employed to save numerous Hebrew boys, who had been sentenced to death at birth, Pharaoh gives a new command. This time it is directed to all the citizens of Egypt: the Hebrews and Egyptians are to kill every male Hebrew baby, on sight. Some Hebrew women surrendered to this horrible fate, while undoubtedly, many others resisted this genocide. Moses' mother, Jochebed, one of the daughters of Levi, was one who resisted. After giving birth to her son, she and her daughter hid him and made sure that he was safe and secure from destruction. By God's grace and sovereign plan, Moses' was floated downriver, toward his divine destiny. He is discovered by a daughter of Pharaoh and becomes a son of the royal household. Amazingly, and during his early formative years, God ensured that Moses' mother, Jochebed was able to nurse her own son, in Pharaoh's house – with pay! It is probable, that at Jochebed's breast, Moses heard the whispered stories and songs of their people. Apparently, Moses was always conscious of his Hebrew roots. It would be this "woke status" that would move Moses to begin standing up against the unjust treatment of his enslaved people.

I thank God for all the mothers, of every color and culture, who have birthed, protected, nurtured, and taught the children of our world from the cradle to adulthood. Both of my sisters are great mothers. One, has a biological son. The other, has served as a caring surrogate for nieces, nephews, and younger cousins. I thank God for all the African, and African American mothers who, though despised and rejected by many, have withstood the hate, and provided much spiritual strength and praying courage, to turn back the destructive plans of their adversaries. In Black America, where five thousand (5,000) preschool children are expelled annually (90% male); where *every day* three (3) children or teens are killed by firearms; where *every day*, ninety-six (96) children are arrested for violent crimes; where *every day,* six hundred and ninety-seven (697) babies are born into poverty; and three hundred and ninety-four (394) babies are born to mothers who are not high school graduates; we need to press the reset button, and learn from our biblical and cultural history so that the next generation of mothers will be equipped to raise and rescue, the next generation of African American children. God helped the Hebrews, and black folks, before, and God is well able and willing to do it again! We need strong mothers, partnering with strong fathers, and both reaching up to God for sustenance and success. We need more mothers who will take radical risks to save their children, like Moses' mother did for him!

My own mother was a priceless jewel. She nurtured me in the faith of our people. She exposed my sister (the eldest sister, of two) and I, to a diversity of religious beliefs and experiences. In fact, before my mother had a conversion experience in Christ, for a few years we were Black Hebrew Israelites (a sect of African Americans in Chicago and in other cities, who believed that blacks in America were the lost tribe of Israel). After her conversion experience, she raised the three of us (including my youngest sister) to love Christ and the church. She taught us the importance of being smart, ethical and kind. With my father as her support and our primary provider, she raised my sisters and I, to be conscious of the struggles and beauty of our people. She also taught us to love all people, no matter their color, or socio-economic particularities. She read and studied the Bible and theology voraciously; she pastored a church in one of the toughest neighborhoods on the southside of Chicago, with love. She earned certification and degrees from Nursing School, DePaul University, and the Chicago Theological Seminary, respectively. She was the quintessential example of an intelligent, godly woman, who had steel in her soul. How much steel? One day, my mother and father were carjacked around their garage. The assailants were not masked. With semi-automatic weapons pointed at my parents, my mother and father surrendered their car keys and other belongings. From what I was told later by my aunt, the thieves had my mother's Bible, which was in a soft case. With guns pointed at her and my dad; with conventional wisdom advising people who find themselves in such a predicament to be quiet and cooperate; my mother broke with convention and boldly asked the gun-toting car-jackers to give her the Bible back! She got it back. She had God's steel in her soul.

Her love for us? unquestioned; her love for my father? thoroughly evident; her love for God? remarkable; her love for God's people? an example for all. She went home to be with God and the ancestors, nearly four years ago. I miss her beyond words, and I look forward to seeing her again.

21. Shouting it Out is Fine, but What About Walking it Out?

Scripture Texts: Ezekiel 1:4-21, and Galatians 5:16-25

Periodically, when my mother took a brief hiatus from our quiet, dignified, Disciples of Christ congregation in Chicago, she would take us to a little storefront Pentecostal congregation, on the near Southwest Side of the city. She was truly ecumenical in her friendships and outlook. The worship services of these smaller, independent, congregations were very different from what I was used to at the Park Manor Christian Church. At Park Manor, if one said, "amen!" with too much volume, one might be confronted by disapproving glances and glares from more than a few of the members. As a ten-year old, I preferred the overall passion and energy level exhibited in the storefront churches, though there were some demonstrations in the service that unnerved me a bit. What I especially noticed was that when the piano player or organ would accompany the preacher's sermon at the climactic point of the message, some of the members and attendees would begin dancing, or would have, what I would have described then, as "convulsions." I was never sure of the source of the strange bucking and kicking movements that were demonstrated by some of the congregants who shouted and jerked themselves out of their seats, sometimes onto the floor. In fact, these manifestations often left me thinking that the person who was shouting, jumping, and jerking, uncontrollably, was being possessed by some overpowering force – a force I did not want to overtake me. When I asked my mother about these disturbing emotional events, if my memory is true, she would tell me, without much explanation that "they believe they are catching the Holy Spirit." Many years later, my mother and I would have many fruitful conversations about some of the phenomena which happens in the corporate worship of some churches; phenomena sometimes attributed, rightly or wrongly, to the Holy Spirit.

Many Christians have been taught, or they have a sense, that the Holy Spirit is a very important part of every believer's spiritual life. In the Gospel of John, chapters 14-17, Jesus taught his first disciples that the Holy Spirit would be the indwelling, advocating, guiding, convicting, and comforting presence, who would function like Jesus functioned while he was physically on earth. But even with the words of Jesus to aid and enlighten us, many Christians also have a hard time articulating the practical role of the Spirit in helping us to be godly. Often, in the mind and testimonies of many, the presence of the Holy Spirit is reduced to a fuzzy, abstruse, subjective, emotional state that makes us feel good or enthusiastic about our faith; for such Christians the presence of the Spirit is known primarily by the way a person responds to a sense of God in public worship on Sunday. For others, the Spirit is understood in a purely intellectual way; the Spirit is understood to be one of the three Persons Who comprise the one Triune God. Those who experience the Spirit primarily through their intellect can often quickly recite the traditional theological formulas about the Trinity – that the *Father/Divine Parent* lives in perfect love with the *Son* and *the Holy Spirit;* the three are one in essence, purpose and action.

While it is sometimes very important to *feel* the Spirit, and it is also very important to have *clear thinking* about the Spirit, as best we can; it is even *more important* to live a life that is *guided by* the Spirit. The New Testament and life teach us that when we apply God's word with Christ's way of being in the world, and we learn to walk in the power and purpose of the Spirit, instead of the lusts and passions of the sinful nature, we are learning to walk with God! Every day, via our choices, we can walk with God. Jesus and the Apostles talked much more about how believers should learn to be guided by the Spirit, than about the ins and the outs related to the emotions and excesses that our truncated understanding of the Holy Spirit can evoke. Also, from reading the sacred texts of scripture, Jesus and the Apostles spent much more time talking about the fruit of the Spirit, and the love that the Spirit works in our hearts, than about the nature of the Spirit's hypostatic (relationship union) position in God's mysterious Triune presence.

In Ezekiel 1, the prophet is given a complex vision of the whirlwinds and wheels of the spirit. With the angelic beings only moving when the Spirit moves them – *they are entirely guided by the Spirit!* They follow the direct leading of the Spirit; they do not turn to the left or to the right of the Spirit's will, motion and travel (vss. 12, 20, 21). This is illustrative and instructive of how we ought to follow the Spirit's leading. One thing though, the Spirit guides us away from the dictates of the sinful nature. Paul echoes this notion. In Galatians 5, Paul instructs his readers that to bear the fruit of the Spirit, they must be *directed by the Spirit*! He clearly delineates the characteristics of the Spirit, from the works of the flesh. The workings of the sinful nature are adultery, fornication, lewdness, idolatry, sorcery, hatred, infighting, jealousy, rage, selfishness, and many other sinful behaviors. The Spirit guides us into love, joy, peace, patience, kindness, goodness, faithfulness, gentleness, and self-control.

How's your Spiritual walk going? Do you move in the Spirit's direction when the Spirit is trying to guide you into producing godly fruit? Do you become still, when the Spirit says, "Be still?" Or have you been yielding to the temptations of the sinful nature? Jesus said that His words are spirit and they are life! A reliance on the leading of the Spirit, cannot be divorced from the words of our Christ and his Apostles. How much word do you know? Your knowledge of the word of God, will help you to discern the voice of the Spirit. What have you noticed about Jesus' actions in the Gospels? Your familiarity with the actions and attitude of Jesus Christ, will help to define how you are to walk in the Spirit.

God does not want us to just talk about the Spirit, as we exult in feeling what we believe to be the Spirit, but God wants us in proper fellowship with the Spirit. So, let us not just talk the talk; but let us learn to walk the walk! If our walk becomes authentic, so then will be our shouts of praise! I do not think that there is anything better to God's ears than a shout of praise, coming from the mouth of someone with Spirit-guided hearts, hands and feet!

Study Questions

1. What can we learn from the example of the angelic beings in Ezekiel 1, as we think about following the Spirit?
2. Is there any connection to how Ezekiel describes the Spirit as a whirlwind, and what Jesus says about the Spirit in the Gospel of John, chapter 4?
3. As you peruse Galatians 5, what are some of the works of the flesh that seem to be your weaknesses? What fruit of the Spirit remains a bit underdeveloped in your life?
4. As you reflect on your spiritual life, have you put more emphasis on *feeling* the Spirit, or *following* the Spirit? Can feeling and following be linked? How?

22. God's Power

Text: Exodus 34

For every believer in Jesus Christ, there is a power at work in us and through us. The power of the Spirit is ultimately the greatest power in and beyond the world. Before the church age, the Spirit would work on, and through various people, especially, certain Jewish prophets, priests, governors, liberators, law-givers, Elders, song writers and poets. Moses was the quintessential example of a person, on whom the Spirit empowered and rested. The Spirit enlightened Moses to receive divine revelation and fellowship. Unfortunately, unlike Moses, many in the church have not tapped into the power of the Spirit as much as God desires. God does not only desire to rest upon a selected few, but God desires to indwell all of God's children; because when we are indwelt by the Spirit, we are given the ability to do the works of God, as we love the world that God loves. How do we better avail ourselves of the Holy Spirit's power?

After accepting Jesus Christ, we have access to the Spirit. It does not matter to what denomination we are connected; it does not matter our social status. When we receive Jesus as Lord, we have unrestricted access to the Holy Ghost. As we learn to walk in the Spirit, we grow in the Spirit. As we grow in the Spirit, the power of the Spirit begins to flow through us consistently and impressively. Before His earthly departure, Jesus tells the disciples that the Spirit will empower us to help challenge and change the world by: 1) convicting the world that its system is sinful. 2) persuading persons that through Christ, all can be made righteous; and 3) convicting the world that evil has an expiration date, because Satan has been judged as a defeated power. When empowered by the Spirit, the church will have this effect, as it preaches, heals, prophesies, does miracles, gives, and loves the neighbor, in a sin-sick world.

We must keep in mind that the Spirit often uses human vessels to accomplish this powerful work of helping to redeem the world. The Spirit doesn't flitter and flutter around, as a disembodied spirit. As we allow the Holy Spirit to work in us and through us, God will use us as agents of conviction — a bold light of love that shines God's truth in a world of spiritual darkness. According to our text in Exodus 34, after an encounter with God, Moses had the illuminating, convicting light of the Spirit reflected on his very face. Later, when the Children of Israel saw Moses' face shining they were convicted by Moses' presence. Likewise, when the church is walking in the Spirit, the Spirit will convict those who live among us that God is real. Has the Spirit been using your presence to convict, convince, and persuade others — folks on the block, within your family, at school, and your place of employment? And that sin is real, but that we can be made righteous, and that the devil is ultimately defeated? Have you ever had others to avoid you or be attracted to your presence, because of the presence of the Spirit in your life? Sisters and brothers, in a world that has gone haywire, we need Christians to be houses of the Holy. When we have faith that we have become such, God will bring about a steady conviction in our lives, and in the lives of those we love, as God persuades them, through us, that there is a better way! Sometimes we don't even have to say a word, because the Spirit, does a strange, but powerful work!

23. A New Kind of Baptism

Text: Acts 2 and 3

What is Holy Spirit baptism? Is it a phenomenon that only happens to those who are gullible and vulnerable emotionally? Is it something akin to a trance, or being possessed by spirits? Baptism in the Spirit is a needed gift of empowerment and ecstasy that God has for every disciple of Jesus Christ. Jesus promised these gifts in the Gospels and in Acts 1. John the Baptist came on the religious scene baptizing the Jews in water; Jesus came to baptize all people in the presence of the Spirit. Baptism in the Holy Spirit is *a next level experience* meant to equip us with all the love and power we need to glorify God, and help our fellow human beings, in a world that is constantly slipping away from God's desired will. This *second baptism* fills one with a heightened awareness of the fiery presence, love and power of God. Some suggest that this baptism is accompanied by "the tongues of angels" (praise and prayer languages), or by the ability to heal, or to work miracles; or to lead others in worship, or to better attend and organize church business, or to preach and counsel with deepened levels of truth, wisdom and discernment, or to interpret the scriptures in ways that powerfully convicts and comforts. More than anything, the experience of being Baptized in the Spirit, *floods followers of Christ with a holy boldness to glorify the name of the Lord, in the midst of great opposition and conflict.* This experience is so powerful that it will spill out of one's personal experience into the public square, affecting lives of close family members, friends, and even strangers, for their good and for God's glory.

Immediately following the initial baptism and filling of the Holy

Spirit, on the day of Pentecost, the Holy Spirit moved the church and its leaders to impact the city of Jerusalem, and beyond. The book of Acts, chapters 3 and 4, serve as today's source of reflection as we discuss and consider how the experience of the baptism in the Holy Spirit helped the early church to: 1) Set captives free (sometimes miraculously) in Jesus' name. 2) Convert new believers to the Lord 3)Possess and speak divine wisdom, even in opposition to the agendas of world leaders and critics. 4) Change the way we pray, because in the Spirit we will be moved to ask God for ridiculous blessings for the church and the unchurched. 5) Give generously to meet the needs of those in our fellowship and beyond. In our text, both the wealthy and the not so wealthy become fountains of blessing (see the last section of Acts 2).

Although the scriptures and some of our experiences reveal that the Spirit moves on many Christians to speak in glossolalia (tongues) today for the purpose of edifying God, we make a colossal mistake if we reduce the power of the Spirit to only speaking in tongues. One can infer from what Paul writes in his Epistle to the Corinthians, that all believers might not necessarily speak in tongues, after being possessed by the Spirit; but he does teach us that those who are baptized and filled with the Spirit will do *something powerful* that glorifies God! I believe that if we allow God to more fully possess our hearts, minds, souls, and our strength, God will do wonders through God's church! That includes you, doesn't it?

Study Questions

1. Have you ever been baptized in the Holy Spirit?
2. What was your experience?
3. Did you speak in tongues? Were you filled with an overwhelming sense of God's love? Were you moved to worship God in Christ?
4. What were the signs of the early church's baptism in the Spirit? How did they treat one another? How did they treat those in their community?
5. Name the times you saw the early church exhibit courage in Acts 2 and 3?

Part 4

Ordinary Time

24. A House Built Upon the Rock

Texts: Deuteronomy 8:1-3 and Matthew 7:24-29

Our First and New Testament readings for this reflection communicate something to readers that we must not overlook. Both texts communicate that the word of God is not just a religious word, limited to the boundaries and precincts of temples, synagogues, and churches, *but it is the word of life!* Much more than merely religious phrases, dusty dogma, and doctrine, the word of the Lord is what undergirds human existence. In Genesis, God spoke, and things came into being; God spoke to form us, and then breathed into us, spirit, and we came alive and made sense of our surroundings. To get his attention in the Midian desert, God helped Moses to see the burning bush that was not consumed; and then grounded his visual experience in divine speech. Moses heard The Voice which makes all other voices possible. This experience began an ongoing, life-affirming, liberating, intimate relationship between Yahweh and Moses. Consequently, in Deuteronomy 8, Moses, reminded a new generation of believers – those who had survived the forty-year, wilderness journey – that God's children are to also cultivate a relationship with Yahweh, by not only *hearing the words of God*, as written and taught to them, but they were to *live according to every word* that proceeded from the mouth of the Lord (vs. 3). In this, our first text, Moses reminds the people that God had indeed revealed God's word through laws, signs, wonders, and miracles, via the Exodus; also, by the way God had sustained them in the wilderness with Manna to eat, and garments to wear – garments which ordinarily would have fallen apart after a few years.

The Hebrews were taught that the word of God was not just a religious category of teachings, meant to be segmented away for a small section of one's life, but the word of God was what ultimately guided and grounded every aspect of their lives, including their miraculous experiences with God. They knew that the words they received, and the amazing experiences they had in life, were undergirded by the one who spoke all things into being.

Many years later, Jesus, who is the embodiment of God's word, echoes this sentiment about the centrality of the creative power of divine speech, in Matthew 7:24-29, as he teaches the multitudes on the Mt. of Olives. In his concluding remarks, he teaches the crowd about how his words, since they originate with the one he calls "Father," are the very foundations for all aspects of life. He expresses that God's words are what we should erect the entirety of our lives upon. And if one reads between the lines of what Jesus says in this text, it is clear that even when brazenly ignored, God's words will continue to work behind the scenes of people's lives, to their possible prosperity or peril. No matter one's culture, color, or country; no matter one's youth or old age, Jesus said that if we do not live the words of God, then we will build shabby, flimsy, lives, that won't be able to endure the storms of life. But, thanks be to God, Jesus also says that if we hear and obey his words, we would build our lives upon the sure foundation of God's eternal power. Though the storms might come, our lives will remain meaningful, powerful, purposeful and indestructible – our "houses" will not be washed away. Because when we live lives built on worship, love, forgiveness, unselfishness, grace, holiness, and truthfulness, we are in harmony with the eternal elements which make life what it actually is. The reason why death, in its various forms, comes as the cessation of life, is because sin was introduced into the equation of existence. Sin is against life, because it is against the word of God; sin tries to disconnect us from our life source. In Judaism and Christianity, the word of God is the life source of all that was, is, and will ever be! And in my life, I am continuing to learn how to rely on the word of God as my source of life, through wilderness experiences; through temptations to sin; through the stormy rains of life; through adversarial attacks; through personal failings; through the popularity of new-fangled philosophies, often rooted in vain words. The longer I live, and the more I am allowed to witness the goings on in our society, the more I am convinced that the words of God, revealed through Moses, and preeminently Christ, are not just religious in nature, but they are the fundamental building blocks of good relationships, communities, societies, and of reality in general.

25. Independence Day, and a Liberated Life!

Then Jesus said to those Jews who believed Him, "If you abide in My word, you are My disciples indeed. And you shall know the truth, and the truth shall make you free." They answered Him, "We are Abraham's descendants, and have never been in bondage to anyone. How can You say, 'You will be made free'?" Jesus answered them, "Most assuredly, I say to you, whoever commits sin is a slave of sin."

Text: John 8:31-33

As Americans celebrate our Independence from Great Britain, I think we should all consider, very deeply, the question: "What does it mean, to be free?" Though the Revolutionary War of 1776, provided a way for our country to help determine its own destiny, free from the monarchal, imperial, and economic tyranny of the British, we must not forget that countless other citizens of this country have not known these same freedoms to the extent of the children of Europe. Many Native and African American citizens of this land have been consistently oppressed and subjugated, since this country's inception. Native Americans and African Americans are still grappling with what it means to be free, in a land of immense opportunity, mixed with what are still profound levels of racism and injustice. This stain on our American history continues to be one of the reasons why African Americans, by and large, have celebrated and supported the quiet pre-game protests of quarterback, Colin Kaepernick; and it cannot be missed that amazingly, many European Americans have angrily vilified him for taking a knee against police brutality and racially motivated injustices, during the singing of the National Anthem.

Midway through the 19ᵗʰ Century, black folk were still enslaved. At the same time, many Native Americans were being systematically killed in a genocidal campaign to eradicate and annihilate them; survivors were segregated and shuttled away to reservations under harsh conditions. Why was this done? Because of a lust for the acquisition of more land and power, coupled with racism, as the new immigrants from Europe, increased the Western expansion of the states. So, given these historical facts, what does it mean to be truly free when your people and communities are being colonized on reservations, or segregated and ghettoized in the poorest areas of the nation, both urban and suburban? ghettoized in the poorest school systems, and lowest paying jobs?

Though we must cry out for freedom in all of its forms, our core definition of what it means to be free must go deeper than materialism, social class rankings, and anything that is easily measurable and tangible. True freedom must mean more than having access to social and material accoutrements, or else there is not much hope for the millions and millions and persons who have lived and died, and will live and die, under deeply sinful and corrupted dictators, governmental systems, and regimes. The core meaning of liberation and freedom must include the capacity to authentically know and be known by God, as we come to know ourselves and our neighbors. When we know and are known by God; and we are empowered to discover who we are, as we bless our neighbors, we are free, despite the presence of evil. There is an inner existential freedom that can give birth to all other notions of freedom. Through one of the oldest texts in the scriptures, we read of a figure, named Job, who seemed to know this kind of freedom. And as readers, we can only see the complexity of this kind of existential freedom, through the great trials he would endure. As we read Job, we can learn about the unusual freedom that is evidenced as human beings are allowed to question and wrestle with God – a God who, behind the scenes, is rooting for us and vouching for us; a God who desires to strengthen us and vindicate us, especially when evil and the Evil

One, have touched and tainted much of what we have deeply cherished and valued on this side of the Jordan River.

In the book of Job, Satan destroys most of what Job had acquired. He seems to lose what made him a free and prosperous man. He loses his wealth, his livestock, his servants, his children, and his health. Beginning in chapter 3, after God allows his life to be devastated, Job questions whether or not it was a good thing for him to have been born. He is so gripped with bad news, that he cannot see the light of any good news. He is oppressed by sad and bad situations; his marriage is very unstable and his body is racked with boils and painful blisters; in the midst of his despair, he longs for what he believes would be the liberating power of death. He just wants to be free from his earthly troubles. He wants to go where: *"…the wicked cease from troubling, And…the weary are at rest."* He says that in Sheol – the grave, *"…the prisoners rest together; They do not hear the voice of the oppressor. The small and great are there. And the servant is free from his master."* Job's sentiments illustrate for us that there are times when life can seem to wrap us up in its awful tentacles, and the only hope for liberty comes in the form of going on to the next life. Thankfully, by the end of the book of Job, Job discovers that God has a plan of freedom which includes what happens to us, and through us, in this life.

Despite life's significant challenges and pain, God ultimately wants us to live a life of freedom, joy, and hope. Job sees this more clearly by the end of this tough season in his life; even though exposed to evil events, he ends up knowing God more deeply and more completely than before his trials, and still chooses to love God, and his tormenting "friends" which opens him up to new expressions of God's grace and mercy – Job ends up receiving double for his trouble!

In a few verses in John's Gospel, in the eighth chapter, Jesus reveals to the reader the heights of this same kind of glorious freedom; a freedom anyone can claim and know. First, He tells his listeners that sin causes all of us to be held in the grips of an evil bondage – no matter our race or genealogy (vs. 21-24); but, despite this terrible fact, there is the hope of a great, incomparable freedom. Jesus says that we are freed up, deep on the inside, when we discover *the truth* about life, God, and people. How do we come into this truth and this rare quality of liberation? By intimately, acquainting ourselves with Jesus' word – His teachings on every subject. It is when we ingest and digest the words of the Messiah; it is when we allow the word of God, in Christ, to shape our thinking, believing, and actions; it is then that we will be freed up to see God, ourselves, and our neighbors more clearly. We will see life better through the lenses of forgiveness and love. It is our consuming and living the word of God, which empowers us to pray for those who have hurt us; we are freed up to keep pressing on, even when life comes with heavy crosses; freed up to keep serving, giving, and loving, even as we are being loved; freed up to say no, to that which would ensnare us, and to say yes, to all that would propel us upward and onward! Greater than any temporal king, Jesus has the power to eternally set God's children free! I'm glad that whomever the Son sets free, is free indeed!

26. Youth Sunday

How can a young man cleanse his way? By taking heed according to Your word.

Text: Psalm 119: 9

According to what is reported by the Children's Defense Fund, under the leadership of its founder, Marion Wright Eldelman, every five seconds, during the school day, a black, public school student is suspended. Every forty-six seconds, during the school day, a black high school student drops out. Every minute, a black child is arrested. Also, every minute a black baby is born to an unmarried mother. Every five hours, a black child is a homicide victim. Every day, a black youth/young adult under the age of twenty-five dies from HIV infection. Though we cannot pin all of the problems of our youth on one neatly boxed factor, which causes so many to spiral downward, we who value the message of the New Testament can easily see that hovering at the top of the list of the reasons why we see so many of our urban youth in peril today is because of the breakdown of our nuclear families; especially the breakdown of healthy covenantal relationships between the parents of the children. We praise God for all the godly single parents (most of the time, mothers) who have done/are doing the best that they can, under very difficult situations (my paternal grandmother was a single parent, who struggled to raise my father, without assistance from my grandfather, who for various reasons was not present). However, we would be in denial, if we did not admit that a trail of broken romantic relationships among parents, has often left children vulnerable and in jeopardy, facing all kinds of difficult problems, without quick and easy solutions.

I believe that one way we can turn the tide is by teaching and mentoring our children and youths to consider wise and godly options regarding dating, sexual activity, pursuing higher education, and of course, pursuing their Christian faith, beyond what I call, *churchianity (a set of religious traditions and rituals practiced in many churches, with hardly any investment in the actual work of the Spirit of Christ in the world). Churchianity* will not be an adequate substitute for a real-talk, and real-discipleship, Christianity, that many of our youth desire to grapple with. Our congregations must become safe houses, where young people can discuss, question, and find answers, related to their doubts, impulses, desires, hopes and dreams.

All of us have grown up in a society and culture which have offered us many wonderful freedoms and choices. Unfortunately, some of our freedoms and the choices we make in our youth can lead us down dangerous pathways for years to come, if we opt to choose wrongly. Certain choices made by us have sometimes placed us in spiritual harm. This is not an entirely new phenomenon. The psalmist, in Psalm 119 raised the question, "How can youths walk in pure ways?" The psalmist's answers his/her own question? "By taking heed according to Your (God's) word." On this Youth Sunday, and many other Sundays, it would behoove us to grapple with the wisdom revealed in God's word. Becoming biblically literate is critical for young people who are dealing with so much deception and fake news in our world today. Knowing the word of God, as one begins to practice what is taught in it (especially what Jesus teaches in the Gospels, along with the supporting teachings of the Apostles), will enable the next generation to stand as godly young men and women, in a world of arrogant, mental and emotional small-mindedness. Because no matter the environment, with the sword of the Spirit in one's possession, one becomes a discerner of God's truth and is empowered to cut away falsehood. With knowledge of the word of God, youth can fight against the many lies of our spiritual adversary. When the devil tries to convince us that we will always be alone, God's word reminds us of Jesus' promise, at the end of Matthew 28, *that he will be with us always, even to the end of the age.* When doubt tries to blind our pathway, we are reminded by Paul, in 2 Corinthians 5:7, that *we walk by faith and not by sight!* When temptations and weaknesses collude together to take us downward, we are reminded by Paul again, *that there is no temptation that is uncommon to other human beings, but God is faithful, and will not allow us to be tested above what we are able, but with the temptation God will make a way of escape that we may bear under the pressure.*

To better arrive at a place of victory and spiritual maturity, we've got to talk, transparently, and biblically, about the issues that are impacting our young people; we've got to have open dialogue about their fears, sexual concerns and attractions; about bullying, cliques, peer-pressure, racism, problems related to a poor self-image, the media, the information web; social media, etc. The word of God must be shared in ways that weave its perspective into the fabric of young lives. When we allow the word of God to be the very word of life, on every issue in life, then and only then, will we grow into the kind of person God desires us to be.

27. Living Between the Promise and the Promised Land

And He said, "The kingdom of God is as if a man should scatter seed on the ground, and should sleep by night and rise by day, and the seed should sprout and grow, he himself does not know how. For the earth yields crops by itself: first the blade, then the head, after that the full grain in the head. But when the grain ripens, immediately he puts in the sickle, because the harvest has come."

Texts: Mark 4:26-29 and the book of Ruth

One of the hardest things for young Christians, and recent converts, to understand is that there is, with rare exception, a delay between God's promises and the fulfilment of those promises. From the moment we exit the waters of baptism, God has promised us a plethora of spiritual blessings: salvation; the authority and anointing that the Holy Spirit grants; gifts of the Spirit; relationships centered in mutual love and forgiveness; peace and a purpose for living; all of our material and spiritual needs met; health and a biblically- based, holistic prosperity; a commission and mission which will empower us to make a significant difference in the lives of the hurting and disconnected all around us. But although God's promises will come to pass for the faithful, many of us fail to realize that before we experience the fullness of these blessings, there is sometimes, a long waiting period of trial and error, hits and misses, which we must endure, before we secure God's promises. We soon learn that to help us to trust and grow in the graces of God, God will often delay the actualization of God's promises. In the mean time we must learn how to conduct ourselves during the delay period.

If we investigate the story of Abraham, we learn that before Abraham became the Father of the Nation, through the promised miracle that was Isaac, he took matters into his own hands and had an Ishmael. Before the nation of Israel experienced joy in the Promised Land, they went through the ordeal of wandering in the wilderness. Before Jesus would fulfill the great promise of saving all who would believe, he had to endure three intense years of spiritual and religious controversy and spiritual warfare, which seemed to only culminate in a cruel cross.

In both of our texts (The book of Ruth and Mark 4:26-29) we see that God gives us a process through which we move from the promise to the fulfillment of God's harvest time blessings. First, the Spirit gives us a word, or an impression of a promise; the impression of a blessing that God wants to get to us/our families/our communities. After the promise has been given, there is a delay in the fulfillment of it. *What we do, or fail to do, during the period of delay, especially when it seems as if nothing is happening, can prove to be the critical determinant of whether we will acquire what has been promised!* When our salvation, liberation, relationships, money, etc., seem to be lying dormant, do you give up hope of God's abundance? Do you stop planting worship, faith, love, faithfulness, study, and ministry in your life? Or do you trust the Lord, diligently serving until your harvest arrives? This is the enduring testimony of the protagonist Ruth, and of the nameless man who keeps planting and watering in Mark 4, until his harvest gradually appears!

Ruth must endure the deaths of loved ones and long hard roads to travel, as she joins her mother-in-law, Naomi, as they relocate to Naomi's people and culture. Ruth is a stranger there. She must work hard in the fields in the heat of the day. She must submit to traditional, but unfamiliar, Jewish courting rituals meant to woo and further persuade an unfamiliar man of wealth and means; but, after her actions and her wait, she fully receives her Boaz blessing! Once her wait has ended, she ends up being co-owner of the wealth, and the acres and acres of land she once worked in; and she becomes the boss, of the workers she once worked with, during the harvesting season. The tail has become the head! But, it took a process to get there.

In Mark 4:26-28, Jesus says that a farmer must first, put in the hard work to plant his potential harvest. After the period of planting, there is a delay of the harvest blessing, during which time the farmer rises and goes to bed, many days, before there are any signs that his labor was not in vain. Finally, under the right weather conditions have nurtured and nourished the seeds, there is a sprouting up of the crop – *first the blade, then the head, after that the full grain in the head.* Notice that the farmer will not fully benefit from the approaching harvest until long after the first sprouting of the crops. It is not until the full grain appears that the farmer can harvest his crops. There is a long wait period before the harvest! And often, it is the same with us as we await the fulfillment of God's promises. In the interim, keep praying; keep praising; keep serving; keep loving; and more than anything, keep planting God's word in your soul!

28. How to Deal with Folks' Stuff

Texts: 2 Samuel 11 and 12 & Galatians 6:1-4

Because Christians are linked together in a spiritual community and are also connected with the broader world culture, there is no way to avoid being impacted by the thinking, actions and choices of others – for good or for bad. The decisions of those who live and rule in Russia, affect those of us who live in the United States; the decisions of those who make policies in the U.S. impact those who live in Russia. The decisions of those who live in the United States, affect those who live in Mexico; the decisions of those who live in Mexico, affect the policies of the local and national government of the U.S. This interdependent dynamic has almost infinite examples, ranging from what happens in our governmental politics, to what happens in business, the ecology, the economy, race relations, and our religions. The call that Jesus extends is not a call to forever live an isolated religious life, secluded away like monks or hermits. Jesus and those first disciples were fully engaged in the lives of others, and so should we be — making a positive and powerful difference in the world. Our faith should touch someone else's faith; our service should inspire someone else to serve; our prophetic proclamations, should shine light in dark spaces. Our religion, and our lives, are intertwined with other people. Dr. King called this fact *an inescapable network of mutuality, tied in a single garment of destiny.*

But this connection we have with others can sometimes cause great disruptions and even chaos. Because of our interconnectedness there are many occasions for the sinful and thoughtless actions of others, or of ourselves, to negatively impact our world and the righteous work of the

Redeemer. In 2 Samuel 12, King David's decision to sin grievous sins, negatively impacted David's household, Israel's peace, and the victorious advance of God's Kingdom. Consequently, the prophet Nathan was directed by God to bring this fact to David's attention so that he could repent of *his stuff.* Many years later, in Galatians 6:1, Paul called on spiritually minded members of God's church located in the region of Galatia, to confront and gently restore persons who found themselves caught in rebellious acts and disobedient lifestyles. Paul instructs the people of God to not just tolerate the sinful acts of others, but to lovingly counsel, deliver and restore, the recalcitrant child of God. In both the First and New Testament scripture texts, we can see the importance of holding our brothers and sisters accountable for their sins and rebellion; especially those acts which are rather blatant and publicly known. This is for the community's good! Persistently sinful actors can ruin the power and effectiveness of an entire faith community. When preachers, elders, and other faith leaders are not practicing what they teach and preach; when choir members and musicians are not living what they are shouting and singing; when ushers are acting up; and deacons are being devilish, the reputation of the whole church suffers. In fact, the neighborhood community suffers. When churches begin to acquire bad reputations because of the ungodly behavior of its members, the community suffers the absence of a spiritual center that is functioning with integrity (As an important caveat, it is also important to note that in efforts to hold accountable our straying members, faith communities should not go to the other extreme and become places of a legalistic judgmentalism, where *the sin police* are always on patrol).

Holding ourselves and others accountable to New Testament standards is a work of love and grace. As we minister God's grace and administer discipline, we must also avoid a hyper legalism which is also sinful and can destroy the Spirit's work of instilling a sense of grace and mercy in the hearts of God's disciples.

The main thrust of today's message is the second part to last week's message, which was about the importance of dealing with *our own individual sinfulness, before* we attempt to address other folks' sins. Today, as we balance last week's emphasis on individual confession, personal integrity, accountability before God, and self-denial, we will grapple with the importance of learning how to hold our sinning sisters and brothers accountable, as we seek how to become our best selves before God together; thus, the provocative title: *"How to deal with other folks' stuff!"* As we focus on how Samuel, the prophet, dealt with David and his stuff (his adultery and murderous actions) and as we hear anew Paul's advice to the Christians of Galatia who had to learn how to deal with those among their ranks who had been discovered in some scandalous act, or who continued to manifest a devilish disposition, we are standing on good ground if we spend our energies in efforts to restore the person to their right relationship with God, themselves, and the church, in general. The prophet Samuel, in efforts to restore David to a posture of spiritual uprightness, *privately appeals* to the wayward King by using a potent and powerful proverb to help David to see the seriousness of his error. Paul, manifesting similar thinking, reminds us in Galatians 6:1, that the Spirit wants us to restore our wandering sisters and brothers, in a *spirit of gentleness,* as we are mindful that we too are often only one or two strong temptations away from yielding and getting caught up in a salacious scandal, or a demonic trap.

Far too many Christians seem to take glee in the downfall of others. This should not be. Neither Samuel or Paul modeled this kind of attitude and neither should we. When people in our faith communities have sinned publicly, we must not excuse the act, but neither should we pick up stones. When persons have persisted in some problematic direction, warnings and a tender church discipline is in order, but a ruthless condemnation is not. When it comes to God's children, and even those who have not been born into God's family, God is a second, third, and forth chance God. If God swatted us away, every time we had made a misstep or a deliberate choice against God's perfectly clear will, then God would have a world absent of people. But, God knows we are but dust – flesh and blood, sometimes fickle and moved by earthy passions. Therefore, God desires us to deal with other folk's stuff, as we would want God to deal with our own stuff. God wants us to view other folk's faults and foibles, in the context of our own faults and foibles. This kind of perspective does not preclude discipline, but it shapes the manner and attitude that is at work in the process of administering discipline.

29. God Can Put it Under Your Feet

Text: Matthew 14:22-33

Have you ever felt so overwhelmed by the events of your life that you felt you were going under? When there are more bills than there is money; when there is more bitterness than there is honey; when at your door, there seems to be more harsh critics than there are loving visits; when there are more obstacles in view, than there are wide open vistas before you; psychologically and emotionally we can feel like we are sinking toward death. The good news for the child of God is that when we seem flooded over by almost unbearable circumstances, God is around us and in us, ready to lift us up above those factors that would seek to drown out our joy and victory.

In Matthew 14:22-33, Jesus strongly compels his disciples to get into one of their fishing boats and go to the other side of the Sea of Galilee. Some of these men were experienced fishermen, and they knew when rough weather was approaching. Given this, it seems (according to the Greek word for "made" in verse 22) that they had to be strongly urged by Jesus to take this trip. As the disciples had imagined they did end up in a stormy situation. They tried with all their strength to row to the other side, but the winds were blowing against them and the forceful and invasive sprays of the sea water was getting in the boat. They were struggling, while Jesus was on land, praying. In the fourth watch of the night (3 am to 6 am) Jesus does the unthinkable. Jesus walks on the storm-tossed sea to rescue the disciples. And even more amazingly, before the day dawns, two men will have done what seems humanly impossible; and almost unfathomably, one of the two will not be the Messiah! According to Matthew's narrative, Peter, the fisherman, turned itinerant preacher, goes down in recorded history, as one of only two people who has defied physical laws of gravity to walk on the sea. Brothers and sisters, this event gives us a parable for what any follower of God can do when their energy and focus are on Jesus. We probably will not be able to walk on the local lake, because such a display is not necessary, and Jesus is not beckoning us to join him out there. But, as we meditate on God's word, we can do what seems impossible; we can become the kind of wives and husbands we never saw modeled by our own parents. With help from God's presence and word, we can sing and speak in front of large audiences, even though in our pasts we have had a debilitating fear of public speaking and performing. As we spend time in intense prayer, with yielded and concerned citizens, we can put our heads together and rid our blocks of drugs and gangs. As we meditate day and night on Jesus' teaching about the Good Samaritan, and His statements about how the first will be last, and the last first, we can challenge structures of class and racial supremacy, and the most negative aspects of gentrification, and make our society more just and equitable – we can walk on water!

Peter was focused on Jesus, and by obeying the words Jesus had spoken to him, was able to briefly master that which should have easily drowned him immediately. And the great thing about Jesus is that our being able to put intimidating realities under our feet, is not a proposition that is wholly dependent on our human abilities; Jesus lifts us even when we stumble and trip, in the process of trying to make God's vision of our lives a reality. Peter is the perfect example. In this same narrative, when in a moment of fear, Peter falters from his amazing posture of having the sea under his feet, Jesus revealed a God Who is willing to rescue us and helps us to put all our problems under our feet, even when our faith gets low! Therefore, especially for risk-taking, boat-leaving Christians, we aren't ever completely *"under bad circumstances,"* but we can trust in a God, who, in God's own way, will put everything that belongs under our feet, under them!

30. Who is Jesus to You?

When Jesus came into the region of Caesarea Philippi, He asked His disciples, saying, "Who do men say that I, the Son of Man, am?"

Matthew 16:13

During the middle of the twentieth century, a new popular game show emerged, called, *"What's My Line?"* I used to watch old reruns of it at my grandparent's home, as they watched me during the summer in Chicago. My uncle Paul, who is just a couple of years older than me, used to turn to it occasionally. One of the objects of the game was for a blind-folded panel to guess the identity of a secret celebrity. To guess the mystery guest's identity, the panel would ask probing questions while listening very carefully to the tone, and tenor of the stranger's voice and answers. Often, the identity of the celebrity would become known through the process of questioning and listening to the answers given. This is a good example of how to unravel a mystery through asking questions, ascertaining clues and employing the gifts of human reason. But, how do we draw important conclusions, and discover critical information, when human reason, and probing questions, and a keen sense of observation, alone, are not enough to crack our most pressing mysteries?

In Matthew 16:13, Jesus confronts his disciples with a question about his own identity: "Whom do men/women say that I, the Son of man, am? As they answer, they rattle off answers based on what people have said about Jesus. After listing all of the possible prophets Jesus seemed to be, in a reincarnated form, Jesus directs the question directly to the disciples:

"But who do you say that I am?" This question is a timeless question for all of us who populate the planet. At some point, we must all reckon with the imposing nature of this question: *Who is Jesus to me*? To you, was Jesus just a prophet? The Leader of the Christian religion? Or is he a personal bridge over troubled water? A being who has answered your prayers? As all of us attempt to answer this question, we must discern how we have arrived at our conclusions, if we have reached one. This is the seat the disciples were sitting in, in our text. Peter has an answer, and according to the one asking the question, Peter gets an A – Peter's right. Jesus told the disciples and Peter, that Peter's insight into Jesus being the Christ, the Son of God, was downloaded directly into Peter's spirit by God the Father. It was a profound revelation; the sure rock of God's self-disclosure to Peter. Once Peter got it, and it was confirmed by Jesus, the other disciples could receive it and run with it!

Human-centered intellectualisms suggest that it is impossible to know with certainty the answer to the question of whether God exists or not; or whether God can be fully incarnate in a human being. There are limits to what the mind can conceive on its own. There are limits to our scientific, Western way of thinking and knowing. But, for those of us who believe in God; and for those who subscribe to a non-Western way of interpreting the world; and for those who advocate for an epistemology which includes supernatural possibilities and categories (the kind of thinking which is consistent with Jewish, African, Native American, and Hispanic conceptions of reality); if we believe in a Creator, whatever our ethnicities, then surely this Creator, by virtue of being the Creator, is free and wise enough to reveal aspects of the Creator's presence to us in ways that are accurate, helpful, and graspable. In our text, Peter blurted out, *"You are the Christ, the Son of the Living God!"* This amazing moment of revelation was granted by God on the edge of Caesarea Philippi; a place which celebrated and reveled in its polytheism and idolatry. Since that time in history, Peter, the disciples, the church and the world, have never been the same! Because on that day, human beings were given a full peek into a profound and life-altering truth. On that day, the secret of Jesus' identity and origin were unveiled. Right on the edge of this Gentile stronghold of idolatry, a few of society's misfits learned that the Son of the Living God was standing in front of them! What an amazing God we serve.

31. The Power of the Ten Commandments - Even those Which Seem Obscure

You shall not take the name of the LORD your God in vain, for the LORD Will not hold him guiltless who takes His name in vain. Remember the Sabbath day, to keep it holy. Six days you shall labor and do all your work, but the seventh day is the Sabbath of the Lord your God....

Exodus 20:7-10a

In most bookstores, there are book sections dealing with a diverse range of topics. If one were to carefully peruse the different titles and categories, it wouldn't be long before one would happen upon the "Self-Help" or "Self-Improvement" section of the store. I have rarely found myself drawn to these kinds of books. I would like to believe that it is not because I am so egotistical and foolish enough believe that I don't have room for self-improvement. Knowing, what I know about myself, I have got plenty of room for personal and spiritual growth. My aversion to this genre of books might have more to do with how I am hardwired. For me, the Holy Scriptures, biographies, sociology, history, and what I learn in familial and collegial relationships, help provide both the fuel and the friction which help me to grow, change, empathize, envision, aim, confess, forgive, and strive for higher heights, and deeper depths.

I must confess that there have been a couple of exceptions to my complete avoidance of the self-improvement genre. In the early 2000s, I found fascinating and informative a book which helps the reader learn how to better discern, interpret, and translate the particular *love languages* in which one's spouse, family members, and friends, are most conversant; and about a decade before that, in the early nineties, I remember reading a book that was considered the quintessential self-help/self-improvement book, at the time. A member of the congregation I was serving gave me a book entitled, *"The Seven Habits of Highly Effective People,"* by Steven Covey. This is now a classic, especially among those who desire to foster and improve relationships, team building dynamics, and the chance of mounting win-win victories in the business sector. The member who shared this book with me worked in a management position for *The Eli Lilly Co.*, a world-renowned pharmaceutical company, headquartered in Indianapolis. As I had already shared a book or two with him about Christ and faith, this member was so excited to put this work in my hands because he cherished the principles revealed in it. *The Seven Habits* teaches readers how to create win-win relationships, especially in business situations; situations which will, in best case scenarios help to improve not only the quality of one's work relationships, and the level of one's business successes, but one's overall quality in life, period. About a year or so ago, as I prepared to preach from the book of Exodus, the section of it which houses the ten commandments, I thought about the aim and content of Steven Covey's work. What is more, I felt led to approach the Ten Commandments, from a certain pedagogical perspective; one that would couch the commandments as self-help and community-help principles which ensure personal and communal levels of success, because of the greatness and wisdom of the God who issued them.

We thank God for other books, but no wisdom is as anointed and potent as the wisdom found in the Book of books – the Bible. In the second book of the Bible -- Exodus -- Moses is given the Decalogue (more commonly known as the Ten Commandments) by the finger of Yahweh. These ten practical and spiritual directives, not only formed the basis for all of Israel's additional laws, mandates, and household and holiness codes, but they also have served as the foundation for the creation for many of the early laws of the United States. In fact, as the colonies formed, many government bodies met in churches. And until the last few decades, many of our courthouses displayed memorials to the Ten Commandments, because of the spiritual and historical position they hold in our judicial system.

Most biblically literate Christians who are familiar with the doctrine of Grace, as taught since the Reformation, know that Yahweh, the Father of our Lord, doesn't grant persons eternal life *only* because one tries one's best to keep the ten commandments, or any other laws associated with religion. While commandments and laws are critical goals and directives for our spiritual practices, Christians have come to know that our justification and righteousness before God is the result of receiving a priceless gift of Grace from God, which is granted as we profess faith in Jesus' atoning death for our sins. Even in the days when the Hebrews tried to follow the entire Mosaic Law, there were practices they observed that pointed to the power of God's grace that was at work to save them both individually and collectively; they practiced an annual Day of Atonement for the benefit of the entire community – for everyone who had disobeyed aspects of the Mosaic Law during the year. The point being that keeping the Decalogue and the other adjoining laws and codes was never the ultimate power that would grant forgiveness and save the people. The grace of God, at work through sacrificial systems – systems of animal sacrifice - was always the seal and sign of God's pardoning of the Hebrews of their sins as attempts to perfectly obey the law had failed. However, though most Christians and Jews understand that our attempts to perfectly keep religious laws does not, and cannot ultimately save us from damnation and lostness, many Jews and Christians recognize that the Ten Commandments were given by God to offer individuals and societies among the Jews and beyond, critical moral pillars – guidelines and standards for living successfully with others, toward which we should aim as we seek to please God and bless our neighbors.

This week, our focus will be on what some of us might consider two of the more obscure of the commandments -- the **third** and **fourth** commandments; the commandments *to not take the Lord's name in vain* and *to sanctify and make holy the Sabbath.* For those of us who have come of age in a culture which has become increasingly comfortable with the use of crude colloquialisms, slothful slang, ethnic influenced Ebonics, cool casual-speak, egregious epithets, and vicious vulgarities and profanities, it might be difficult to see the importance of obeying a commandment to not take the Lord's name in vain; especially if we have certain popular and capricious notions about what that means, running around in our heads. Because as distasteful as it might be, we are no longer shocked to hear what our *culture deems* is taking the Lord's name in vain. Our ears have become desensitized to hearing someone utter under their breath an exasperated *"God-damn-it!"* or a frustration-filled, *"Jesus! won't you get off the couch and do something?"* Also, for those of us who are not Jewish and do not observe Saturday, or any day, as our Sabbath (a day when we cease from all our labors to reflect on and honor our faith), it might seem ridiculous to esteem any day of the week, as a holy day. We have work to do; places to go; and people to meet every day. Sundays are no longer sacrosanct substitutes for the Jewish Sabbath. The first day of the week, that only a generation or two ago in American culture was recognized as the Lord's Day, commemorating the day when Jesus was raised from the dead, is no longer the Sunday it was in 1955; it is no longer a day when almost all stores and businesses are closed for business. Today we worship our sports teams, which wear our colors in huge cathedrals dedicated to the pigskin carried by running-backs, or the round leather projected upward into rims and nets. We shop, build, design, and go to our kids' football, soccer and basketball games on Sundays, especially when our children's playoff games begin.

For many, these two commandments are not the big-ticket ones. Many of us give no serious thought to breaking them. They are unlike the ones which prohibit lying, idolatry, dishonoring parents, adultery, stealing, covetousness, and murder. Mistakenly, we tend to think that the other commandments, are infinitely more important in God's view, not realizing the interrelated aspect of all the commandments (Family members and friends have often said, "If you will lie, you will steal; and if you will steal, you will kill." Maybe it could also be added that if one will not regularly rest, one is more vulnerable to being tempted to steal, commit adultery, covet, etc. And, if one will easily use the Lord's name in vain, then one will not truly respect any other name, or the person behind the name.). But, the fact is that these two commandments are not ones which send us into a panic as we imagine feeling the heat of God's nostrils of judgment ready to blow the hot fires of destruction down upon us! Taking the Lord's name in vain, though still considered a bit uncouth among Christians, no longer sets the religious alarm bells off, quite like other violations do, because we misunderstand its meaning. Likewise, not honoring the Sabbath today, does not cause many Christians to lose much sleep today (in an ironic twist), though it can indeed throw off the rhythm of one's entire spiritual life. Let's take a closer look at the meaning of these commandments.

First, as one considers what it means to take the Lord's name in vain, it is important to understand that *t*he purpose of the command is significant. By what is commanded here, whatever the commandment truly means, it is clear that God has a strong desire for all human beings to honor, respect, and use appropriately, and with integrity, all that the name of God (Yahweh, Jesus) represents, which is Yahweh's very person. In Jewish thought, the name of God encapsulates the character and presence of God. The name of God contains and reveals aspects of the nature of God. The Jewish theologians, philosophers, and prophets, would not even spell out the full name of Yahweh as they wrote their literature. Consequently, when we as church and synagogue, claim to be children of all that the name of God represents (e.g. faithfulness, power, goodness, holiness, love, forgiveness, wisdom, strength, grace, etc.), *and we live contrary to God's name*, we are taking the name of the Lord in vain in one of the worst ways. When we worship Yahweh with the dance, and praise Jesus on strings, wind instruments, and drums, in our worship settings, and offer up vocal praises to God, on Saturday, or Sunday, but on Monday through Friday, we act like atheists, or bullies, or miscreants, we are taking the name of the Lord in vain. When we claim to be a people of prayer, and pray in the name of the Father, Son, and Holy Spirit; or we pray to Yahweh, or Jehovah Jirah, and then once off our knees we go about not believing that we have been heard by God, we are using the Lord's name in vain. When we mention Yahweh, or "God," or utter the name "Jesus," without a sense of the sacred, or we use the name as a part of a negative pejorative, we are using the Lord's name in vain.

When we love a person, their name is important to us. When we are engaged in a serious courtship, we are sometimes ready to put on boxing gloves, and resort to pugilistic protestations if anyone tries to sully the name of our beloved. Not that God ultimately craves or needs us to defend God's name and character in a similar way, but should not we who claim to love God, feel somewhat protective of, and heavily invested in, the sacredness of God's name?

It is important for us not to use God's name in vain, not just because we have loving affections for the Lord's name, but also the Lord's name is the one name we must call on for help, deliverance, assistance, relief, healing, and most importantly, salvation! God's name is foundational to our spiritual consciousness. Ideally, we pray our casual and most fervent prayers in the context of God's name. We do our acts of service in God's name. We establish our relationships in the name of the Lord. Ideally, we spend our money, plan our travel, receive important counsel, raise children, and choose our spouses, all in the name of the Lord. To do anything in God's name, means that we are conscious of, and desire to invoke the presence, and the character and power of God's name into the details of our circumstances. When faced with threats, devils and haters, the name of the Lord is a strong tower that we run into. We use the name of God with faith, like a shield, as we expect protection, deliverance, exorcisms, and swift turn arounds. Therefore, it stands to reason that if we love God, and are grateful for God's power being released into every aspect of our lives, we should not want to ever take the Lord's name in vain, as though it were something common or profane. For it is in God that we live, move, and have our being. And by chance, if we do find ourselves drifting off into such vanities of expression, we ought to confess it quickly and soberly; and then, because of the name of Jesus, we can ready ourselves to receive the forgiveness and grace that is attendant in that glorious name!

Secondly, *Keeping the Sabbath Day* means much more than what we have reduced it to mean in our modern culture. Observing the Sabbath means more than debating whether the day falls on Saturday, or on Sunday; it means much more than creating a laundry list of what should be considered work and not work. In fact, Jesus said to those who loved to engage in debates regarding the Sabbath, that they should never forget that the Sabbath is to be understood as a gift from God to benefit human beings. *Human beings weren't made for the Sabbath, but the Sabbath was made for human beings!* This command to keep Shabbat was not given to enslave us to old, dead, stifling, meaningless, religious traditions and rituals. Jesus taught that Sabbath day observances were made to serve humanity – providing for us a way to rest in the holiness of God's grace and love, as we reflect on all the reasons we are to be grateful to God. Humanity was not made to slavishly serve under a wrong concept of the Sabbath, but the day was meant to bless us by putting all other days into proper perspective. From what we have in both the First and New Testaments, keeping the Sabbath means finding a day to freely and regularly connect with God, self, and family, so that one can find that soul's rest that is absent from the urgent demands of trying to meet the deadlines, obligations, and the anxieties related to the hectic existence of our lives.

How are you doing with the third and fourth commandments in your life? We are living in an age of rebellion. Far too many are no longer committed to following the laws and mores of our society. Rebellion is nothing new, and it is not always bad. Our country was birthed through the seeds of a certain kind of rebellion. When evil men and women and institutions seek to oppress and squash the freedoms of others, a rebellion, or a revolution, can be an indication that people still have goodness inside, and that many desire justice and righteousness for their society. Led by God, Moses prophetically, stood against the imperial powers of Egypt. But when our society rebels against goodness, decency, wisdom, and godliness, the entire society is in danger of anarchy and self-destruction. When we refuse to honor God's name and treat the name of God as something common; and when we fail to make sacrosanct, at least one day for the purposes of honoring God, family, friendships, and ourselves, we are losing the benefits and blessings, inherent in keeping these important commandments.

If you consistently honor God's name with your lips, your life, and find ways to sanctify a day to connect with God, family, friends, and self, *at least* once a week, then you are well on your way to living the abundant life!

32. Making Room at the Wall

Scripture Texts: Nehemiah 3 and Matthew 9:37-38

In our New Testament text, Jesus is concerned about the cities and villages which have not yet fully encountered God's love and sustaining power. Clearly there were too many Galilean villages and hamlets which had not yet heard about, or experienced God's abundant life. Matthew records that as Jesus went preaching in a circuit around the region of Galilee, He observes that people around the community were confused, in bondage, and harassed by demons and life's pressing issues. Looking into the not-so-distant future, through divine eyes of compassion, Jesus sees that a larger number of more committed disciples (laborers) would be needed to tackle the formidable task of helping to liberate and guide God's people to the abundant life. Consequently, in Matthew 9:37- 38, Jesus tells His disciples to put a prayer request at the top of their lists because:

The harvest truly is plentiful, but the laborers are few.
Therefore, pray the Lord of the harvest to send out laborers
into His harvest.

Our sermonic meditation for the week will focus on answering the question: *"What will be required of us if God were to answer this prayer in our faith village, as soon as tomorrow?"* What would happen if God were to flood us with sanctified laborers who were ready to learn and then lead? Most church folk say they desire to see new members added to their fellowship. Often the real hope behind such a sentiment is that the empty pews would become filled with tithers who would also be willing to fill in for *a few* of the ministry positions of the church that are open – positions which do not hold great decision-making power.

With true growth comes the need for a true spiritual and social stretching. Often, if God were to send in a flood of *on-fire* laborers who are excited about witnessing, and saving souls; mentoring, feeding the hungry, speaking out against injustice, and starting new ministries, the current members would not be able to handle. It has been my experience, that unfortunately, when this kind of growth occurs, the real power struggles begin. I wonder, if confronted with the problem, would most of our well-meaning congregations provide a true welcome and a place to rise and shine, for a flood of new laborers? Or would most of the long-time members be intimidated by a potential shift in power? From what I have seen, the latter is more common than the former. But, with help from the Spirit, we can be up to the challenges which come with growth and change!

In the third chapter of the book of Nehemiah, Nehemiah and the Jews, fresh out of Babylonian captivity, tried to employ as many workers as they could to rebuild the dilapidated walls of Jerusalem. Every available and willing worker was given the space and the honor to serve with significance and distinction at the wall. A record of the names of the diverse workers was kept by Nehemiah. There were those of the priestly class, contractors, women, men, artisans, brick masons, goldsmiths, politicians, older and younger folks, who put their hands to the work of rebuilding the walls. There was enough work for everyone to lend a hand in helping to secure the city against attacks from its enemies; enemies like Mr. Sanballat of Samaria, and an Ammonite named Tobiah, and a coalition of Arabs and Ashdodites (see chapter 4). The only group among the returning Jews who refused to work at the wall, were those of the nobility – the upper class (vs. 9). Unfortunately, this is often how systems and institutions work, or fail to work. Those who feel the most entitled, and privileged because of their money, race, social status, etc., will sometimes, intentionally, not make room for others to serve in positions of power; or because of their elitism and arrogance, they will not join with the new, excited and eager workers who are ready to help shoulder the hard work of building up the congregation, social organization, or business institution. For over three decades of ministry engagement, I have been privileged to serve more than a half-dozen congregations at various levels of responsibility, and have seen the charter members, or the children of charter members, or those who seem to have the most money, power, and influence, constrict the entry ways to power and vital positions of service, even when the newer member of the organization has obvious gifts, and a certain level of spiritual maturity. This problem of those in power not making room for others to serve, contribute ideas, be involved in decision making aspects of the institution, seems almost universal. But this kind of systems ethos is in opposition to the will of God, given that Jesus said that we should be praying to the Lord so that God would send more laborers – willing servants of the Lord, to help win souls and revolutionize our churches, neighborhoods, and the society in general. But how can this happen, if we intentionally, and politically, restrict God's new laborers from being all that they can be in Christ? Today, with help from the Word and the Spirit, we will grapple with this issue and these questions, and will listen to hear God's answers, as we seek to *make room at the wall for everyone!*

33. Marriage: Don't Lose Your Mind in the Institution

Scripture Text: 1 Corinthians 7

It seems like nothing twists us in knots quite like our romantic entanglements. Whether we are married or single, the subject of what constitutes a powerful covenantal love, and how we express or withhold the blessings of love, is one of the most important subjects for human beings to consider. Most religions teach its followers that God wants us to express some form of love to those around us. In the Christian revelation of agape' of love, we are taught to love, the seemingly unlovable, because God is love. But, even with agape' as the goal, many blood- bought Christians struggle with learning how to properly navigate and negotiate neighborly, romantic, erotic, and especially agape, love. As we consider what arrests our attention, ignites our passions, and moves us toward fidelity or infidelity, it must be acknowledged that our love engagements are a tricky subject. The subject of our romantic relationships – our lusts, loves, attractions, eroticism, and romances - take up much of our energies during our waking hours, even if primarily at a subconscious level. If we are not in a relationship, many of us are wondering somewhere in the back of our minds, will we ever find love and fidelity with someone to whom we are attracted. If we are in a relationship, a lot of our energies are spent either enduring or enjoying our love connections, or we are entranced and enthralled by the possibility of a new relationship that we hope will capture our hearts and imaginations. Dating, marriage, and our sexuality make up the witch's brew sometimes.

All one has to do is watch, or read, the many tragic news stories about all the people who have failed to learn how to properly manage their loves, romances and emotional passions under the auspices of the Spirit, and a good human therapist; who have divorced, abused, abandoned, stalked, and resorted to criminal behavior.

In my life, I have been immensely blessed to be married to my wife, Crystal. I have known her most of my adult life. In the early '80s, she and I attended Chicago's well known, Lindblom Technical High School, located on the Southwest side. During this time, by her own account, she was not in a vibrant relationship with Christ, though she regularly attended church. During this same period, I was not a Christian, or religious, in any way. Though, we did not date in any serious way while at Lindblom, four years later we rediscovered each other. When our paths crossed again in a Chicago health club, it was as if the Lord had orchestrated the reunion. When we met up again, she was a committed follower of Christ, and so was I. I had gone to the club with a friend. While my friend was in another part of the facility, I was in the track room. While starting to lift weights in an area of room, I noticed a pretty young lady running around the track; she had a familiar silhouette. It was Crystal. I called out to her, and we struck up a conversation. As we talked, we both testified about our new faith in Christ. She was not dating anyone at the time, and neither was I. Five years after that reunion, after I finished college out of state, we married after I had completed my first year of seminary. She was a beautiful bride (and still is); radiant, effervescent as she walked down the aisle of my home church. After that hot wedding day in July, more than twenty-seven years ago, we still have been discovering and rediscovering new layers of our relationship. Some of what we have found over the years has been a confirmation of the wonderful blessings that we suspected God had designed for our mutual well-being all along. We have learned, laughed, and prayed together; shared our faith together; raised three wonderful children together; encouraged each other, when life has thrown us curveballs. But also, like all agape' love connections, there have been a few other things we have discovered about each other that has required much prayer, patience, forgiveness, and grace. Even when two committed Christians come together, there is, in the words of R & B singer, Frankie Beverly, a lot of "Joy *and pain… sunshine and rain.*" But, as

I reflect on what marriage really is, neither one of us would have grown in our faith, or into the people we have become, quite the same way, if we had not experienced the warm love and laughter of the sun-shiny experiences of our union, as well as the drizzling miserableness of the rainy parts of it. Love is a tricky thing. It is not an easy undertaking over the long-haul; and if a couple, are going to walk in the precincts of agape' love for a life time, then it requires a strength that comes from God alone. God is committed to making the two, one. God is more than willing to give us that insight and strength, if we will stop relying on our strength alone. The Spirit and the Bible help to mediate that strength.

The Bible (especially the New Testament) is replete with helpful instructions about how to discern the proper paths to follow when we become intimately involved with those whom we love, or *think we love*. Too many times we fail to learn the lessons presented in the stories of the First Testament, the Gospels and the pedagogical aspect of the Epistles, on the topics of romance, jealousy, faithfulness, infidelity, bitterness, and marriage, because we are too blinded by human-centered advice, wisdom and philosophies. Most secular ways of knowing about intimacy, lust, love and romance are rooted in a conviction and pedagogical agenda which emphasize how we can better achieve levels of personal happiness and individual pleasure, with not much emphasis placed on virtues like sacrifice, self-denial, a willingness to endure sometimes painful dynamics (not physical abuse) for a time, for the greater good, even if we seem to be temporarily diminished in our hopes. Many secular based resources make no reference to the divine Word and the Lord of love, as we seek to love and be loved. Conversely, from the very start of the canon, the scriptures are helpful in giving us a vision about the potential power and joy, as well as the disappointments and pain, that are a part of our romantic relationships and love connections. According to Genesis 1 and 2, God created everything good; and a part of God's good creation includes the triune gifts of intelligence, love, and a desire for intimacy. God walks with humankind in the "cool of the day." Observing the need for man to have companionship, compatibility, and sexual intimacy, God created the institution we now call "marriage." God created the binary genders for us to find complimentary spiritual, emotional, and anatomical unity – through fellowship, conversation, and sex which was and is to be enjoyed for our pleasure and the miracle of human procreation. Men and women were originally created to find joy and fulfillment in God, and in each another, through the Lordship of God, and the covenantal bonds of marriage and family; unless God has blessed a person to enjoy the fulness of life through singleness and celibacy. Adam and Eve are the prototypical symbols of the male and female who unite together in the paradise and struggle of holy matrimony. But, even in that first marriage, sin sabotaged the institution, and pushed them and us somewhere far south of Eden.

Since the beginning of human societies and cultures, sin has always affected our marriages. Adam and Eve ate of The Tree of the Knowledge of Good and Evil, which opened a Pandora's box of rebellion, alienation, and pain. Since that time, we have struggled to get along with our lovers and spouses. In this country alone, many of us have heard the often-quoted statistical data on marriage: *five/ six out of every ten marriages end in divorce court; nearly seven out of ten, in the black community.* Sadly, these numbers don't vary much based on the couple's religious affiliations. God doesn't want broken vows, homes, or hearts; God never intended for us to go crazy in the institution of marriage! Contained in the many principles and proclamations located in the Gospels and the Epistles, there is great wisdom made available to every God-seeking, unity-seeking, holiness-seeking couple. In 1 Corinthians 7, The Apostle Paul gives us some helpful godly wisdom. The entire chapter is dedicated to answering questions about marriage that have been posed by the Corinthian Church and given to the great Apostle. The Corinthian Christians had been socialized in a Hellenistic culture which held idolatrous views of sexuality and sensuality. A wanton and blatant sexual licentiousness was the norm for the citizens of Corinth, and this fact was known throughout the Empire. Many of the citizens of Corinth were known for mixing temple religion, with prostitution and orgies, as they worshiped their idols. Once a citizen of Corinth was converted to Christ, they often wanted to know from church leaders what were the acceptable norms for expressing their feelings, sensual urges, and romantic desires.

In the opening verse of chapter 7, Paul initially relies on his limited experience as a celibate Pharisee. Paul was not married (he could have been, at one time) and consequently shares his own prejudiced perspective and states that if Christians can remain celibate like him, they will be able to dedicate more of themselves to God, like Paul had done. But, by the time he pens *the second verse*, it is as if Paul realizes anew that not everyone has been gifted with the kind of discipline and calling with which he was gifted; and Paul begins to reach far beyond his personal experience and acknowledges that marriage is a good and godly institution because, among other things, it provides the right, covenantal context for human sexuality. In verses 2-9, Paul elaborates on how God's gift of sexuality should be exercised liberally and unselfishly between marriage partners. Neither the wife, nor the husband, should think of their bodies in selfish terms, sexually. The two are one flesh, just as the writer of Genesis and Jesus state. Therefore, the husband and wife are to engage in sexual intimacy, without refusing their partner, unless for an agreed upon time period. Toward the end of this section of the text, Paul puts in one more plug for celibacy, and then moves the reader into a robust discussion of the right and wrong conditions for divorce.

Beginning at verse 10, Paul tackles the subject of divorce. As he answers the concerns of the Corinthian Christians, Paul, like Jesus, shares with the faith community, God's prohibition of divorce. For a variety of reasons, couples become estranged, and even hostile adversaries. Paul advises that if the wife or the husband decides to leave the marriage, that wife or husband is to remain unmarried. Reconciliation should be the goal. Paul also teaches that if a Christian has a non-Christian spouse, they should not initiate a divorce just because their spouse is an unbeliever (vss. 12-14). In fact, Paul implies that the Christian in the relationship, should have a sanctifying effect on the entire family, spouse included. But, Paul is clear on what should take place if the unbelieving spouse is intent on leaving the marriage- the believing spouse *should let them go.* Paul asserts that God has not obligated the Christian spouse to try to force someone to remain in a marriage they hate. This would be a futile attempt to bind someone up in a relationship they no longer value. Paul admonishes the saints to remember that above all, God has called us to live in peace with our spouses or former spouses, as best we can.

In the remaining verses, Paul gives answers to some of the questions the Christians in Corinth probably had about various practical concerns about marriage in general. In verses 17-39, Paul explicates that for those who are unmarried and are contemplating marriage, their primary concern should be about serving the Lord and humanity vis a vis the calling God has extended. They should be chiefly focused on their commitment to Christ, no matter what marital state they are in; whether bound in the covenant of marriage, or without a spouse, there is still much kingdom/ kin-dom work to do. Paul says:

> "You were bought at a price; do not become slaves of men (human beings). Brethren (and sisters), let each one remain with God in that state in which he (and she) was called." (*inclusive language additions are mine*).

The more he shares his heart on the matter, the more Paul begins to speak again from his earlier position – his default position – He desires for the saints to remain celibate, if possible; especially widows and widowers. Paul emphasizes that the time is short; Jesus will return soon; persecutions are coming. In verse 34, he sums up his undergirding conviction on the matter: *The unmarried......cares about the things of the Lord.....the married...cares about the things of this world.....*

It is obvious that Paul feels ambivalent about the institution of marriage. Since Paul was always unmarried, or widowed, he sees being unmarried – celibate for Christ - as a supreme virtue. This is how he begins his discourse on the subject. This is also how he ends his advice, as chapter 7 concludes. Like the teachings of the Catholic Church related to the priesthood, Paul tries to persuade the Corinthian listeners and us, the modern reader, that though marriage is a gift for men and women who are in love and desire to be in covenant, the ideal is for the crème de la crème of the church to avoid its onerous impact on the soul. In Paul's mind, marriage is a somewhat burdensome institution that potentially weakens one's pastoral call; it can keep Christians from living life unencumbered, fully dedicated to the Lord. His closing advice to widows who might contemplate remarriage, says it all:

> "...she is happier if she remains as she is, according to my judgment –and I think I also have the Spirit of God."

Though I respect much of the advice that the Apostle gives to the

Corinthian Christians about their romances, marriages, widowhood, and divorce, I think Paul misses the mark with his intermittent suggestion that it is better for Christians to remain single, than to marry, or remarry. While taking preaching classes at the Christian Theological Seminary, in Indianapolis, my homiletics professor, Ron Allen, would periodically tell the students that when it comes to interpreting and proclaiming certain biblical texts, it was more than appropriate, in light of the gospel, to *preach against certain texts*. In other words, professor Allen was sharing with us an important, and maybe controversial, hermeneutical method: *If what is contained in a certain text doesn't harmonize with the Gospel of Jesus Christ*, and I would add, or with what seems to be the consensus view among most of the Bible's New Testament authors, then we were to bring these points out in our sermons and preach against whatever text which seems to be at odds with principles revealed in the teachings, behavior, and works of Jesus Christ, along with the Apostles as they taught in harmony with Jesus. I think Allen's teaching advice is helpful in the light of Paul's expressed reservations about the spiritual necessity of marriage. Though Paul doesn't prohibit marriage, he doesn't give the institution a glowing review. And while in many ways his advice to potential married couples is practical and powerful, Paul's personal preferences bleed through the pages of the letter. While there can undoubtedly be a sacredness in the kind of singleness and celibacy that is dedicated to pleasing the Lord, without any "distractions," Jesus never puts marriage in a negative light. In fact, marriage is the central metaphor for the consummation and union of God, Christ, and the Spirit, with humanity. In Matthew 19, Jesus extolls the sacredness of marriage, as he warns God's children to restrict divorce only for the most egregious breaches in the marital covenant. So, I think in the eyesight of God, marriage is a wonderful, dynamic, life-altering, and character transforming institution. The only thing is, it can be both so rewarding and challenging, that it can cause some folk to go almost coo-coo! Through the love stories in the Bible; and in the teachings of Jesus, and through the practical advice of the Apostles, God gives us some Holy Spirit handles on the matter, so that we won't go insane in the institution of marriage. God desires for men and women to become one flesh, healthy and whole.

34. Letting Go of the Chains

Genesis 19:16-26 and Philippians 3:12-14

In the Books of Genesis and Philippians we have warnings about the dangers of looking back with nostalgia and longing for the old way, when God has a special calling on us to set a new path forward in Jesus Christ. This is hopeful word for those of us who are occasionally, chased down by our past choices. In Genesis 19 we have the account of the destruction of the popular, yet notorious cities of Sodom and Gomorrah; destroyed because of the citizens' sexual immorality, violence, and brutal predatory practices. Mr. Lot (Abraham's nephew) and his family were instructed by angels to leave the area and not look back toward the fire and brimstone judgement that would be meted out. As they left with the angels, Lot's wife, for whatever reason, decided to disobey and she looked behind her toward the cities. Consequently, she turned into a pillar of salt.

In Paul's letter to the church at Philippi, the imprisoned Apostle to the Gentiles warns the early Christians and us that it would be a mistake to not only look back at our past failures, but to also rely solely on our past religiosity, cultural heritage, and ethnic pedigree, as a means of having a satisfying and liberating relationship with the Lord. In the early portion of chapter three, Paul recounts how he was one of the most religious Pharisees to ever live; and how he had come from wonderful religious and ethnic stock. In his and other folks' minds, these facts seemed to insure his position as a religious and spiritual giant in his community; but one day Paul met the Lord on a Damascus Road, and came to realize in an instant that his *right standing* with God had been based on a faulty premise – a premise which had him convinced that his religious and cultural history, and his own righteousness, would justify him in God's sight. After a revelation of Jesus Christ, Paul lets go of his old perspective of Christ and God's dealings in the world, while looking ahead to his new calling as God's servant and friend – saved by God's grace through Jesus' blood, to minister Jesus to the Gentiles.

We praise God for what has been passed down to us. We should remember that we stand on the shoulders of giants. There are great truths about our failures and missteps; our faith, and our cultural and personal histories that can help us run, with courage, into our futures; this is in harmony with the African concept of *Sankofa*. However, we are reminded through this morning's biblical texts that there are some things in our histories that we shouldn't recall. There are some memories, good and bad; some traditions and legacies good and bad, that will enslave us, if we are not careful and prayerful. The past can become a museum of death, instead of a house of life, from which we launch new creative energy. The past can also become a ghost which haunts us to the point that we fail to see and know the new thing to which God is calling us! Cherish the treasures from your past – learn from the good and the bad - but also subject your faculties to your today and tomorrow! Christ is alive, today! God has a calling on your life, today! And the best, is yet to come!

35. God Has Done More than Wake us Up this Morning!

Text: Exodus 15 and Revelation 7

Christians from every cultural, racial, and national persuasion have praised the Lord for all the wondrous things the Lord has done for humanity. If we were to take the time to count all the blessings the Lord has given to us, we would soon run out of reasons to be sad and depressed. The Lord has not only *awakened us this morning; the Lord has not only started us on our way*, as many in the black church testify in our churches; but the Lord has given us the ability to do and enjoy the good, the better, and the best, in a society which is often trying to negotiate between bad news and worse news. Because of the redemptive love of God, revealed to us through Jesus Christ, our sins are forgiven, our present circumstances are hopeful, and we are empowered by the Spirit to help turn our godly dreams into concrete reality! We can become, whomever God intends for us to become. We can build and leave a legacy of courage, faith, kindness, and altruism. We can start businesses, in Jesus' name. We can author books and works of poetry, in Jesus' name. We can become teachers, preachers, and politicians in Jesus' name. We can start new charitable organizations in Jesus' name. We can win our family members and friends to the Lord, in Jesus' name. We can make stronger, organizations like *Black Lives Matter*, and the *MeToo* movement, in Jesus' name. What a glorious God we serve!

We have countless good reasons to cross the threshold of our worship sanctuaries, as we exit, with smiles on our faces, praises on our lips, and joy in our hearts. In fact, heart-felt and thankful worship, not only blesses God, and us, *but it runs away evil too.* Praise and worship are some of the greatest weapons that we have against the forces of darkness, and they enable us to chase away feelings of gloom and doom. It is not that we should harbor selfish motives for worshipping God, but the fact remains that authentic, joyful worship, greatly benefits us in a variety of ways; it not only touches the heart of God when God's children express gratitude, but as we come eagerly before the presence of God, with the people of God, we becoming light wielding, spiritual aggressors, utilizing spiritual weaponry against our adversaries; as we begin to reflect upon how big God is such thoughts give us the courage to do great things for God's glory and our good. Such considerations make burdens lighter, sometimes to the point of pouring over effusively in vocal ecstasy.

There is something else that is empowering about enthusiastic corporate worship -- it is not only efficacious in blessing God, us, and giving us spiritual empowerment, but the act of joyful and enthusiastic worship also carries an element of being contagious. When the Body of Christ gathers to lend heart, voice, and music, in adoration to God, the observing Christian novice, or the unbeliever who is visiting a faith community, is often greatly impacted by the palpable elation and words of thanksgiving uttered by the congregation, via its rhapsodic singing and testifying. At United Christian Church, our mission is to *unite people with God through our worship, witness, outreach, in-reach, and discipleship.* We believe that our first obligation and privilege is to worship God with our lives. As a congregation we are growing in our understanding of just how much our passionate, or dispassionate and blasé attitudes in public worship, affects those who walk through our sanctuary's doors. When guests come into our worship space, and sense that the overwhelming majority of our members, are thankful to God for a long list of blessings that the Lord has given to them; when they come to check out our worship services and they hear testimonies, and see smiles on the singers' and musicians' faces; when they detect in the congregational prayer, an attitude of gratitude for health, wisdom, protection, sanity, our culture, financial miracles, and above all, salvation, then there is a certain level of inner conviction that begins to well-up in our guests' hearts. I believe there are good questions, and a mindset of self-reflection which surfaces in those who visit us; and they ask themselves: "Why are these folks so happy and so thankful, and I am not?" or "What might they have, that I do not?" "Maybe God is real and worth serving." It is my belief that authentic, corporate and vocal worship to God can become contagious and empowering!

In the books of Exodus and Revelation, we have two wonderful examples of the infectious effects of heart-felt, spirit-led, enthusiastic praise and worship. In Exodus 15, immediately following the drowning of Pharaoh and the Egyptian army, oppressors who had been brutalizing the Hebrews for many years, Moses leads the people in what seems to be a spontaneous praise service to God. He and the people sing and shout out: *"I will sing to the Lord, for He has triumphed gloriously! The horse and its rider He has thrown into the sea! The Lord is my strength and song, and He has become my salvation!"* They were singing with a joyous gusto because they had been saved from terrible slavery, bondage, and destruction. Moses' leadership in guiding the people into joyous praise to Yahweh for their deliverance from Egyptian terrorism, had such an impact on Moses' sister, Miriam, that according to verse 20, she is moved to pick up her tambourine and start dancing and singing to the Lord. As if by a powerful spiritual contagion, thousands of Hebrew women, of various levels of spiritual perception and commitment, see her doing this and they too grab their percussive instruments and begin dancing and singing about God's exploits. What can we learn from this? We can learn that *emotive, God-directed praise, rooted in deep gratitude for God's many acts of deliverance, is empowering and infectious!*

This idea is also supported in Revelation 7. In this apocalyptic text, we are given a glimpse into the heavenly realm, by the Apostle John. God and the Lamb are enthroned. Women and men from every ethnic group, are clothed in pure white robes, and are standing, crying out with loud voices, testifying about how good their Redeemer is. Consequently, the heavenly angels and the ethereal Elders decide to join in on the praises too (vs.11). They fall on their faces and worship the Lord, shouting out blessings and *amens* to God. Sisters and brothers, as we have noted, God desires that we would offer this kind of worship and praise; a kind of expression of love that is not too cool, dignified and respectable to be vulnerable.

As we worship and praise the Lord, evil is turned back. A shout, from a set-apart heart, can knock down walls, open prison doors, and give the fire needed to start new ministry endeavors. Authentic worship is a weapon for God's good. There is a glorious and fascinating quality that flows out of our high, corporate praises – vibrant corporate praise can influence others to become worshipers. Our texts in Exodus and Revelation, along with many other scriptures, reveal that true praise, in the assembly, is often infectious and contagious. Those who authentically praise God with their mouths, with the dance, and with their lives, will soon be joined by others who want to get in on the holy fun! Oh, you did know that it can be fun to praise God, didn't you? I have heard certain youthful worship leaders, when caught up in the moment saying, *"There aint no party, like a Holy Ghost party, because a Holy Ghost party don't stop!"* Though the statement might not express the king's best English, I think it captures the King's sentiment and desire for His people.

36. Is Your All on the Altar?

Text: Genesis 22

Elisha A. Hoffman was the son of a minister and would soon follow in his father's footsteps after the Civil War. Hoffman became a Presbyterian pastor who served primarily in the Midwest in the middle nineteenth century, to the early twentieth century. During the zenith of his career, which was served while in Benton Harbor, Michigan, not only did he pastor his congregation, but he wrote hymns at a prolific pace. Hoffman wrote over two thousand hymns! While in Michigan he wrote some our nation's most beloved spiritual songs, many of which are known and sung all over the world to this day; hymns like: *Leaning on the Everlasting Arms; What a Wonderful Savior;* and of course, *Are you Washed in the Blood?,* a song which in graphic language, confronts the listener with the salvific question of the ages; a question which asks us whether we have applied the marks of Christ's suffering and death to our need for spiritual covering and divine forgiveness. Addressing our chief concern this week, Hoffman also wrote the hymn entitled, *"Is Your All on the Altar?"* a question through song which pierces through our spiritual laziness and stubbornness; a question which lovingly and persistently interrogates us so that we might probe deeper in our commitment to worshipping, serving, and loving our God. God already loves us at such profound depths, and then some; therefore, what is, and what will be our response to God's suffering and passionate love? Hoffman's lyrics illustrate that there is a special blessedness that accompanies a person who dares to take the journey to love God with all that they have and are. The lyrics are melodic, yet penetrating:

> *Is your all on the altar of sacrifice laid? Your heart does the*
> *Spirit control? You can only be blessed, and have peace and*
> *sweet rest, as you yield Him your body and soul.......*

It is from this song that we sharpen the focus of today's message. As we reflect upon God's great and expansive love for us, we are challenged to reciprocate back to God this self-sacrificial love, which has been inspired by God's love. True love will often require (especially, in the one extending love) a sacrifice of one's personal ambitions; it requires a willingness to give up our own long-cherished dreams for the long-term benefit of the kingdom, our families, and our communities. Throughout the gospels, Jesus promises if we lose our lives for his sake, we will find our *real lives*. In Genesis 22, we have the remarkable, strange, and troubling story of Abraham and Isaac's journey to Mt. Moriah. This is a story that fleshes out this principle mentioned in our song. God tests and reveals the quality of Abraham's love, as Abraham senses the call to lay down all his future hopes, in Isaac, on the altar of sacrifice. But, thanks be to God, once Abraham makes the commitment to yield his all, in the person of his beloved son, God makes it very clear that God is the greatest giver; and God makes it plain to both Abraham, and those who would follow in his path, that God is not a God who delights in the killing of our children, and other human beings, to appease God. A ram caught in the thicket is God's acceptable sacrifice – not Isaac.

Since the beginning of human history, God has seemed to be temporarily satisfied with animal sacrifices; such sacrifices have been a startling and awful reminder of how much sin hurts creation and has within it, a principle of punishment and death; but in Genesis 22, God reminded Abraham, the Jews, and through them, all humanity, that God is not blood thirsty for physical, human sacrifices, like the pagan deities of the ages. Since Abraham discovered the Ram, in Isaac's place, and since the death of Christ on the cross, God is much more impressed with our willing, and painful, sacrifices of the heart; things we give up which help us to filter out and know our true loves – along with identifying where those shadowy places of idolatry, selfishness, and sin, lie.

This song of Hoffman's continues to interrogate us, through the spirit of God's love and concern; and the questions he raises, push us to keep wrestling with our need to clarify our commitments to God. So, what is your response to Hoffman and God's question: *Is your all.........on the Altar of Sacrifice laid?*

Study Questions

1. What does "all" really mean for you?
2. Have your emotions, intellect, and will, been given over to the limitless love of God?
3. Are your plans for your choice of a mate, submitted to the word, and wisdom of God?
4. Have you committed money, and energies to the work of God?
5. Your heart, does the Spirit control?

37. Do Not Forget to Share Your Gifts in the Summer Time!

Give, and it will be given to you: good measure, pressed down, shaken together, and running over will be put into your bosom. For with the same measure that you use, it will be measured back to you.

Texts: Luke 6:38, coupled with 2 Corinthians 8

In both Luke 6 and 2 Corinthians 8, God's people are encouraged to live with open hands, instead of clenched fists. When times are tight, and resources are few; when the blessings are bountiful, and the fun is too, there is the all too human tendency to *forget* that we have been blessed *so that we might be a blessing!* We get caught up in our own press clippings. We hone in on our BMW and Mercedes Benz cars; we become enraptured with our three-car garages with maximum square footage. When we are only focused on our trips and travel; when we are only counting every penny in efforts to save up for the latest flat screen television, the newest Gucci shoes, or simply the new hair weave, we tend to tighten down the financial hatches to get the next gadget. Up to a point, there is some wisdom in this approach; for if we desire something, it is better to save for it, than to use that plastic monster kept hidden in our purses and wallets. We are to be good stewards who are very prayerful about the gifts and resources we have received from God. So, depending on the objects of our desires, there is something very smart about saving our resources, and being thrifty. But this is not the whole picture of how Christians should operate when we are stewards over our financial resources. Sometimes, this holding on to our financial resources for something we *just have to have*, spills over into the level of support that we contribute (or often fail to contribute) to the Reign of God, and the ministry of God's church. In other words, before we are even fully aware of it, as our closets and garages become fuller, the treasury of the church, which is for the purposes of manifesting the love and care of God for people, becomes an afterthought, or a postscript to the expanding evidences of our material wealth.

In both Luke 6, and 2 Corinthians, it is clear that God calls us even in tough times, and also especially during those hazy hot summer months, to continue to be a people of faith who are willing to give and live generously in the support of kingdom work, like evangelism and marketing; like undergirding the needs of mentoring and charitable ministries. In Luke 6, Jesus was teaching a large multitude of followers several truths related to how the kingdom of God operates, including how we should open our clenched fists, and wisely and freely give away our possessions when life and human need demand such sacrifices. Jesus even intimates that such acts of generosity opens the floodgates for reciprocal blessings. Also, in 2 Corinthians 8, Paul commended a church, located in the impoverished, or "the ghetto section" of Macedonia, for its penchant for giving joyously and liberally from their repository of humble monetary gifts, to bless the ministry of God. Looking at our giving trends for the last month or so, our level of giving is rising. This is a wonderful sign as we seek to offer the best to you and the community. Congratulations! Let's continue to give and live with an open hand, and not clinched fists!

38. Do Not Let a Bad History, Stop Your Good Destiny!

Text: John 5:1-15

President Barack Obama, more than a decade before he would become the President of the United States, wrote a book entitled, *Dreams from My Father: A Story of Race and Inheritance.* I started reading this book around the time of the beginning of his second term in office, as President. I was drawn to it, not only because I had heard so much about it and wanted to learn more about what made our president the great man he had become, but I also wanted to read it because I believed it might have something to say to me about the importance of God's destiny impinging upon what many might consider, an unremarkable history. Barack Obama wrote the book, at age thirty-three, spurred on by a publisher who wanted the then, lawyer and community organizer, to chronicle the fascinating story of how an African American of mixed parentage, who grew up in Hawaii, and educated in New York, who eventually came of age in Chicago, seemingly with no silver spoon in his mouth, ended up becoming the first African American president of *the Harvard Law Review* (a prestigious, legal periodical issued at Harvard). The story recounts his life from the time he was a child who grew up in a home, painfully, and greatly impacted by divorce (he was an impressionable boy and teen, out of touch with his Kenyan father, and seemingly out of place racially and socially, growing up in white and Asian culture), to his maturation of becoming a community leader and political savant. He admits that he could have become stuck by the separation which existed between him and his biological father; he could have become paralyzed by his own tendency to loaf through life, as he experimented with drugs, seemingly on track to sabotage his purpose and potential. Amazingly, with the help of his faith in God, and good mentors, he shakes off the spiritual atrophy that was trying to settle in the bones and muscles of his potential, and he becomes the young man who would successfully run for a State Senate seat, in Illinois, surprising pundits and establishment politicians. As I was reading through some of the early sections of the book, it was clear to me that his story is a testimony about the importance of *not allowing a potentially paralyzing history, to block an amazing, God-ordained, destiny.*

In John 5, we have a story which contains many of these same themes. We are introduced to a man who is paralyzed and held captive by his own body; his life is depressing, and frustrating, because he has not managed well with his infirmity; and given the protracted time of his torment, this is understandable. It appears he has given up when we meet him in John 5. He seems to no longer believe that his present circumstances will be any different from his long past of having to deal with a crippling, paralysis. He lives in a section of Jerusalem populated by a throng of other people with disabilities and sicknesses, not far from the central location of temple life. But unlike some who are depicted in the narrative as still being ambitious and hopeful in spite of their limitations, his hopes of a better life have been dashed – he is paralyzed both physically and psychologically. Near the Sheep Gate of the city, there was a network of five major outdoor spaces surrounded by terraces and pools for ritual cleansing. These spaces were known as "the five porches of Bethesda." This was the man's main address for a number of years. He stayed here, because he had heard, as many others had, about a powerful legend. It was rumored that at some point in the unspecified past, an angel had come down and stirred up the waters with healing properties. It was believed that the first person who descended into the swirling troubled water would be healed. This unnamed man seems to have lost hope that he could beat anyone to the pool first. He had no use of his limbs and had to deal with this illness for nearly forty years. But one day, by the grace of God, Jesus shows up in his life and asks him a question, not about his past, but about his destiny: *"Do you want to be made whole?"* By the way the man answers this pivotal question, it is clear that the man's focus was on his tough history and on the lack of aid and help he had received. He was sedated by the hopelessness of his circumstances. It seems his negative self-perception, and his very real problems, were all-consuming and quite possibly could have blocked his glorious destiny. Instead, and mercifully, Jesus shows up; and when Jesus shows up, Jesus overrides the man's negative self-perception, and his focus on his years of suffering, and he commands the man to do, what had previously been an impossibility. Jesus commands the man: "Take up your bed and walk!" The man is somehow moved in his soul, spirit, and imagination, and agrees to respond to Jesus' seemingly impossible directive. His will is given a spark. Lo and behold, the man's body responds. Strength and support are given to his pelvis, hips, and legs; strength that was not previous there (or which was there, but untapped)!

For this man, who had been infirmed for so long, to even muster up enough faith, to even *try* to move his atrophied muscles, is miraculous. At the command of Jesus, he forgets about his paralyzed, stuck, and sad past, and he is challenged to do something that will set in motion a new future. At the end of the narrative, the man ends up carrying that which had carried him for so long. His bed becomes a basis for his testimony! He leaves from an area mired in pain and pathos, and he is able to walk into uncharted territories, praising God!

In light of this word, we must all pay close attention to the wonderful destiny God has ordained for each of us. At the command of Jesus, a past failure, indiscretion, or mistake; a history filled with pain, sickness, abuse and addiction can be reversed! As we hear the words of the Master, we can learn how to stand in a new hope. We can get up from whatever had us down, with the result being that we end up carrying what used to carry us, via our witness! I think this is what a God-glorifying testimony is all about.

39. Forgiven!

Text: John 8:1-11

I witnessed one of the greatest baseball games in history. It was game seven of the 2016 World Series. The Chicago Cubs were going against the Cleveland Indians. It was a ten-inning game filled with excitement, drama, and excruciating tension. Over the decades, these two Midwestern titans had suffered much disappointment and defeat. The Cleveland Indians had not won a World Series in over 60-70 years. The Chicago Cubs had not won a World Series since 1908. As we Detroiters know very well (because of the records of the Lions and Tigers over the years), having a losing team, a bad sports product representing one's city, with the millions and millions of dollars, emotional capital, attention, and hope, invested --- to have to root for a losing team, almost seems unforgivable to the passionate fan. We love our teams and grow emotionally attached to them, but with decades of losing as a long legacy, some of our teams don't seem to love us back. This was the case with the Chicago Cubs and their fan base. As a boy, I remember my grandfather faithfully listening to countless Cubs games, while he sat on his front porch in the tough Englewood neighborhood of Chicago. His love for baseball and the Cubbies spilled over to my young uncle and me, as we played the game in vacant lots. We would imagine that we were the Cub's best players: Ernie Banks, Jose Cardinal, and Ron Santo. But, my grandfather's love, and our love, for the Cubs *never seemed rewarded with winning seasons.* Many fans, like my grandfather, lived their entire lives and died supporting a team that never seemed to be able to consistently put it all together on the field. Some might say such a sports failure was unforgivable. But Thursday morning, I heard something interesting. After the Cubs became champions, I heard an announcer say, *"As bad as things have been, and for as long as things have been bad; even as it seemed as if the owners and management did not know how to rebuild this team, all has been erased now. With this kind of win, they have been justified and all is forgiven!"* Sisters and brothers, in one fell swoop, one night in early November, the Cubs had been redeemed, and all had been forgiven.

Forgiveness is a powerful gift. Most of us have had failures and faults that we would like to forget. Some of us have risen high in life, only to have come crashing to the ground, in shambles. Others of us have always seemed to struggle at the point of take- off – never seeming to get off the runway of life with much success. When sin, disappointment and failure add up in the bank of our life's experiences, we can begin to lose hope. Or, sometimes, it is not the many little failures that take their toll on us, but one big mistake; one moment of misadventure; one poor decision can totally shift the trajectory of our lives. Concerning our biblical text (John 8:1-11), we don't know if the unnamed woman in our scripture, was shaped by many little sins, or whether, or not, her life was lived morally, until she made one colossal error, but we do know she had been suddenly thrust into having to account for her sin. From the scriptures, we do not know much about her history, other than that she had been in an illicit, adulterous liaison. But, what we do know is that she got caught in the very act of her sin and was turned over to the top preachers and church folk of the city. Following the Mosaic Law (Leviticus 20:10), she and her partner were to be condemned and executed, together. For reasons that can only be attributable to her powerless status in a male-dominated society, the man was not brought with her to the stoning pit; only she was dragged there. The good news is that Jesus was also there!

In attempts to set-up Jesus, and pit him against the teachings of Moses, the merciless religious leaders of the day were using this woman to trap Jesus. But they could not trap Jesus, who is determined to offer forgiveness to all who have sinned. This event/story is a reminder to all of us. No matter what we've done in the past, or how long we have failed to be all that God has intended us to be, God is determined to forgive our sins. Forgiveness is the blessing that gives and keeps on giving. There are practical benefits from it. Forgiveness takes the sting out of our past defeats and opens the door to a whole new beginning. When we are forgiven, we can begin to forgive ourselves. When we are forgiven by God, and truly realize the price that was paid to secure our new lives, then, we want to go forward, living a new kind of life, hesitant to condemn anyone else. Forgiven, we can live a life of victory, not condemning others, as we walk with God and make better choices. I praise God for the countless times he has forgiven me. Many of you praise God for the many times, God has forgiven you. Now, let us work to extend this same blessing of forgiveness to others. Because if once notorious losers, like the Cubs, can become champions, we all can!

40. We Need King Jesus to Keep Us from Chaos!

Text: Judges 19-21

In Judges 19-21, we have one of the most inglorious moments in Israel's history. During the time of the judges, a town called *Gibeah,* which was controlled by the Tribe of Benjamin (one of the twelve tribes of Israel), was overrun by a spirit of violent wickedness. Many of the men of that town had become violent sexual predators. One day, a particularly terrible crime is committed against a young woman who had been travelling through the town, with her husband, a Levite. Initially, the men wanted to sexually violate the Levite, but unable to do so, they settle for his wife, who was exposed. Consequently, she dies after the abuse. Once dead, in the radical act of dismembering her dead body, her husband literally brings his case (and her divided body) before all of the tribes of Israel, as evidence and testimony against the Benjamites of Gibeah. As a result of the evil that had infiltrated the community through the souls and actions of the men of the tribe of Benjamin, the other eleven tribes aligned themselves against the Benjamites. Despite this powerful confederation of tribes, aligned to seek justice against the men of Benjamin, the Benjamites would not self-prosecute and punish the rapists and murderers among them. In modern parlance, the Benjamites employed a "no snitch" campaign among their own people. Eventually, a civil war broke out. During this war, the entire Tribe of Benjamin is brutally decimated by the other tribes. Justice has been re-established. The surviving men of Benjamin were now few in number; and the surviving women of Benjamin were even less. In fact, there were not enough women remaining to repopulate the cities and towns which had been under the control of their tribe for years. This terrible state of affairs had grieved the members of all the tribes. Chapter 21, records how Israel devised a solution which offered grace, sympathy and a new beginning for the Benjamites. The book of Judges closes this tragic story, with an indictment against the spiritual and moral chaos which had enveloped the people and caused such tragedies:

"In those days there was no king in Israel; everyone did what was right in his own eyes."

Sisters and brothers, we might be living thousands of years from these events which mark Israel's sin and spiritual confusion, but the depths of our nation's sexual decadence and violence are similar today. Unfortunately, this wickedness is an integral part of the tattered and torn fabric of American culture. We, like the remnant of the righteous who lived in Gibeah, are living during a time when lust, rape, confusion about our sexuality, and a willingness to murder, make it difficult for us to negotiate the chaos we see. Recently, I heard the news report about a couple, who were out for a walk on a major thoroughfare in Detroit; they were accosted by a group of young men, and driven to a nearby alley, where the woman was gang-raped in front of her badly beaten boyfriend. During this same period, I also heard about several men, who had kidnapped, and gang-raped another young man, in an East Coast city. Also, not long after these tragedies, I heard about a man who was parked over on the shoulder of the Southfield Highway (in Detroit), and from that vantage point, began shooting at other drivers for reasons that are still not very clear. Not long after this report, I heard about the tragedy of another man who was shot and killed in his home, in front of his family, which included young children. About the time of these news stories, the Democrats staged a sit-in protest on the floor of the House of Representatives, to protest the Republican-run House, because they would not allow for an up and down vote on commonsense, gun legislation. And while these stories represent just a few of the latest sad, confusing and controversial events happening in our local and national news, there are many more similar stories which never get mentioned nationally. Just as in the days of the Judges, many people – even some of those who claim to be God's people - are living life as though *there is no King – no Jesus – no God, to Whom we will give an account; consequently, many in this society and even in the church, are doing what is right, in their own eyes.*

The good news today, is that no matter how much chaos and anarchy seem to be colluding together to invade and ruin our peace, there is a king who ultimately reigns over us, the church, the world, and the universe; but He reigns in the context of God's schedule, and human free-will. Much of the New Testament is about Jesus revealing to the world that there is a King, who reigns above all evil and good; all obedience and rebellion. Because of our sinful proclivities, we might not always see clear signs of this Kingdom, but if we look closely enough, there are indications that it is here. Whenever, and wherever, we see people submitting their minds, their affections, their intentions, and their decisions to goodness, kindness, holiness, forgiveness, charity, and worship, we are seeing signs of the presence of the King, and of His Kingdom. Whenever we see churches filled with people who love God's word; God's neighborhoods; God's co-laborers; God's pastors and leaders; and God's least, lost, and left out, we are seeing signs of the presence of the King. Today, I pray that we will all accept the challenge of learning to live our lives, under the authority of the King, who reigns over all other powers. Jesus is the King of Kings, and Lord of Lords! Our challenge in our homes and hearts, our communities and churches, is to submit to His Royal Lordship. We do not want it to be said of us in this hour that: "they persisted in doing, what was right in their own eyes, because they were not aware that there was a King!" Jesus has a better plan for you and me; better than the ones we conjure up on our own.

41. Look and See what God has Done!

Texts: Psalm 34 and Matthew 20

In his book, *God of the Oppressed*, the late James H. Cone, called by many, *The Father of Black Liberation Theology*, writes from personal experience about how God, more than anyone, identifies with the struggle of oppressed people in general, and the struggle of Africans and Africans in the Americas, in particular. Cone explained that theology (our God-talk and ideas about God) doesn't take place in a vacuum, but we come to know what we know about God, through the experience of our internal and external struggles against nefarious forces which attempt to oppress and suppress us. For example, Moses came to know God as he was running from an Egyptian system that was oppressing the Hebrews and seeking to imprison/execute him for fighting against a brutal enslaver. Another example is how the disciples came to know God. All of the disciples came to know God in a culture that was dominated by the Roman Empire, poverty, sickness, disease, and demonic oppression. Jesus revealed Himself to a people who had come out of Babylonian captivity, and now were living in the shadows of Rome, and of a religious system which majored in the superficialities of Judaism, and propagated legalism over against freedom in the Spirit. For Cone, this is the God revealed in both the First, and New Testaments. Cone is quite clear: Divine revelation happens in the midst of this universal struggle of those who are oppressed and must contend against forces of hatred. Reaching this conclusion, Cone suggests that God is most definitely on the side of black folks, because God is on the side of the oppressed.

In Cone's estimation, no one on earth has been as oppressed as those who have been thoroughly kissed by nature's sun. He pushes the point even further by saying that, in fact, *God is black.* Not that God necessarily has ebony dark skin (or any skin, for that matter), but God is black in the sense that God is willing to completely identify with the brutalized of the world; God has chosen to be submerged in the struggle of those treated as the scum of the earth, as God works against all forms of racial, ethnic, and economic supremacy. For Cone, scripture has played a key role in revealing this aspect of God's core nature. For example, as alluded to above, Cone often cited the most powerful liberation narrative of the Hebrew scriptures to prove his point about God being a God of the oppressed. The story of the Jews' Exodus from Egyptian bondage. Cone states that Yahweh was revealed to Moses, as One Who had decisively chosen to side with his enslaved people. God is not neutral, but God empathizes and feels what God's children feel, to the point that God felt enslaved with them. Cone wrote *God of the Oppressed* in 1975, on the heels of the Black Power movement, as he defended some of his earlier works that were written in the late 60s.

While, one might not agree with all of the radical imagery and controversial points that Cone used in his books to communicate his conviction about God's way of working in the world (I think it is important, as Cone wrote in his more recent works, to hold in tension God's work in particular communities, like the African American community, with God's universal work to liberate all who are oppressed, *even those who engage in acts of oppression*), every serious student of the scripture should agree in principle with the notion that among the many glorious works of God, God chooses to side with those who seek righteousness, against unrighteous forces, systems and people. God loves us all, even those who use power in very bad ways, but the Bible reveals to us a God who challenges persons of power to repent, and learn to walk justly, and lovingly with others; if they will not, God's justice will deal judgment. In this manner, the biblical record from our texts in Psalm 34, to Matthew 20; from Egypt, to Rome; from Babylon, to America, cries out that God is working to set captives free; heal broken hearts; and flip the story line, so that those who were once last, will become first, and the first, will become last. God has revealed Himself to be One Who is working to right wrongs that have happened and heal those who have been crushed under boots of systemic oppression. Throughout the First Testament, God flipped the script against the Egyptians, the Canaanites, the Midianites, the Assyrians, and the Babylonians. In the New Testament, on behalf of oppressed people who were crying out to God, God overturned the power of the Pharisees, Sadducees, and eventually, the Romans. The same has been true in this country, regarding the plight of black folk. God is working to flip the racist script of the legacy and mythology of white supremacy, so that our society and world will be more loving and equitable. The destruction of this myth is critical for the salvation of blacks and whites. Ultimately, because of God, the Ku Klux Klan, and all of its offspring movements, are doomed; and Christians are overcomers.

When many African Americans made the trip northward from the south, though they found jobs, they also found discrimination and segregation. In the midst of this struggle, Reverend Robert L. Jordan, a preacher, scholar, and historian, along with other saints, felt led to ensure that African Americans in Detroit, and in Michigan, would not be last and left out, when it came to persons in city having an opportunity to benefit from a Disciples of Christ congregation in the area. Though many believed this was a pipe dream, because they did not think that African Americans could organize or come up with enough funding to establish a new Disciples of Christ congregation, the dream would become reality. Eventually, United Christian Church, was birthed and became one of the largest Christian Church congregations in the region. It became the Mother congregation for most African American Disciples congregations in the Southeast portion of Michigan. God can work out God's will among and through the oppressed, helping them to become overcomers in Christ! There are many stories like our story. Why? Because God has been working, and is working, to make the last first, and the first last!

42. A Few Thoughts on Stewardship

But this I say: He who sows sparingly will also reap sparingly, and he who sows bountifully will also reap bountifully. So let each one give as he purposes in his hear, not grudgingly or of necessity; for God loves a cheerful giver.

(2 Corinthians 9:6-7)

October is Stewardship Month at the United Christian Church of Detroit. Our focus for the month is to learn how to be faithful and grateful stewards of all that God has given us, as we put God first! A critical part of putting God first in our lives involves us learning how to count the cost of discipleship, as we make spiritual and material sacrifices for the good of the kingdom and the prosperity of the ministry of God's church. True discipleship means first hearing the word of Christ, which helps receptive, church-going, Christians to differentiate between what it means to be a mere church attendee and a true follower of the Lord. Disciples are those who have counted the cost, and are willing to pay the cost (time, talent, treasure, idols, sin, etc.) of following Jesus Christ and God's Kingdom agenda. Paul taught the Corinthian church that each follower of Christ must come to an inner resolution regarding their attitude about giving generously to bless the church, as the church blesses our sisters and brothers in the community. The apostle taught the saints that God does not want believers to give their energy or their material blessings, if their giving causes them to nurse deep resentments. Instead, God desires God's children to give cheerfully, with joy, and out of a sense of love – a love for God, the church, and our neighbors.

While salvation has been freely given to us by God's grace (Ephesians 2:8), following the Lord in faithfulness will eventually cost us many things -- relationships, selfish ambitions and at times comfort, and even "our" financial resources. Ultimately, nothing is off the table, if God asks us to give up something for the spread of God's influence in our lives, and in the world; though, in our most honest moments, all of us would have to admit that sometimes giving up what we have is not always an easy act.

More than anything, this biblical notion of "following the Lord" is a mindset; one which prioritizes our relationship with Christ, as the greatest and most important relationship in life. Ideally, our relationship with the risen Christ is *THE relationship* around which all others revolve. It is grounded in the fact that God has already given God's greatest gift to us (Himself, incarnate in Christ), and in response to God's altruism and grace, we are challenged to give our best to the Lord, sometimes at great cost to our personal comfort. If we only follow the Lord when blessings and favor seem to be flowing our way; and as long as our following Jesus doesn't ever stir up controversy with family members, loved ones and friends; if we follow the Lord only when it is convenient, are we ***actually following the Lord? Or*** are we following a Santa Claus God? Jesus states in our text that we cannot authentically be His disciples, and become faithful, joyful stewards of all that God has given to us (health, strength, time, talent, treasure), if we are not ever willing to count the costs and leave behind the old life, which includes some problematic people; some old and odd places; and maybe even an irresponsible handling of some valued possession; or a tight-fisted view of money; all of which can block true discipleship and the advancement of God's reign on earth, as it already is in heaven. Come on church, let's count the cost of discipleship! Let's be cheerful givers! The song writer wrote, "***Where ever He leads me, I will follow . . . I'll go with Him, with Him, all the way!***"

43. Men of God, Rise!

Text: Luke 15:11-32

Today is Men's Day at United! Over the centuries numerous black men have responded to the call to follow Christ and through their lives and testimonies, have provided godly examples of what it means to be a courageous, servant leader, in a world filled with people who champion and nurse a me-first attitude. A few names that quickly come to mind are: Frederick Douglass, Booker T. Washington, William J. Seymour, Richard Allen, W. E. B. Dubois, Jackie Robinson, Thurgood Marshall, Martin Luther King, Jr., Jessie Jackson, Earvin (Magic) Johnson, Cornel West, Charles Ogletree, Jr. and President Barack Obama. If you carefully read their bios, many of these towering figures would never have become the men God intended them to become, if God had not used other men to help mentor and inspire them. Through the power of the gospel, coupled with strong male role models, these men enjoyed personal awakenings which prepared them to serve God and the world. This idea is the overall thrust of this year's Men's Day theme: ***Men, It's Time to Wake Up!*** *If men are going to wake up spiritually, we need Christ, and we need other men to inspire us and hold us accountable.* This inspiration and system of accountability must begin early though. It begins with the older men teaching their sons and other boys in the community how important it is to respect God, momma, their sisters, and of course, other men. An important aspect of African tradition and culture can teach us something about this.

In the eyes of the African boy, the father, or some other respected older male, *is* a revered figure. Besides the child's breast-connection with the mother, this is where the seeds/value of respecting others in society begins. African religious scholar, Benezet Bujo reveals something very important that happens in African culture to support this idea. He notes that in various places, throughout Africa, sons and other young males, since toddlerhood, have been socialized to *never sit in their father's/older male's chair, while they are alive*; to do so, displays a breathtaking lack of spiritual respect. In essence, to sit in a father's or elder male's chair is to **count as dead the influence of that father or male elder.** Unfortunately, in our culture today, many men (younger and older) live by an "I'll sit anywhere I damn well choose!" personal philosophy. They no longer respect or seek to learn from good men. The reasons for this are legion. Chief among these are that many adult men have been absent and irresponsible in relationship to their sons and other youths. This absenteeism in our culture can breed contempt. Whatever the reasons are for this growing lack of reverence for its men, whenever a community loses respect for and a connection to the wise men of that community, all the people of that community forfeit a part of the group success God intends and envisions for that community.

There is an aspect of this in the story of the prodigal son. In Jesus' parable (Luke 15:11-32), the prodigal boy does not respect the key male figure in his life – his father! The self-centered youngest son could not wait for the natural unfolding of time and events to bring him to the time when he would receive the secondary portion of his father's inheritance. He demanded that even before his older brother received his portion; even before his father had died, that he would get, now, what would have been coming to him later! Whenever we as men can't wait for God's timing, and we try to rush the fulfillment of God's promises, we can find ourselves in danger of rushing out into some *far country experience*. It was not until this young man hits rock bottom and wakes up in a pig sty that he comes to his senses. But the *good news for him and us is that he does wake up!* Once he wakes up, he rises and returns back home.

Once home, there is another interesting dynamic to Jesus' tale, the older son, is not at all happy that their father is celebrating the younger son's return. In fact, the older son is incensed and filled with indignation. After hearing of their father's plans to restore the younger son, the first born, fuming with anger, retorts, "He wasted all the money you gave him on parties, pimping and prostitution!" "How can you celebrate him?" The older brother, at no time, claims his younger brother, as his brother. He speaks about his brother as if he were a complete stranger. His perspective and attitude had become warped with self-righteousness, envy, and rage. Men, there is an additional lesson for us in these details. We must be careful not to become too judgmental when some young male among our ranks, falters and fails, or just chooses a pathway that is downright, selfish, stupid, and self-destructive. We have been called to be mature mentors, not the ultimate judges and the wielders of swords of condemnation. It is not easy to discern what particular demons lurk in the minds and on the shoulders of one individual, in comparison to another. As we hold one another accountable to God's standards, we do not want to think that just because we might be more disciplined, that our value to God is greater than our prodigal brothers. The forces of evil seek to tempt and destroy all who have been made in God's image; and make no mistake about it, the devil comes after men so that they will harm women, their families, and themselves. Without men who are rooted in God's goodness and holiness, our entire society and world, is in eminent danger. The adversary of our souls is a long-time strategic thinker; and though not anywhere close to God's level, the devil is a formidable enemy for human beings who are not covered by the blood and empowered by the spirit and name of Jesus. The older brother confused his obedience to his father, with a notion of some inherent moral superiority to his younger brother. The older brother was sinning too. His sin was the sin of living in the far country of a destructive self-righteousness, which reduces grace, to nothing more than a little insignificant factor in our spiritual success. Consequently, his father, had to help him to wake up; he reminded his eldest son, that the younger son was indeed his brother, and that it was more than right to celebrate a boy who was becoming a man!

Men, with God as our source, and other godly men to help hold us accountable, awakenings are possible for us today too! Resurrections are possible. But, we have to be willing to trust God, and wait on God's process to unfold, in God's timing and way. To make it happen (whatever it is) using manipulation and worldly tactics cause us to fall and fail; but if we let God's process of maturation and preparation run its course, we will come to ourselves like the prodigal and be given a new perspective like the older brother; and together, brother to brother, we will enjoy our Father's love!

44. What Can We do After this Presidential Election? We must Speak Out!

Texts: Portions of Isaiah 65 and Luke 21:5-15

What can the people of God do, when the old order of things – dynamics that are spiritual, social, and political – seem to be winning out against, and crowding out the possibility of, God's new order? This has been the existential struggle of the followers of God in every age, especially during certain periods in history; periods when the elite few are satisfied with the old status quo, while the masses are so discontent with the tyranny of the old that the entire fabric of society is in danger of being ripped apart by the forces of discontent and outrage.

In our lectionary texts, we have two very different passages of scripture, which point to one powerful reality: **God is at work to overthrow the old order, because God's agenda is to make all things perfected, new and whole!** In our First Testament text, in Isaiah 65, we are given a vision of what Isaiah sees in his societal context, and in the spirit. Earlier in the chapter, Isaiah describes a rebellious people; a people who are not seeking God, a people clearly engaged in evil and idolatry. According to verses 4 and 5, theirs is a culture of death and darkness. But, as the chapter progresses, Isaiah shares with the reader that God will ultimately protect and nurture his people, while those who live lives of defiance and sin will encounter judgment. God's servants will enjoy God's newness; they will be satisfied, have joy, and prosper, while idolaters will be trapped in their old patterns of living, until they are cursed. It is a hopeful message for God's children; it is also a very tough message for those who refuse to repent. Beginning at verse 17, Isaiah describes God's plans for His remnant people. The prophet says that God will totally overturn the old order, and the former things will not be remembered because the new order will be just that glorious! The fear of death, or the anxiety associated with living an unfulfilled, unproductive life will pass away. The wolf and the lamb shall feed together (vs. 25). This new age of serenity will usher in a society that heals, and doesn't hurt; that creates, and doesn't destroy!

In our New Testament lectionary, Luke 21:5-15, Jesus describes a global atmosphere which reflects something similar to what Isaiah describes in the early portion of Isaiah 65. Jesus speaks of how, not only will there be conflicts around Jerusalem, but also, around the world; the entire global community will be in conflict. The nations of the world, both Jews and Gentiles, will forsake God and will give themselves over to idolatry, violence, dead religious practices, and false Messiahs. Consequently, as the world drifts towards the last, of the last days, there will be a continuous stream of "wars and rumors of wars." Those who are God's elect will be ultimately blessed and protected from the wrath of God, but they will also be called upon to give witness and testimony in some very difficult circumstances; possibly exposing themselves to the wrath of earthly leaders. Jesus says that His disciples will be moved by the Holy Spirit to speak God's words about Jesus, justice, and judgement, in the presence of unjust kings and magistrates (verses 12 and 13). But, in verse 14, he also offers a powerful word of assurance to his followers for the task at hand: *"...do not meditate beforehand on how you will answer your adversaries; for I will give you a mouth of wisdom which all your adversaries will not be able to contradict or resist."* In essence, Jesus counsels his disciples to trust that God has given them (at just the right time) an inner power; an inner faith; an inner joy; an inner testimony; a powerful God-given message, that they will speak out boldly, and unashamedly, a word which announces God's new way and new day, in the presence of many despotic rulers stubbornly committed to the old order!

What is God's *new* all about? God's *new* is about having old sins forgiven and washed away, so that we can look forward and not backward in guilt; God's new is about having the very life of God coursing through our being, in the presence of the Holy Spirit; God's new is about knowing and sharing a love, creativity and intimacy, that only God can give – as we share the gospel of Jesus Christ; God's new is about being deeply concerned for those who seem to have the least in our world; God's new is about creating opportunities for the hurting to be healed and the voiceless to have a say in the precincts of power; God's new is about helping to create the Kingdom/Kin-dom of God on earth as it is in heaven! This is always a timely message for us, as human beings. Ironically, we must be reminded again, and again, of God's new, because it is the devil's job to help us to forget. Today, more than ever, we need to be trying to spread God's new order - telling someone about Jesus, and His way of justice and mercy; faith and hope; love and equity; holiness and healing! His new way should be trumpeted before paupers and royalty.

Spreading and promoting the new today, has never been more important in this country, especially given what seems to be the emergence of a slippery slope backwards towards the old. After President Trump's ascendancy to the Whitehouse, many African Americans and immigrants from Latin American countries, are being confronted with an old bigotry. With the election of Donald Trump to the United States presidency, many feel like the old ways of white supremacy, sexism, with the rich getting richer and the poor often despised and forgotten, have been given a powerful platform again. Many decry what seems to be a regressive move back to the worst aspects of the 1940s and 50s. Because of the very incendiary, insensitive, and even hostile statements, President Elect Trump has repeatedly made, many minorities fear that the clocks of progress against past racist policies and anti-immigrant sentiments, have been turned backwards to a terrible era we hoped was gone forever.

Despite these troubling events, we are reminded, by Isaiah and Jesus, that no matter who is in public office; no matter who currently seems to be holding all the cards of power and legislative agency, *God's new is coming!* It cannot be stopped, because God wills it so. Therefore, as we wait for the full manifestation of God's new order, our charge is to be prepared for conflict, pray for our enemies, as we declare God's coming reign. Now is the time to draw closer to the Lord than we ever have before. Now is the time to pray and commit to loving others, like never before! We are called to pray for our elected officials, and practice non-violent resistance when necessary, like never before. Now, like never before, is the time to learn and share about the many good things God has done in Jesus Christ, and that God has deposited in people of color – our history, our gifts, our faith – and celebrate these cultural gifts, as we also honor the gifts of all people! When we prepare like this, God will grant God's wisdom to those who are good stewards of the message of God's kingdom. The Spirit will bless us with a timely word that afflicts the comfortable and comforts the afflicted.

Our faith is a testifying faith; a prophetic and holy faith; a talking and walking faith; it is a faith which has always challenged wayward kings, queens, presidents, governors and sheriffs, to be godly and just; it has always challenged and comforted those who have been oppressed, encouraging them to remain faithful in tough times, as they wait for God to do exploits on their behalf. Sisters and brothers, I am glad that the witness of our scriptures, and the history of Israel and the church, confirm that the Spirit has made sure that we have a faith that this old world's system will not be able to shut up!

45. Youth Sunday

Text: 1 Kings 15-18

During the reign of the wicked and wayward King Ahab, and his evil, Phoenician wife, Jezebel, Israel and Judah had fallen so far from God's ways and will that it was mind boggling. Much of the blame can be placed at the feet of this terrible twosome. The King, Ahab, was a weak, evil, leader, who was prone to get involved in ungodly alliances, and idolatry. When introduced to us in 1 Kings 16, the text says that he did great evil in the sight of the Lord, more than all who came before him. His strong-willed, pagan wife, Jezebel, worshiped Baal, which culminated in the worship and deification of calves all over the land. She used her influence and power to try to completely, destroy the influence of Yahweh over the people of Israel, so that God's people would worship cows, and engage in forbidden sensual and sexual practices! She was so devoted to her pagan and violent impulses, that she had even commissioned the execution of all the prophets of Yahweh. She and her husband exalted the spirituality and theology of the false god Baal, while doing all in their power to sinfully silence the voice, commandments, and power of Yahweh in the land. *But why?* Why had these two prominent leaders of Israel, chosen to use their "swagger" to disconnect the people of God from their history, spiritual practices, and faith in the God who had brought them out of Egyptian slavery? *Could it have been because both of them had failed to commit to the One true God, when they were much younger?* I believe that this issue of Ahab and Jezebel having given themselves over to their ungodly impulses, needs to be analyzed.

People don't usually become as evil as Jezebel and Ahab had become, overnight. I would bet that their wickedness came from years of practice. At some point during Ahab and Jezebel's spiritual development, while still youths, they kept making choices to follow voices, behaviors, and trends, which did not mesh with the revelation of God, which came through the teachings connected with the Mosaic Law. Ahab ignored the teachings which reveal to us God's holiness and goodness, and he was more attracted to learning how to grasp political and social power for his own gain. Jezebel was a foreigner who grew up in the same region as the Jews; she was probably well acquainted with the stories, music, and theology, associated with the worship of Yahweh. She had heard of what Yahweh had done through King David, only a little more than a century earlier, but she wouldn't relinquish what she had learned from childhood (as other foreigners like Ruth had done) about the gods of her own people. Jezebel preferred the violence, prostitution, drunken sexual orgies, and even human sacrifices, connected with worshiping Baal, and Astoreth (Baal's female counterpart). As young people, both Ahab and Jezebel kept making choices to heed voices which gave advice, messages, and a spirit, different from the One True God's advice, message, and spirit. This was how things went in Israel, until the prophet Elijah showed up.

Elijah was led by God to pronounce a drought over the land of Israel and Judah, because of the sins of the King, Queen, and people. It didn't rain for three years. Even so, Ahab and Jezebel wouldn't repent. Finally, God orchestrates a showdown on Mt. Carmel; a confrontation between Ahab/Jezebel and God; between the prophets of Baal and Elijah; between many false voices, and the One True Voice! On this Youth Sunday, our task will be to challenge ourselves and our youth to learn to tune in to the voice of Christ, in an age when many voices are vying for our attention through friends, television, movies, videos, Instagram, Facebook, Facetime, games, and other mediums. What influences are truly guiding our decisions? Are we persuaded by the voices of our peers; by the actions of athletes; by the advice of our parents; by the teachings of our faith; by the lifestyles and messages of talented hip-hop artists like Drake, Chris Breezy, Rhianna, and Young Thug; or is it some new-age philosophy, or a hybrid of religions that is mesmerizing your mind? religions which claim to offer something better for youth, than faith in Christ; or something better for black folk;

or city folk; or for folk who want to become wealthy, or for folk who want to live a life without moral restraints? I think God's question, through Elijah, in 1 Kings 18, is still a great one for us to consider today -- *"How long will you waver between two opinions?"* Let's talk about it, as we consider our youth, Ahab, Jezebel, Elijah, and most importantly, God.

46. Thanksgiving

Text: Colossians 1:1-20

Beginning in verse 9, of the first chapter to the Colossians, Paul is sharing with the Christians in Colossae, the details of what he and other prayer warriors had been praying over the people's lives. He reveals that they had been endlessly praying that the Colossians would be filled with divine insight; that they would be filled with wisdom and spiritual understanding; and that the Colossians would walk right – walking worthy of their relationship with the Lord. Paul and other leaders had been praying that every good ministry work in which the Colossians engaged, would flourish and bear good fruit. Lastly, Paul adds in verse 12, that as the Colossian Christians experience answers to these prayers, they should live with an attitude of gratitude to God, the Father/Parent! They should give thanks, because God has qualified them as God's children, to partake of an inheritance that comes from the realm of a bright, dynamic, mind-blowing, life-transforming, light.

As we reflect upon Paul's words, it seems as if Paul was building a case as to why the Colossian Christians should be thankful. First, they were going to receive the multiple blessings that Paul and other leaders had been praying to God for them to receive. That was a reason to be grateful. Next, they had been qualified to receive the greatest inheritance – eternal life, with God and the saints! That was a definite reason to be thankful! But, as I contemplated what Paul was writing, I couldn't help but to think to myself, "To whom do we owe, this great connection we now have with the

Father and the Spirit? And as I read the rest of our text, the answer was easy to find – Jesus! Let me explain.

In verses 13-20, Paul gives us one of the strongest Christological statements in the entire Bible. Paul says that we have been translated from a kingdom of darkness, into a kingdom of light, simply because it was the will of the Son of God's love. We have been redeemed from the penalty of our sins, because of the blood of the Son. He (the Son) is the very image of the invisible God, Paul boldly declares in verse 15. He is one by Whom all things were created. He, as the very Word of God, is the means by which all things, seen and unseen, exist. There are no powers, nor thrones, nor principalities and dominions, that are outside his ultimate purview. He also predates all things, Paul says. He holds all things together. Better still, he is not just some distant abstraction; he is not an impersonal force. According to Paul, he is the head of the church – the first one, out of many, to rise from the dead!

Sisters and brothers, we might not have experienced the answers to all of our prayers yet. We might not have all the resources – monetarily, socially, romantically, or vocationally - that we trust will eventually make it to our doorstops. During a season when strange, dark, political and societal winds are blowing, and our personal trials and tribulations might eclipse our view of the kingdom of God, it might not seem as if we have instant access to pure, perfect, light and joy. Despite this, I submit to you that each one of us has a reason to shout out a thanksgiving of praise from the rooftops of our souls! Why? Because Jesus is here and available to meet your needs; because Jesus is bigger than whatever you might be grappling with today; because Jesus is the Co-Creator of things seen and unseen; and because Jesus is not only the all-powerful Lord, but can become your Friend; the Friend, who will never leave you, nor forsake you! Alas, in light of who He is, how can we not say, "Thank You! Thank You! Thank You! Thank You!!"

Part 5

Advent and Christmas

47. Do We Really "Get" Advent?

Text: Mark 6:1-7

At the religious and commercial intersection of the Christmas holiday season, it is sometimes easy to misinterpret who Jesus really is to us, and all that God wants to do for us, through Christ. Jesus is more than a Savior who exists primarily within the brick and mortar structure, framed with stained glass windows, cushioned pews, prominently positioned pulpits, and choir lofts. Jesus is much more than the one whose life is domesticated on the pages of the Bible, and in the stories of Joseph and Mary making the difficult trek to Bethlehem. The New Testament reveals a Jesus who has come to save us in every dimension of life. Jesus has come to shine divine light in our hearts, and on our spiritual, moral, and social darkness. Jesus was sent by God, as the Son of God, to spark a love fire within us that burns bright and long, and strong. Because we have become aware of God's deep love for us, we are set free from forces that are at work, within us, around us, and beyond us, to destroy all that is good and godly. Jesus has come to reveal to us, that God is present with us, as "Emmanuel" and that God loves us, unconditionally and is willing to prosper, purify, and heal us. Jesus has come to demonstrate that those hateful forces that are at work to destroy our lives, our homes, and our society, can be made subject to God's power, in Jesus' name. But when we only see Christ's coming to humanity as an occasion to have *good church, in church*; or as an opportunity to shop and wrap gifts, we have gotten the purpose of Jesus' coming, *twisted*. It is sometimes easy for those who should be closest to Jesus, to misinterpret Jesus. This is the key problem in what unfolds in the early portion of the Gospel of Mark, chapter six.

In Mark 6:1-7, we have Mark's account of Jesus and His disciples' trip back to Jesus' hometown of Nazareth. Jesus probably heads home to reconnect with his earthly family. He loves them. Upon returning to Nazareth, it is clear his reputation has preceded him. He has been asked by the local Rabbi, in charge of worship in the synagogue, to preach and teach on the Sabbath. He agrees. The day has arrived, and while he's teaching, all of the hometown folk are astounded by the power and wisdom flowing from his orations. This is quite a homecoming for our Lord. The people of Nazareth are not certain of the source of his power. They are not entirely convinced that God is actually the One flowing through him, because they remember a young teen-aged Jesus; they remember the pre-teen version of Jesus; they are too well acquainted with him, and the household in which he had grown up – they knew Jesus' momma and 'nem. They had used the services of the family carpentry business. They remembered what Nazareth Public Schools he and his siblings had attended. Ultimately, though awestruck by his amazing oratorical gifts, they were offended by Jesus. They were tripped up by Him; they were too familiar with him, though they didn't really know him; consequently, in their own hearts *they got his identity twisted*. Because of their inaccurate view of the totality of who Christ was and is, Mark notes that, "…He could do no mighty work there." Because they had a warped view, they lacked the faith to ask the Lord to answer their most pressing needs; answers to their requests that Jesus could have easily provided; blessings that could have blessed their lives beyond the synagogue, and their religious celebrations. Jesus approached his hometown ready and well-able to heal broken bodies, hearts and minds, in Nazareth. They did not see Jesus in this light though.

As we approach this Christmas holiday, and as we allow the Spirit of Christ to approach us this Advent season, let's pray that God would clear up any significant misperceptions we might have about our Savior. Let's pray that we would really "get" Advent. We celebrate this season of the Christian Year because it reminds us that Jesus has come once, and is coming again with all power, immeasurable love, profound justice, great mercies, and a desire to make all that is wrong, right. His life, his presence, is what we need. Today, the Lord can do mighty works in and through us. The Lord would do more in our world, if we would only "get" that with God, nothing good is impossible!

Study Questions

1. What do you think Jesus desired to do for his hometown, as he and the disciples approached the border of Nazareth?

2. What do you think God desires to do in your family's life; in your community's life; in the life of your city or town? Do you actually believe God can do it, whatever "it" is? In order to accomplish the desired goal, will God need your cooperation, and participation?

3. How can we attain a more comprehensive perspective of Jesus Christ? How much time do you spend meditating in the Gospels, per week? How has the content of the Gospels reshaped your views about God?

4. As you reflect on the purpose of Advent, are you anticipating the second coming of the Lord? If so, why? If you're not, why not?

5. Most Christians, and even many non-Christians, enjoy the festive character of Christmas. What are you anticipating most about Christmas as the day approaches?

48. Christmas – The Day When God Messed Up Someone's Plans

Text: Matthew 1:18-25

Have you ever had the experience of planning for some event, accomplishment, relationship, vocation, ministry, social status, or educational pursuit, only to have your plans disrupted, dislodged, or virtually destroyed? In our text, this is what Mary and Joseph experience nine months before the world's first Christmas. Their notion of what it meant to be married, and to have a family, would become inverted by the announcement of a strange addition to their lives.

Think about it carefully. Joseph and Mary had planned to be married – they had their own ideas of what a future, as a couple, would mean. They were betrothed to each other, which was an act more serious than our modern-day marital engagements. In the days of the New Testament, in Jewish culture, a betrothal meant that the couple was practically married before the final formalities. Both families were fully involved in the betrothal. Money had exchanged hands between groom and bride's families. Money had been spent to organize the coming wedding ceremony, celebration, and feast. Plans had been put into place. There was no backing out, except in the rare case of a serious moral breach, especially on the bride's part. Betrothal was a serious thing.

Can you imagine the kind of plans Mary and Joseph had made? He was a carpenter, he had spent years honing his skills as a cutter and shaper of woods and metals. He would turn these raw materials into useful items.

Joseph was to a degree, settled, because he had mastered a trade and had begun making his mark in the world. Though he might never become wealthy, he had prepared himself to be a husband and father who would have the means to support a family. And one great day, when cupid's music was in the air, Joseph was smitten by the sight of a woman named Mary. When he saw Mary coming, something within Joseph said, "This is the one!" Many scholars and historians depict Mary as being much younger than Joseph, based on acceptable cultural practices at the time. So, it is quite possible that when Mary first became aware of Joseph's interests, in her youthful excitement, she might have idealized Joseph as the perfect husband/father figure; one who would not only make a great father for the coming children, but one who would be a mentor, protector, and source of spiritual security for her.

Both Mary and Joseph had many plans and hopes about how their godly union would pan out. They had many dreams about their future family. This probably included the number of children they would have; their financial, spiritual, and social status, in Nazareth. They, like most God-fearing couples, also had hopes that what they would make of their lives would thoroughly please and glorify God. They had a lot of plans, but they did not yet realize how *God was about to mess up their plans!* In Matthew 1:18-25, we are told how God messed up Mary and Joseph's plans. God's Spirit, through a divine word that was sown in her heart via an angel's announcement, impregnates Mary, before she had intimate relations with Joseph. She is pregnant before the honeymoon and Joseph's not the father! Mary's explanation to Joseph is not credible. In fact, it probably sounded to Joseph as if Mary, in a panic, had lapsed into a pathological emotional state that led her to concoct an insane lie about visiting angels and miracle pregnancies. Consequently, Joseph begins to make new plans – he plans to annul the betrothal. Joseph would be on a new trek to find someone else, someone worthy of his love. This relationship, which had seemed to be on good, calm, happy, peaceful ground, had now been totally upended by God's plans. God did not ask Mary and Joseph whether the Spirit could interrupt their plans. God did not ask this couple if they would be okay with being the parents of the Son of God. God did not instantly give them all the answers to their many questions (Although, thankfully, in verse 20, through an angel's visit to

Joseph's troubled mind, God calms some of Joseph's inner turmoil). But, make no mistake about it, in a very real sense, God had messed up *their plans*. What Mary and Joseph did not yet realize was that God had only messed up their plans, because their plans were not worthy enough of the high calling to which they had been summoned. God wanted to use them to mess up all of the devil's plans for humanity. God thought enough of the character, integrity, and wisdom of this couple, that God had a special mission for them. Again, their mission: *Give birth to; and love, nurture, provide for, raise, and teach, the Savior of the world!* Their plans would take them places, no young couple in Nazareth (or anywhere, for that matter) had ever travelled mentally, emotionally, and spiritually. They would be stretched to their limits. Soon, they would be heading to Bethlehem, and then to Egypt, and then back home to Nazareth. God's plans would see to it that the doorway to our salvation would abide under their roof. God's plans would ensure that their names would go down in history, as arguably, the most admired couple in the world.

What is the lesson here? There are several. *First,* God will mess up our plans. *Second,* when we are really going through the wringer, we must distinguish between what is God's work, and what is simply the messiness of the devil's work. *Finally,* once we discern it is God messing up our plans, we must learn to let God do, what God is doing! Because when God is the one messing up our plans, then we must come to believe that our own plans were not worthy to match up with who God is shaping us to become.

Study Questions

1. Have you ever had your eyes set on reaching some goal, or accomplishing an important task, only to have your plans interrupted and or changed by events greater than your control?

2. Both the most famous and anonymous among us have had to recalibrate their routes in life; aging, sickness, loss of a job, the death of a loved one, a change in a relationship, can alter anyone's plans. Can you recount the experience of someone you know, or have heard about, who seemed, in the long run, to benefit from a change in the trajectory of their life?

3. Mary and Joseph had to shift gears, individually and as a couple. Do you think it is more difficult to adapt to changes that God authors, if God is moving on an individual to make that change, or if God is moving a couple, or a group, to shift directions? In other words, do you think it is easier for God to guide one person in a new direction, or several persons?

4. Do you think Mary, or Joseph, could have resisted God's will? And, if so, how do you think God would have brought Jesus to the world? If not, what does this say about human free will?

5. Mary and Joseph's mission in life became one of birthing and raising the Messiah. Because God chose them to do this, what does this say to you about the character of this couple?

49. A Scandal in Nazareth

Luke 1: 26-35

The network television series, *Scandal*, is one of the highest rated shows on television today, in terms of its viewership numbers. It is a political thriller and soap opera. It follows the romantic and political machinations of a powerful and beautiful African American woman named Olivia Pope (who is played by Actress Kerri Washington), and a host of other characters – political power players, and wannabes, who orbit the fictionalized, Washington D. C. universe. Miss Pope is a woman of immense skill and intelligence. She is a lawyer, who owns her own crisis management firm, and in the recent past, was the White House Communications Director for the President of the United States, Fitzgerald Grant. Miss Pope has major drama in her life, and at the top of her list of complicated issues is that she is occasionally involved in an illicit affair with President Fitzgerald, who is white and very married. Around their on-again, off-again romance, is a swirling mess of other selfish characters, secrets, lies, plot twists, immoral choices, sexual debauchery, revenge, double-crosses, schemes, assassination attempts and even murder. The show boasts a large viewership of African American women (and many men too); many of them who attend and serve in churches; some even serve as pastors.

It seems as if there is nothing like a good scandal to get our attention, and move us toward conversation, contemplation, and a response. Maybe this is one of the reasons why God created one of the greatest scandals of all time, albeit one of a very different sort.

In first century Nazareth, God created a scandal which involved a

234

romance that quickly went rocky because of a poorly explained pregnancy. It involved the possibility of fornication, or adultery, the latter of which could have been punishable by death. It involved a man who owned his own carpentry business, and was known in the Nazareth community, and who felt betrayed and stabbed in the back by the woman he loved most; a young woman, who, on the surface, seemed to have mental issues and problems with promiscuity. To the uninformed, it sounded like a tale of immorality, which could have, and would have ended in public shame, at best, or domestic and judicial violence, at worst. But, unlike television's *Scandal*, God was the author of what was at work in this real dilemma. In real time, a divine Child had been given to us through the Holy Spirit; a sinless Savior would be born; and because of this couple's faith, love, and desire to please God, Mary and Joseph would go down in history as one of the greatest couples who ever lived. But things would not have ended well, at all, if Joseph and Mary had not been people of faith, who learned how to properly handle being thrust into the throes of the salvation scandal.

Today, in a world rife with scandals and salacious happenings, with God's help, we can survive a scandal, or several scandals, whether they be personal, familial, social, national, and or international. God can help us to overcome a personal failure, known by the public; or a tawdry association with a company or institution that got caught in unethical business dealings; or the nation being subjected to a national or international crisis because of a politician's erratic, or unstable behavior. The ability to recover from scandals is part and parcel, of what makes the message of Christmas so good.

The human family has found itself, caught in the web of a complicated and dangerous spiritual scandal. The earliest human beings became embroiled in a sad conundrum when we thought we could be as smart and wise as God, without God. We thought that we could easily disobey God and listen to the voice of the lowest fallen angel, and still ascend to the highest heights of our own power and glory. Instead of rising, we fell – we mucked everything up. In the years following that fateful day, the human race has trafficked in all kinds of scandals, from family breakups, to personal betrayals, murders, physical and emotional abuses, the organizing of criminal enterprises, wars between the first city-states, antipathy and violence between ethnic and tribal groups, and even the horror associated with the offering up of human sacrifices. Christmas reminds us that God loved us so much that He created God's own scandal to rescue us from ourselves. God desired to put on human flesh and sacrifice God's self, in ways we cannot even imagine. In order to reach the depths of human depravity, God, in the form of Christ, submitted to the violence and depravity of wicked people, in order to save the very people, who were given over to evil. Through the birth of Christ, God out-scandaled the devil. Forgiveness was made available to all, through this Child; and now, even when we, or others, do the unthinkable, God is not shocked, because a way out has been vouchsafed. The Way is here! Christ, the Savior, was born in Bethlehem today!

Study Questions

1. Have you ever been caught up in a scandal? How did you survive it?
2. What is it about scandals that repulses you? What is it about someone else's scandals that attracts you?
3. How can a careless decision end in a scandal? Can you give a couple examples from what you have observed? What about from the Bible?
4. Is it appropriate for Christians to enjoy television characters and shows that seem to relish scandalous scenarios, as they immerse the viewer in the drama of sordid behavior? Should it be written off as escapism and harmless entertainment? Or should we never watch anything controversial, or that which depicts sinful actions, on television shows?
5. How did God create a scandal to solve all scandals? The birth, life, and death of Jesus all included scandalous aspects. How did God use this one life, to provide a remedy for all other scandals in life?
6. I am glad that God decided to be involved in the scandal that is the redemption of the human family. If God had not revealed God's saving love to us, where do you think we would be as a global society?
7. Do you find it strange to associate Christmas, with a scandal?

50. The Praises Go Up, Because the Blessing Has Come Down

Luke 2:4-14

The most unique baby that had ever been born was coming! Mary and Joseph had to make, what seemed to be, an ill-timed trip, to satisfy the Roman government's demand that every person in this part of the Empire register in a census, for taxation purposes. Because of his lineage, Joseph's place of registration was Bethlehem. Among several meanings, the name Bethlehem meant "the house of bread." It was located in the district of Judah (which means praise). Mary and Joseph were carrying the greatest baby ever born, while they made their way to the house of bread, in a district of praise! Years later, an adult Jesus, would claim to be the bread of life, sent down by God for the salvation and sustenance of the world; and years later, Jesus would be praised for all of the wondrous works that God wrought through His hands. But in Luke 2, none of these future events are known by human minds. Yet, in this morning's text we see a foreshadowing of how Jesus was set to be the bread of heaven, to whom we should give praise.

Finally, after making the 80-mile trek to this little town, about six miles south of Jerusalem, Jesus is born in what many archeologists suggests was nothing more than a large, attached room in a house, filled with a family's animals; a room which doubled as a make-shift barn. The Word made flesh, the King of Kings, the Lamb of God, the Bread of Life, has come down from heaven, to this little town and makes His entry, and is born in this modest space! He was not born into a palace, as He deserved. But, in spite of such humble and ignominious beginnings, soon praises would ascend to glory, because of His birth. Luke says that a domino-like succession of praises begins to travel outward and upward, on the outskirts of the town, in a field where shepherds are tending their flock of sheep. Late into a silent and holy night, as tiredness sets in, suddenly an angel of the Lord appears. The angel is shining, with the glory of God, and after calming the shepherd's fears, announces that something glorious has happened! Something earth-shattering, and cosmic-shifting has occurred! Luke notes it like this:

> *"For there is born to you this day in the city of David a Savior, who is Christ the Lord. And this will be a sign to you: You will find a Babe wrapped in swaddling clothes, lying in a manger."*

Soon, the announcement that the Savior of the world has been born in their city, is accompanied by the shocking, yet serene appearance of a heavenly choir – a large host of heavenly beings, begins to send their praises up to God, in the presence of the shepherds. The shepherds hear melodious voices that are literally out-of-this-world! These heavenly beings are not sending up praises, *so that blessings will come down* (Often we propagate this kind of theology in our worship services today, when we encourage God's people to offer up vocal and visible praises to God, with the expectation that if we do such acts alone, special blessings will be dispensed to us). The heavenly host is praising God, *because The Blessing has already come down!!* Later, after seeing the infant Jesus, the shepherds, go about the town of Bethlehem, praising God, just like angels and heavenly beings did. They go about, giving vocal and exuberant praises, in proper response to what God had already done. In the House of Bread, God had sent the Best Bread - salvation bread – to feed a world, starving for love, peace, and righteousness!

United, on this Christmas day, I am not suggesting that we never praise God in advance of some wonderful thing we believe God is going to do in our tomorrows. Neither am I suggesting that it is entirely bad theology to believe that when sincere and authentic praises go up to God in worship, that some kind of benefit won't follow suit; but what I am saying is that God has already done the most wonderful thing ever by making God available to us, in Jesus Christ. Such a gift cannot be topped. In Christ, salvation became clearer; God became more tangible and touchable; love became more understandable; our sins were forgiven, and our faith was given a strong anchor, revealed through the strongest person! So, this Christmas, instead of praising God with the expectation that as our voices go upward to the ceiling, new blessings will come down to satiate our fleshly appetites, why not choose to simply praise God for *The Blessing* who has already come down!

Merry Christmas, peace on earth, and goodwill toward women and men.

Study Questions

1. In your mind, have you ever linked your worship on Sunday with your blessings on Monday? This kind of thinking might not be entirely wrong-headed, but it is important to remember that just because we sing Sunday songs, and offer up holy hallelujahs, it does not mean that God is going to suddenly rain down all the toys for which we have been praying.

2. In the Lukan narrative, the heavenly "choir" gives a praise performance for some tired, smelly shepherds in some forlorn field. Why do you think God chooses such a place to be the setting for heaven to announce to humankind the good news of Jesus' birth?

3. God enjoys the praises of God's people. How do you think God feels when our motive to praise God, is primarily to ensure that we get superficial goodies from God?

4. Is it okay to offer up praises to God, with several motives at work in our hearts? Deep gratitude to our Creator, for all God has done, and because praise is therapeutic and spiritually healthy on many levels?

5. When was the last time you praised God for Jesus Christ, simply because you wanted to bless God, for the greatest blessing the world has ever known?

51. Jesus has Come, Now What?

I John 1:1-7

The central focus of our message is inspired by the writings of the Apostle John. In John's first letter to the early church, which many scholars believe was composed close to the end of the first century, John explains to his readers that the disciples had indeed met Jesus, in the flesh. He is writing this letter, in part, to dispel the doctrines of false teachers, especially the Gnostics, who were teaching that Jesus never actually was fully human – fully flesh, bones and blood, as well as soul and spirit. The Gnostics also believed that the way we reach a divine-like status is by attaining a secret, mystical knowledge that makes one, one of the Elite in society; a part of an intellectual remnant, better and smarter than the average human being. John is writing to challenge these heresies. In his opening verses, he explains that Jesus was fully human, and that the disciples had touched the Lord with their hands and had been touched by his human qualities (1 John 1:1-3). Later in this letter, as John had done in his other writings, John begins to address the perennial question of what kind of lives Christians should live. To do so, John uses one of his favorite literary devices - the light vs. darkness trope. He explains that to live a life of sin and immorality, is to live against God's light – it is to live in darkness. In chapter 2, John reveals to his readers that when we live lives that are immoral, or full of bitterness, revenge, and character assassination (all various forms of hatred), we are living in darkness, and not in the light of God's love.

This Sunday, the title of our message is "Love Power." In this message, I hope to share with our church, especially our youths that God's love is what gives us true light! We thank God for Christmas lights and celebrations. We thank God for unwrapped gifts, ham, turkey, eggnog, pumpkin pie, and the anticipation of the coming new year. We thank God for the beginning of Kwanzaa; but if we have not yet learned why God sent Jesus to the world; if we don't appreciate why God grants us additional years, after all the foolishness we were involved in this past year; if we have not grasped the real reason why God grants us purpose and faith, we have not learned the greatest reason for the season. We have been so privileged simply, and profoundly because God loves us. God loves us individually; God loves our towns, cities, and countries; God loves our particular racial category; God loves our unique languages; God loves us with a love that is hard to figure out, but impossible to defeat. Without God's love power which burns as a light toward us, in us and through us, we are existing in an aimless and selfish darkness, which will become a horrible prison. Without an awareness of God's holy love, we are living in gross darkness. On the other side of Christmas, we are called to share this light with the world. As the song writer wrote: *Jesus gave it to me......I'm going to let it shine, let it shine, let it shine, let it shine!*

This past week, because of a strong thunderstorm, our part of Detroit experienced a power outage. For over twenty-four hours, many, on our side of town, had no air conditioning, no ability to use appliances, and no light! It was a miserable experience; so is living a life filled with hatred. Hatred zaps our power; compromises our integrity; jeopardizes our light. Someone much wiser than me said that to hold in bitterness and think that one's bitterness is going to harm someone else, is like drinking poison and waiting for one's neighbor to die. I'm so glad that through a very real, and human, Jesus Christ, God has given us the power to love, which is the power of light – it is the power to see all things anew!

Study Questions

1. Have you ever wondered whether Jesus was, and is real?

2. There are a lot of doctrines and philosophies circulating in society that have a lot to say about Jesus. Can you think of any that you have read in a book or on the internet that have caused you to question what you've learned about Jesus in church?

3. The central message about God according to the Bible is that God sent Jesus into the world to establish a New Covenant, between a sinning humanity and a holy God. The love of God was the impetus for Jesus' coming to our world. John, often contrasts, light and darkness in his letters. Now that Christmas has come, are you engaging sharing with others the benefits of the New Covenant, and spreading the light of God's love?

4. Now that Jesus has revealed to us the depths of God's love, it is important to witness to others about the love we have received from God. The hymn writer wrote how we ought to "Go tell it on the mountain, over the hills and everywhere…that Jesus Christ was born!" Have you at least shared about your faith in Christ with family members and friends? What about your neighbor on the block?

5. One of the most loving things a person can do is to share the love of Christ with someone else. Encourage someone; walk through a valley of suffering with someone; meet a need that someone has. How has the living out of your faith, made your world a better place.

52. New Year's Eve/ Kwanzaa: Celebrating A God Who is a Part of Us

Text: Matthew 2

Because this New Year's Day fell on a Sunday, many churches in the area canceled their New Year's Eve services, which would have taken place on Saturday night. United Christian Church elected to do the same. We recognized that our congregation has many elderly members, and also knew that the weekend would be a very busy time for our members, as people in the congregation would be preparing to host New Year's Day meals with family. The unfortunate thing was, in doing so, we also canceled our annual Kwanzaa worship service. I must confess that I felt a bit ambivalent about not holding our New Year's/Kwanzaa celebration, though logistically, I believe it was the right thing to do. The reason I had strong mixed emotions was because I know that for African Americans, it is critically important to celebrate our faith in light of our African cultural roots. In many black communities, our faith in Christ has often been coupled with a celebration of black history and freedom. The black church has been where we have been able to affirm African-influenced ways of worship, preaching, and building community. As quiet as it is kept, the black church has always been one of the strongest protectors, incubators, arbiters and transmitters, of African values in the United States; values like those celebrated during Kwanzaa; with the inclusion of the Nguzo Saba (The Seven Principles):

1) **Unity**
2) **Collective work**
3) **Cooperative Economics**
4) **Self-Determination** (under God's purview)
5) **Purpose**
6) **Creativity**
7) **Faith**.

Our New Year's/Kwanzaa services have been a way to intentionally, remind us of these seven principles at the outset of a new year, as we rejoice in the knowledge that God has chosen to identify with Africa and its people. In a lecture I heard a year or so ago, the Reverend Dr. Jeremiah Wright Jr., the globally known, former pastor of Chicago's Trinity United Church of Christ, told his audience that all of the events recorded in the many texts of the Hebrew Bible, happened in the context of the darker skinned peoples of the continent of Africa; a continent, which some Afrocentric scholars believe should include the Middle East and the region of Mesopotamia. Wright shares this view about the Hebrew Bible to help his audience understand that God intentionally chose to disclose the divine presence, and all of God's holy covenants, among and through a people who looked more like Egypt's former president, the late Anwar Sadat, and those darker than him, as opposed to the Charlton Hestons of the world. To deny that God is connected to Africans and darker Mesopotamians, is to deny the truth. Such scriptural and archeological facts, discussed by Wright, and many other scholars, anthropologists, linguists, prophets, preachers, and poets, remind us that history and culture should not be forgotten -- for the good of future generations; and that cultural celebrations, like Kwanzaa, can help boost the esteem of a people, who have been caricatured and despised; *buked* and *scorned, and talked about as sure as you're born!*

Obviously, especially given what we have in the First Testament biblical account, God is the God of the particular. Sometimes, as we hurry to honor the God who has universal and general appeal, and who expresses concern about the totality of humanity, we forget that God is also the God of the particular. For example, Matthew's Gospel chronicles very particular events that happened to a particular people: God impregnates a particular Jewish woman, of a particular cultural and genealogical background.

God sends Jesus through and to these people first. God then leads Jesus' parents to hide and raise their infant son, for a time, in the midst of another culture – a Kemetic Culture (Matthew 2:13-15); an Egyptian African culture, which had ascended to its cultural zenith point. It was no accident that God uses the people, culture, and customs of Africans in Egypt, as a hiding, educational, and nurturing place to protect Mary, Joseph, and Jesus. Egypt was all of that and more. It was full of fascinating sights and sounds. The people were beautiful and amazing. Jesus spends his earliest, formative years, seeing the sites, and hearing the particular music and language of these first century, Egyptians. Jesus slept on African cots, located on African soil. It is probable, that as a toddler, Jesus took his first physical steps on some floor or ground in Egypt. Along with the region of Judea and Galilee, it seems God has held, and holds, very dear, the geographical location and the people of Africa.

Today's sermon, from Matthew 2, will prompt us to think about God's work among those who come from Africa (really all of us). Our text will also move us to consider how much effort the Magi (popularly, known as the Three Wise Men) expended, as they exhaustively looked to find the baby Messiah. We can learn important lessons from them, as we keep the new year in view.

To make the biblical connection to our faith and culture, we should note that Matthew reinterprets a text found in Hosea 11, and exclaims that among many believers in the Messiah, Jesus would become known as the Son who was called by God out of Egypt (*see Matthew 2:15*). I can imagine that as a very young Jesus grew up, his parents recounted their harrowing, and yet exciting experience as they trekked from Bethlehem, to Egypt, to Nazareth – running for their lives. Through this scripture text, we can imagine how God used Egypt to help protect the young Christ, providing the earliest, societal influences on the developing Child, as Herod sought to destroy him. This placement of our young Lord among a highly advanced African culture, was no accident. God would use this event, many years later, to help connect with the hearts and cultural importance of Africans. If one analyzes the history of Gentile conversions, the earliest of which begins in the book of Acts, this story of Mary, Joseph, and Jesus' sojourn in Egypt, the placement of Jesus in the bosom of Africa, helped later African God-seekers to know that God wanted to work with and through the African people and continent. I also believe we can draw parallels from this sojourning event, and argue that God continues to use Africans, and African American peoples, to nurse and protect a dynamic brand of the Christian faith; a faith, that might otherwise have been killed off by a European Enlightenment-based skepticism, and a rigid, stifling, misguided, fundamentalism. In other words, God continues to connect with Africans, and African Americans with Christ in ways that have produced a passionate, true-to-the-biblical texts faith; a faith in Christ that is narrative-rooted, but not in a way that can be used to argue for, or against various scientific hypotheses. In the African and African American branch of the church, what we have is a lively, tenacious faith, that is joyful, even in the face of that which should cause great sorrow. God continues to link with black folks in ways that have graciously given the world a form and practice of Christianity that greatly contributes good to the world. Today, I know of truly amazing situations where Swedes are willing to invest in, learn from, and participate in performing gospel music concerts; concerts led and taught by African American experts in the field; experts who do not just teach notes and gesticulation, but who also teach about the sacredness of the Jesus, about whom they will be singing. I know of white preachers and pastors, all over the world, who are studying under and learning from the gifts of great African American preachers, and African scholars.

Connecting our faith traditions to our culture, is not the completed task of the disciple of Jesus Christ. Along with acknowledging how much God has been at work for, through and with Africa, Africans and African Americans, as we enter the new year, our first sermon of the year will be crafted to encourage us to tirelessly pursue Jesus this year, like the Magi did. They pursued the Lord until they found him and worshiped him with their precious gifts. This is the primary task of the disciple of Jesus Christ. I hope that this first message will encourage all disciples, no matter our color or culture, to remember how important it is to pursue Jesus. We have been saved, to do some saving; we have been called, to do some calling; we worship, that others may worship; we love, that others might love; but we cannot do any of these wonderful things, with integrity, if we are not actively following the Lord. The Magi were caught up in a vision of the Lord which they pursued. The positioning of the stars had inspired them and intrigued them. The prophesies from God's word, had moved them and energized their journey. When they had finally located the young Messiah, and after offering gifts to him in worship, they left their encounter with him with good news to tell anyone within earshot of them.

As we follow the Lord, and as we recall how much God has invested in Africans, African Americans and all people, we will become flooded with good news. When equipped with good news, we can change the world. But, the question we are left with is: Practically, what does this kind of celebration and pursuit of God look like, as we stand at the starting line of a new year? It simply looks like this: When we encounter people on the highways and byways of life -- folks who have a *Habari Gani* question (Swahili for *What's the news?*), we should respond by answering, *"Jesus! Jesus is God's best news that has ever happened to me, and to this world!"* But, even in this, the celebration of our faith must go beyond mere words of thanksgiving and testifying. African American Christians have been called to live their lives in light of the resurrection, from the perspective of a profound new birth and transformation; and we are called to celebrate the great things God has done and is doing through humanity, but especially those who have been long-kissed by nature's sun. If we have no love of self, how we will have authentic love for others? When we think about what it means to follow God, it involves loving ourselves, just as God has created us; and diligently and faithfully studying, dialoguing with, and following the teachings and views of our Christ, January through December. His words are living and sharp, yesterday, today, and forevermore. His voice speaks to us, through the Spirit, every season of the year.

God loves us and wants God's children to love God in return. When we love God, and our neighbors, as we love ourselves, it benefits us and blesses God. God desires us to pursue God, as we thank the Lord for the good heritage of a people who have overcome very steep obstacles. As we continue to seek God's face, we will discover that every new month and every new year, we are being empowered from above to become more and more like the One who is already connected to us!

Study Questions

1. The Magi searched for the Christ Child, travelling over arduous terrain and many miles to locate the prophesied Messiah. In what ways are you searching diligently for the Messiah's presence and power in your life, today?

2. How much time do you spend in prayer, versus the time spent on social media?

3. As you anticipate a new year, what are you hoping God will do for you and through you; or for those in your life, or through those in your life? Pray for God to give you a ministry focus for the year. Pray that God would give your loved ones, who are Christians a ministry focus for the year.

4. Matthew notes that Mary and Joseph fled from King Herod and traveled to Egypt to escape the genocide/infanticide Herod was sadistically imposing, in efforts to abort the life of the Messiah – the King of Kings. Why do think Matthew includes this detail about the early life of Jesus?

5. Since Joseph's family was hiding in Egypt, among black, and browner-skinned Africans, what does this say about the color of Jesus' family?

6. Do you think that Jesus heard Egyptian music; ate Egyptian food; wore Egyptian influenced clothing, as a toddler?

7. Jesus might have even had his native, Semitic language, to become slightly shaped by a Coptic accent. What are some other ways you think Jesus and his family were influenced by their time in Egypt?

8. In what ways do you think Africans and African American Christians are "protecting" and representing strong versions of the Messianic legacy of Jesus today?

9. How will you celebrate and follow God this year?

Bibliography

Alcantara, Jared E. *Crossover Preaching: Intercultural-Improvisational Homiletics in Conversation with Gardner C. Taylor.* (Downers Grove: IVP Academic/Intervarsity Press, 2015).

Baker-Fletcher, Garth. *Somebodyness: Martin Luther King Jr. and the Theory.* (New York: Fortress, 1993).

Bonhoeffer, Dietrich. *Christ the Center: A New Translation.* (New York, NY: Harper & Row paperback edition, 1978).

Cone, James H. *God of the Oppressed.* (New York: Orbis Books, 1975).

Douglass, Frederick. *Slaveholding Religion and the Christianity of Christ, in Afro-American Religious History: A Documentary Witness.* ed. Milton C. Sernett. Durham (North Carolina: Duke University Press, 1985).

Dubois, W.E.B. *The Souls of Black Folk.* (Chicago: A.C. McClurg & Co., 1909).

King Jr., Martin Luther. *Strength to Love.* (New York: Fortress, 2010).

Obama, Barack. *Dreams from My Father: A Story of Race and Inheritance.* (New York: Crown Publishers, 2004).

Oden, Thomas C. *The African Memory of Mark: Reassessing Early Church Tradition.* (Downers Grove, Illinois: InterVarsity, 2011).

Taylor, Edward L. *The Words of Gardner Taylor, Volume 1: NBC Radio Sermons 1959-1970.* (Valley Vorge, PA: Judson, 2004).

Walton, Johnathan L. *Lecture: The Du Boisian Dilemma: Sacrificing the Faith in Order to Save the Race.* (Published on *Youtube*, from Chicago Technological Seminary, Chicago; at the 7th Annual C. Shelby Rooks' Lecture Series, October 24, 2013).